AROUND
ENGLAND
with a DOG

AROUND ENGLAND WITH A DOG

by Lesley Choyce

RMB

Several of these chapters have appeared in slightly different form in *Celtic Life International*.

For information on purchasing bulk quantities of this book, or to obtain media excerpts or invite the author to speak at an event, please visit rmbooks.com and select the "Contact" tab.

RMB | Rocky Mountain Books Ltd.
rmbooks.com
@rmbooks
facebook.com/rmbooks

Cataloguing data available from Library and Archives Canada
ISBN 9781771604512 (paperback)
ISBN 9781771604529 (electronic)

Cover and interior design by Colin Parks
Cover photo credit: dog image by GlobalP (iStock); background map image by BardoczPeter (iStock)

Printed and bound in Canada

We would like to also take this opportunity to acknowledge the traditional territories upon which we live and work. In Calgary, Alberta, we acknowledge the Niitsítapi (Blackfoot) and the people of the Treaty 7 region in Southern Alberta, which includes the Siksika, the Piikuni, the Kainai, the Tsuut'ina, and the Stoney Nakoda First Nations, including Chiniki, Bearpaw, and Wesley First Nations. The City of Calgary is also home to Métis Nation of Alberta, Region III. In Victoria, British Columbia, we acknowledge the traditional territories of the Lkwungen (Esquimalt and Songhees), Malahat, Pacheedaht, Scia'new, T'Sou-ke, and W̱SÁNEĆ (Pauquachin, Tsartlip, Tsawout, Tseycum) peoples.

We acknowledge the financial support of the Government of Canada through the Canada Book Fund and the Canada Council for the Arts, and of the province of British Columbia through the British Columbia Arts Council and the Book Publishing Tax Credit.

CONTENTS

For Genevieve, Scarlett,
Ailis and Carys

LOCATIONS

1. Bexhill-on-Sea
2. Bradford-on-Avon
3. Bath
4. London
5. Saffron-Walden
6. The Thetford Forest
7. Leicestershire
8. Betws-y-Coed
9. The Dartmoor
10. Cornwall
11. Cumbria
12. Edinburgh
13. Yorkshire
14. Canterbury
15. The White Cliffs of Dover
16. The Lake District
17. Argyll
18. Southend-on-sea

PROLOGUE

Linda and I were probably sharing a bottle of wine on a Friday afternoon after I had finished teaching my university creative writing class when the idea first came to me. I had decided to take the upcoming fall semester off and wanted a "project" — which usually meant writing a new book. We were also looking for some form of adventure — an extended trip somewhere, somewhere that we knew we already liked. We narrowed it down to Italy, France, England, Scotland or Ireland. A full month in a foreign country.

"But what about Kelty?" Linda asked. "Do we really want to leave our dog for that long?"

That put a wrench in the works. "No," I said, bolstered by the glass of Apothic Red. "We'll take the dog with us."

"Could be complicated."

"We'll sort it out," I said. "How complicated can it be?"

"It's settled, then," Linda said. "Which country?"

"Well, if we're taking the dog, we should keep it simple. No flight connections. One nonstop flight."

"Agreed."

"Then it's England," I said. "We're going to England. We'll get a camper and circumnavigate as much of England as we can. And I'll write a book about it. Call it *Around England with a Dog*."

And that was more or less that.

But it wasn't that simple.

INTRODUCTION

It all *seemed* so simple at first. Around England with a dog. Our dog, of course. Our nearly 2-year-old West Highland White Terrier — a Westie known to the world as Kelty. I'd travelled to England many times but never with a dog. I'd met many a friendly mutt in English pubs and on hikes had run into hikers who too liked to take their dog everywhere. So why not me? Why not us?

"Us" would be my wife Linda and myself. The two of us and our feisty little dog, who had once been labelled a West Highland terrorist by the owner of Country Critters, where we'd send him to stay on our previous jaunts to Europe. But not this time. Kelty was going to have his first trip to the UK. And I was going to write a book about it.

That's what I do. I write books about travel, ideas, life and history. I'm not really much of a researcher or historian, but instead I allow myself to stumble onto things, unearth historical connections and connect them to me somehow. Staring at William Wordsworth's socks in a glass case at the Wordsworth Museum in Grasmere. Standing at the foot of Jim Morrison's grave in Père Lachaise Cemetery in Paris. Gazing at the shiny walls of the room where Mozart played his first concert at the age of 7. That sort of thing. I write novels and poetry, too, but won't bore you with any of that this time round.

My plan was to fly us into Heathrow with Kelty snug in his Sherpa doggy carrier under the seat (probably mildly sedated to keep his terrorist aspects suppressed) and off we'd go in a rental ... um ... camper. At least that was the original plan. We'd drive around the perimeter of England — south, east, north and west. We'd poke in here and there, meet wonderfully funny, wise and eccentric citizens and I'd have a wealth of material to write about.

We wouldn't stick strictly to the perimeter, but you get the idea. It would mostly be a rural thing. Easier to find patches of green grass where a road-weary dog (and his master) could take a pee. I had already started circling on our map towns with names like Ninfield, Saffron Walden, Osgathorpe and Troutbeck Bridge. Surely something of note would happen as soon as we pulled into Bexhill-on-Sea or Bury St Edmunds. Fascinating historic discoveries were certain to be had in Ashby-de-la-Zouch and Bovey Tracey. And because we had a friendly Westie with us, people would want to stop and talk to us. They'd ask us if we were American and we'd have to tell them no, we were Canadian. Maybe we should stitch Canadian flags on our coats, I had already suggested to Linda. The dog himself would sniff out interesting places and the whole operation would be this grand peripatetic journey, a real adventure.

I have a half-time job teaching creative writing and English at Dalhousie University in Halifax, Nova Scotia. Halifax was founded by the British in 1749. It was a military operation and the British did some of the nastiest things they could possibly do there, as they did in most parts of the world where they planted their flag. I knew enough British history to know that it had been a very messy business, trying to conquer the world. And the men in charge were about as ugly and cruel as humans could possibly be.

So, why, I often pondered, did the English always treat me so kindly whenever I asked for directions or queried the

3

location of the nearest loo? Why did they preserve such a tidy and stunningly beautiful countryside and not muck it completely up like we North Americans do whenever we get the chance? Why so many paradoxes?

Well, that, my friends, was part of the quest.

So I applied for a sabbatical from my teaching job at the university — the one that was named for a Scottish lord. George Ramsay was the ninth Earl of Dalhousie and governor of Nova Scotia from 1816 to 1820. He had seen his fair share of battles. In one of the more difficult ones, he had been accused of insubordination by none other than the Duke of Wellington when he declared the road ahead was "too long and too wet." Wellington had later complained about Dalhousie, "It is impossible to prevent incapable men from being sent to the army." But the good earl and former lord must have redeemed himself somehow as he was later given full charge of Nova Scotia, then became Governor General of British North America and finally Commander-in-Chief of India. On our travels, we would walk past his alma mater, the Royal High School in Edinburgh, dating back to 1128, prompting me to wonder what high school would have been like in 1128 or even in Dalhousie's day.

I had to explain the purpose of my paid leave, of course, to my academic superiors, and in the official document I wrote that I was doing research for my next book and made some comments about the depth and scope of my historical inquiries involving Lord Dalhousie, the Romantic poets, Celtic lore, the Second World War and English dialects. I left out any details about taking a dog, surfing, drinking beer or loafing and rambling about the green countryside.

Our travels would encompass a full month at least and would not be confined to England proper. Linda thought we should visit Wales as well, although I wasn't sure I trusted

Wales. I once had a rather unpleasant experience in a pub in Coedpoeth involving being short-changed on a pint of bitter. For a long time I believed the snarly barman was representative of the entire Welsh but, in our itinerary discussions, Linda expressed her opinion that I was wrong. So I was persuaded that Wales might be graced with our presence yet and we would see how Kelty liked it.

We'd visit places that, for the most part, neither one of us had visited before, and I would include in my book the back-story of the chunks we had previously explored — Cornwall, Yorkshire, Kent and Devon.

Having applied for a sabbatical, and realizing that I had little interest in really writing an academic book about anything, I knew I needed a more cohesive theme for our trip, some kind of grand scheme to pull the threads of our odyssey together. Sure, it could just be the perimeter thing, but it needed to be, wanted to be, something more. A quest, of course, a noble quest in search of answers to grand questions.

No, wait. That seemed way too serious.

I had once read a very funny book called *Round Ireland with a Fridge* by the British writer Tony Hawks. Having lost a beery bet with a friend, he decided to hitchhike the perimeter of Ireland with a small refrigerator and see what would happen. He succeeded and had many fine encounters and wrote a very successful book.

Maybe I could do something similar. Write something both serious and funny at the same time so readers would find me clever and amusing. A scrap of history here and there but no footnotes, of course.

England was a shade bigger than Ireland but doable. We would travel around the kingdom and we would take our dog. We would visit towns where my father was stationed in the Second World War, we would travel to Leicestershire to the origins of the Choyce clan, we would walk in the footsteps of English poets who have inspired me, I would surf my first man-made wave in Wales. And more.

And so the journey would begin. It would most certainly be *around* England and *beyond* with a dog, this very dog sitting on my lap.

We'd left the beast behind far too many times, although recently we had successfully taken him out of Canada on a trip to Mount Desert Island in Maine. There a woman in the ShopRite parking lot spied me walking Kelty and rushed toward us. "Great looking dog," she said as she knelt down on the pavement to inspect his undercarriage. "Is he fixed?" she asked. "Yes," I answered. She shook her head, stood up and brushed off her hands. "Too bad for that," she told me. "You could have made some good money and he could have had a good time." After that she lost interest immediately and walked back to her husband, who was loading groceries in the car. The incident made me realize I'd have to keep a fairly tight rein on my pet and be wary of strangers wanting stud privileges or other favours from a man with a dog.

That experimental trip had gone reasonably well. The dog had been no problem at all at borders or otherwise. So England it would be. I'd seen small dogs prancing through airports on the leashes of owners — mostly rich people, or at least people who looked like what I perceived rich people to be. But we weren't rich. What would it cost to take a dog on a plane? A quick check of several airlines revealed it was not expensive to take your pet as long as it was under 20 pounds. Kelty was 18 pounds. But I still wasn't sure he'd settle down for the flight and be willing to stay in his soft-sided kennel. We'd have to work that out later.

With the dog sitting in my lap and staring at me, I asked him if he wanted to visit England and possibly even his ancestral home. And was he willing to be a good dog and follow any instructions we gave him? He immediately licked my face as if to answer in the affirmative most emphatically. So it was a done deal.

In more sober moments I had second thoughts. No, maybe it would be easier to leave the dog back at Country Critters and explore around England with something else. I thought of English history again and the rotten things the British military had undertaken in Nova Scotia — the scalping of Mi'kmaq people, the expulsion of the Acadians, for starters. What about simply writing a book called *Around England with a Grudge*?

"No," Linda said, "it doesn't have quite the same ring to it."

What if we went to places that inspired poets and fiction writers and sought out those vortices of creativity that fostered geniuses like Charles Darwin, Isaac Newton and Stephen Hawking?

"Yes," she said, "we should do that to some degree but it's not quite enough. The dog thing would get a wider readership."

"But he's going to be trouble," I said, losing confidence in the overall canine plan. "What if we fly there and adopt a pet of some sort instead? We could find a nice home for it before we left. Around England with a ferret, maybe. Around England with a budgie? Around England with a hedgehog? Or maybe it could be an injured animal from an animal rescue centre. Something easy to travel around England with. An injured pigeon, maybe, or a sparrow with a broken wing?"

She shook her head. I was being silly. It seemed too artificial, and it just wasn't the same. We needed the dog if it was going to be an honest book. So Kelty was back in the picture, of course.

But where exactly would we go, and why? Well, my ancestors came from England in the eighteenth century.

They came from a tiny hamlet called Sibson in Leicestershire. James Choyce had been a weaver there and eventually took his large family to America, ending up in New Jersey, where, several generations after, I was ultimately born into this world. Sibson did not sound particularly exciting, but I bet that if we went there with a dog, interesting stuff would happen.

My father spent a fair chunk of the war as a truck driver stationed at US airfields near Cambridge and Bedford, and he had kept a journal about it. Those locales were certainly on the itinerary. And I wanted to go back to the Lake District and have another good look at Wordsworth's socks, so the dog might have to wait in the car there, but we could take him hiking for sure on trails trod by the lucky feet of both William and Dorothy. I had a few other poets of interest on my list. I thought I should see Coleridge's cottage where he wrote "Kubla Khan." And if we made a side trip to Scotland, there would be a house or two where Robbie Burns had slept and no doubt written a verse or two for lovely accommodating women. And there was a Choyce family connection to Beatrix Potter worth exploring. Maybe if I threw enough of that in, the sabbatical committee wouldn't totally frown on my "research" and literary endeavours in the end.

My son-in-law got wind of our plans and gave me a book called *The Good Guide to Dog Friendly Pubs, Hotels and B&Bs in England*. Well, that truly fit in with my vision of travels. Find interesting pubs that allowed dogs and take Kelty into the watering holes to await epiphanies aplenty. And beyond that, new and important themes would emerge as they always did. We would discover whatever there was to be discovered when one goes to a foreign land with a canine in tow.

As noted, Linda and I originally thought this would be a camping odyssey. We envisioned the three of us intrepid travellers flying into Heathrow on the overnight Air Canada fight from Halifax and renting a largish camper van. I discovered that one rental agency would even drive it right to the airport for us and off we'd go, south to Lyme Regis and hang a left at the English Channel.

As a boy, my parents had taken my brother and me on a journey from New Jersey to Alaska, north and west across the wide continent, and it had been a wonderful experience. So I had fond memories of RV travel. To get a feel for what it would be like driving such a vehicle, Linda, Kelty and I went to a couple of dealers and looked at several models of Class B and C vehicles — campers mounted on truck or van chassis. Some had big-screen satellite TVs and king-size beds, and what's not to like?

But then I tried driving one of the more modest models down Highway 7 on the Eastern Shore. Really? Was I going to manoeuvre one of these suckers through those dozen or so roundabouts just outside Heathrow without taking out a handful of Morris Minis and Opel Corsas? Worse yet, how would I drive any one of these monsters down those narrow rural English back roads we so loved — the ones about as wide as the sidewalk leading up to my front door? In our travels, it had become our habit to find the most obscure and alluring skinny back road to nowhere along the English or Irish coasts and drive it to the end to discover tiny pocket beaches of stone and sand where curious sheep would stare down at us from clifftops. If we had our wetsuits and boogie boards, we'd jump in the ocean and catch wave after wave until we were exhausted. How would we get to such places in a big camper?

Sometimes, we would return to the car to discover there was no possible place to turn around, the vehicle wedged between rock walls built centuries before by inconsiderate sheep herders who didn't have the forethought that Canadian boogie boarders would one day park here and find it so difficult to turn their rental vehicle around. On such occasions, I'd have to drive backwards down those walled laneways laced with massive thorned blackberry vines, scratching the hell out of the virtually new (500 kilometres on the odie) rented Peugeot, or denting it even, in an attempt to return us to the main highway and back to civilization.

In order to stave off regular damage charges at Avis and Dollar, Linda found a tube of scratch buffing compound at a car repair shop near Sligo and we travelled with it wherever we went. I did once put a sizeable dent in a rented Vauxhall that could not be masked in any way and that provided a more serious challenge. So I stopped in a woods and found a sturdy broken tree limb that I used to push out the dent from the inside of the trunk. Unfortunately, as soon as I took the stick out, the darned dent returned and I was flummoxed until I simply decided to leave the trusty branch in place and return the car at twilight. That seemed to do the trick.

Alas, driving that camper beast around Nova Scotia on wide and nearly empty roads and learning it had ten (count 'em, ten!) cylinders and that it got roughly eight miles to the gallon on gas ... well, it threw a wrench into the camper dream plan.

I still thought that driving around England in a very modest camper van was possibly doable, but then I started googling images of where we would be spending the nights: caravan parks. We had come across caravan parks in coastal towns on the North Sea and on the English Channel before and, much as I tried to convince myself that they were just what the lower-middle-class urban Brits needed to escape from their gritty city apartments and get some fresh air by the sea, they still struck me as a blight on the landscape. Were they really where we wanted to spend our nights while trying to experience "the real" UK of the twenty-first century? Probably not.

So plans kept changing. We needed transportation for us and the dog. And we very much needed to explore those twisty turns and oh-so-narrow back roads where you'd encounter an oncoming car and one of us would have to pop it into reverse and drive backwards for great distances until a pull-off was found. Or even more fun than that was both cars sidling into muddy ditches and inching forward, rear-view mirrors tapping as if in a gentle kiss and then driving on with a smile and a wave of the hand. No sir, we wouldn't give that up for any ole camper van and a night in a crowded caravan park with snot-nosed British wannabe skinhead children playing video games on the picnic tables. Not in this lifetime anyway. So a simple rental car would have to do for a Canadian adventurer and his wife and their scrappy little white dog.

CHAPTER ONE

CROSSING THE ATLANTIC AND STARVING IN FRANCE

There were three writers, really, who inspired me to want to write a book about a modern-day pilgrimage. The first was Bill Bryson, who'd written *Notes from a Small Island* and *The Road to Little Dribbling*. Both were funny, insightful and quirky. I wanted my tome to be all three as well. I thought that Bill Bryson was still living in New Hampshire, where he'd written *A Walk in the Woods*, and that state was within two days of driving from my home in Nova Scotia. I'd write to him, explain about my project and ask for a one-hour interview. I thought any author worth their mettle wouldn't mind lending some thoughts to another fellow scribe. So we started planning a pre-England springtime jaunt in the near future to New Hampshire, travelling with the dog again as a bit of warming up for the big trip ahead.

Before the afternoon was over, we'd booked a cottage in North Conway for early April when my classes ended. Then I sent an email to Bill right away.

Lucky for me, Mr. Bryson answered my query the next day. Unfortunately for me, he wasn't living in New Hampshire and he wasn't doing interviews. To use his exact words:

> Dear Lesley,
>
> Thanks for your inquiry. I am afraid I haven't lived in New Hampshire for 15 years, which kind of suggests that

you haven't been following my work terribly closely for quite some time.

At all events, I am afraid I am not able to give interviews at present, so I must beg you to excuse me, but I do wish you every success with your book.

Best wishes,

Bill Bryson

In other words, Dear Lesley, please fuck off.

We drove to New Hampshire anyway and the dog came along.

We had one good day of weather whereby we visited Madison Boulder, which *Atlas Obscura* states "is thought to be the largest glacial erratic — an erratic being a boulder of a certain type of rock that was transported by glacial ice and deposited on bedrock of different type of rock — in North America. At 23 feet high, 37 feet front-to-back, and 85 feet left-to-right Madison Boulder is estimated to weigh almost 12 million pounds, roughly the weight of 36 blue whales."

I really liked rocks, and this was a big one, although I had never thought of comparing rocks to whales. It was a good hike to the Madison Boulder as Kelty ran free. It was a mild spring day, but *real* spring — the kind where deciduous trees sprout leaves and ferns poke up like green fairies from the forest floor — was a long way off.

It snowed after that. Often. North Conway was a wonderland of slushy streets and depressing outlet stores. It rained and then snowed some more. My brother Gordy and his wife came up from New Jersey to visit and we shared our plans for England with them. Gordy gave me the kind of look he used to give me when we were adolescents and I informed him that one day I would walk on the moon or take a trip around the sun.

The skies started to clear on the way back to Nova Scotia, which turned out to be milder than the mountains of New Hampshire. But we had yet another preparatory road trip with Kelty under our belts that had taken him across at least one foreign border. But no Bill Bryson. I'd learn later he was nearly 3,000 miles away in, where else, England. *East* Hampshire as it turned out, not *New* Hampshire.

This leads me to my second inspiring author: Tony Hawks. No, not Tony Hawk, the world famous skateboarder. Tony Hawks had written that wonderfully funny book about Ireland. He had lost a bet with a friend — naturally, drinking was involved — and agreed to hitchhike around the perimeter of Ireland with a small refrigerator. It turned out to be a wonderful experience and a fine book emerged and, if I remember correctly, virtually no one who picked him up asked him about *why* he was hitchhiking with a fridge.

Well, we weren't hitchhiking and we had a dog, not a refrigerator, and we would be renting houses for three or four nights at a stay to get the feel of different locales. But an interview with Tony would help spark things in our pilgrimage, I was sure. So I wrote to Tony and he obliged by answering in a somewhat more convivial tone than William Bryson. Tony said he lived "not far from Exeter" somewhere near Moretonhampstead in Devon. Linda and I had once stood in a crowd before Exeter Cathedral as Prince Charles and Camilla arrived in a motorcade. We liked Devon very much and put it on our list of places to stay. Tony said to check in with him when we were in the UK and I said I would.

Later I would read Tony's *Once Upon a Time in the West... Country* and learn of his own rural adventures, including an electric bicycle trek across Devon, south to north, with a small pig. Travelling with a dog, I realized, was a bit tame compared to the fridge circumnavigation and the pig pedal, but I remained certain that if I had the right attitude, weird and interesting (and ultimately insightful!) things would come our way. And I looked forward very much to interviewing Tony Hawks as part of the quest.

The third author on my inspiration list was Chris Nelson, who had once come to Nova Scotia from Cornwall to interview me for his book *Cold Water Souls*, about surfers around the world who surfed in winter (in very, very cold water). Along with a handful of other young men, I had been one of the first surfers to ride waves year round in the North Atlantic off our coast here in Canada. Chris was living in St Agnes and said I should drop by to be introduced to some "local characters." Well, the literary side of our travels was shaping up.

And then things went a bit off the rails. When I started to book a flight on WestJet, I soon learned that you could not fly into the UK with a dog in the passenger cabin. Not just WestJet but all airlines, I was told. You had to put the pooch in with the luggage.

No way. I knew we had to get rabies shots and a tapeworm treatment and paperwork up the yin yang but didn't know about dogs forced into the cargo area. Flying, then, to London or anywhere else in the UK was out. I wondered if I should just give up on the whole idea or find another country. I soon learned that WestJet had just opened up a new route to Paris and when I called again, lo and behold, I was told we could indeed fly to Charles de Gaulle International with a doggy in his approved doggy bag under the seat for a very small fee.

That was it, then. No giving up. We'd fly to Paris, rent a car, drive north to the Channel and take Le Shuttle through the Eurotunnel to Folkestone and set off from there. It would just add to the adventure. *Around England with a Dog* would have to begin in France. We'd arrive ashore not far from where William the Conqueror stepped on English soil as part of the Norman Invasion in 1066. The Canadians (and their dog) are coming: watch out!

And then people started getting pregnant. My daughter Pamela announced she was with child and soon after that told us she was having twins — due in August. Not long after that, at the Bowlarama bowling alley (just behind Mike's No Frills store) in Spryfield, Linda's daughter Laura announced that she was pregnant and her baby was due in late September or early October.

The news was all good and we were thrilled about the idea of three more grandchildren on the way but, darn, we'd already booked our pilgrimage for September and that was now incredibly bad timing to be away. As grandparents, we wanted to be around, not only to see the new arrivals but to help out in any way we could. Bloody hell.

We decided to either give up the journey altogether or find a better time. June would do it. It had to be June, which was only a few months away. So we cancelled September flights and rebooked for June. We wouldn't give up. The Around England with a Dog concept had hooked me. We'd come this far. We couldn't turn back. We'd make it happen.

I had a deadline coming up sooner, however, for several magazine articles about the Lake District and Scotland. One more wrinkle. A couple of pints of IPA helped me sort out the dilemma. We'd do two trips. Back to back. The first would be a foray — without the dog — to the north to suss out the origins of the West Highland White Terrier in Argyll, with a quick trek over to Edinburgh and then a visit to the Lake District, which was not far south from our point of entry — Glasgow Airport. True, it made the whole process a bit more convoluted and complicated, but as we well knew, travelling with or without a dog always involved shifting plans and complications. But more on that first spring trip later.

As the departure date for our much-anticipated June trip *with* Kelty drew near, I staked out a route. Once we drove out of the Eurotunnel we'd go west to Bexhill-on-Sea and then north and west to some place near Bath, then east, bypassing London altogether to somewhere near Cambridge, possibly farther out into the Fens, then north and central a bit into the Midlands and Leicestershire, west again to Wales (why not?) and back south to Devon before scooting across the lower length of England to put the car on the train back to France. We started booking houses that were pet friendly and began racking up the bills. One pound sterling was equal to roughly $1.78 Canadian. It was going to be one hell of an expensive trip.

The day before we left Nova Scotia, we had to go to our vet to get Kelty's tapeworm pill. (Is there a good reason that Brits are leery of tapeworms when much of the rest of the Western world is not?) We also had to drive to Kentville, two hours away, to get an official document from Agriculture Canada stating we had a healthy dog. Dr. Shane Hood was a man who knew about details. He told us that the form needed to be filled in with blue ink. "The French insist it's blue ink," he said. We would possibly be scrutinized, he said, in both

France and England much as if we were hauling livestock into their countries. Bureaucracy is rarely pretty, but we'd come this far and we'd do whatever it took for the dog to come with us. We had no tapeworms and we had blue ink and a file with medical records aplenty. I was hoping we were armed with what we needed to breach borders in a proper way.

But would the dog settle down enough to sleep on the plane? He didn't really like his carrier and wasn't used to being confined. We had Benadryl and high hopes. If he decided to yelp, we could only pray there was a crying baby on the plane that was louder than him.

June 9 arrived and Linda wrote this in her notebook: "We took Kelty to the beach this morning and hiked the trail to Crowbar Lake in the afternoon. Haddock for supper and then taxi to the airport." We flew overnight to France. Every time I take an overnight flight from Halifax to the other side of the Atlantic, it seems like a miracle to just wake up in the morning on a plane and realize you've left North America behind like that.

On the flight, the dog slept, I slept, Linda dozed sporadically and we landed on a bright morning at Charles de Gaulle in Roissy, just north of Paris.

Going through immigration, not a word was asked about the dog. He was happy to be out of his kennel and pranced lightly along the shiny floors of the French airport with passengers from around the world smiling at a cute little Westie whose tail was straight up in the air. The adventure had begun.

Hertz was kind enough to have a black Fiat waiting as we requested. In France, the driver sits on the left. English cars have the steering wheel on the right but drive, of course, on the left side of the road. French driving — driver on left, driving on right — would be a piece of cake. But how exactly would I adapt once we crossed the Channel? Left-hand drive on the left side of the road. The rules would change as soon as we drove off the tunnel train. Hmm.

We had planned to spend a night in Giverny, a small artsy town in Normandy, most famously home of Claude Monet from 1883 to 1926. We rolled into town, road weary and jet-lagged, and found our way to a strange little bed and break-fast accommodation called Les Rouges Gorges. Our room was in an old stone building that felt much like a cave, and the man renting to us was (surprise, surprise) very French. Our host, Gils, knew a little English and I knew even less French, so we mostly used hand signals and pointed at things. Despite the fact I've travelled to foreign lands dozens of times in my life, I'm hopeless at learning languages. I'm adept at pointing and gesturing, though, and making facial expressions that have universal meanings. So who really needs to bother to become multilingual?

It turned out there was no place to buy beer to bring back to our room, but our host sold me several tiny bottles of Leffe for five euros each. After scouring the beautiful little town, we also discovered there was nowhere to buy any food except for pastries. As we had walked through Giverny with our dog, we saw throngs of people eating at outdoor cafés, but as soon as the town clock struck 4:00 p.m. it was all over. You could drink wine and snack on pastries and desserts maybe, but no real food. We hadn't eaten all day.

There are many things I love about the French, but, to my way of thinking, they tend to eat at the wrong times of the day. Or maybe it was just good fun for them (in a French sort of way) to laugh at visitors like us who were famished. "Look," I could almost hear one waiter saying, "here come some foreigners. Quick, let's close the kitchen." In fact, as we sat down at a lovely outdoor café with garlands of wisteria drooping down all around us, the time was exactly 4:01 when we asked the waiter for a menu. "*Le menu, por favour, monsieur*?" I asked, mixing up my French with a bit of Spanish. He smiled and gave a hearty laugh. "No, no, no no," he said. "Kitchen closes at four. But it will reopen at eight p.m." We would be dead asleep by then.

The only stores in town sold artwork, tourist trinkets or clothing. No food. Disheartened and starving, we trudged back through the beautiful little village to our cave. Seeing the look on our faces, Gils asked what was wrong. I explained about the curfew on food and he waved his hand in the air, which could have meant anything. And then, God love him, he pointed to an outdoor propane tank hooked up to a cooker on an old wooden bench in an open shed. "*Moules et frites*," he said.

"Moules et frites?" I repeated, believing that saying the words out loud myself would give them meaning. But it didn't. Frites sounded like Frito Lay so I thought maybe it was potato chips. "Moules?" I asked.

He used his fingers to create a shape of something that seemed almost obscene. Noting the scowl on my face, he walked into his house and brought out a single mussel to show me. I smiled. "Moules," I said.

"Et frites," he said, holding up a potato and then grabbing a knife and making a cutting motion in the air.

So moules and frites it was. Our first meal in France. Actually our first meal on the trip. Steamed mussels and freshly cooked French fries. Superb. My admiration for the

French ascended dramatically. We ate our fill, I gulped down two tiny bottles of Leffe and we both fell sound asleep at 7:00 p.m. in our little cave, our dog at our feet on the bed and all well in the world. If the ghost of Claude Monet had been in our chamber, he would have looked at the serenity here and painted his most masterful work.

CHAPTER TWO

IMPRESSIONISTS AND FIRST IMPRESSIONS OF THE EUROTUNNEL

It was no surprise that we were up early and wandering the quiet flowered streets of Giverny before the hordes of tourists had arrived. It really is a touristy town, but I guess if you get up early enough in such towns, you can catch a hint of the "real" place that once existed here. Also not surprising is that Giverny is quaint, lush and well cared for and, for the most part, the centuries have been kind to it and the people who live here have respected and preserved many things from the past.

A soft mist hung over the cobbled street as we walked the dog. The branches of the weeping willows did not sway. There was not a hint of wind. In the park there were ash trees, quinces and gingkos. But it was the flowers that ruled the morning. Springtime flowers were on the wane but still in bloom: irises, tulips, pansies and wisteria to entertain us. Summer flowers were beginning to take over, begging for admirers: dahlias, clematis, anemone, marigold, delphinium and roses of many colours.

If you were an artist and flowers were your thing, Giverny then was your version of paradise. And it was here that Claude Monet had painted some very famous paintings, including *Le*

Bassin aux Nymphéas — those water lilies still blooming behind the wall to his garden. That particular painting had sold to a Swiss buyer in 2013 for US$23 million. I left Linda at the door to the Monet Museum and Gardens minutes before it opened. Dogs were not allowed inside so we left Linda to tour on her own. Kelty and I had an hour to ourselves to ramble about, so I walked to the edge of town and down a narrow country lane leading to some pasture land. It was quiet and peaceful as I awaited revelations like those experienced by the impressionist artists in days gone by.

According the Metropolitan Museum of Art, Monet and his cronies were "rejecting the rigid rules of the beaux-arts ('fine arts'). Impressionist artists showcased a new way to observe and depict the world in their work, foregoing realistic portrayals for fleeting impressions of their surroundings." I rather liked the idea of forgoing realistic portrayals and vowed to do my best in our travels to capture "fleeting impressions." As if on cue, a hawk with a red tail flew over us, casting his shadow on Kelty and me. "Hawk Shadow on Man and Dog just outside Giverny," the painting or poem would be titled.

Monet came to settle in Giverny after looking out on the town from a train window. He liked what he saw, got off the train and then moved here to live. As his fame increased, wannabe impressionists too came to his hometown to follow in his footsteps, but then things got a bit out of control when American artists started moving there. Claude found them overly annoying and eventually avoided them as best he could.

The artist had a stepdaughter who married his son, Jean Monet, which must have set local tongues wagging, but Papa Monet probably found it better than her previous beau, who was one of those irritating American painters who had come to town. Photos of Monet show a man with an ambitious beard and piercing eyes. He insisted on a small funeral at his death and it was attended by a mere 50 people. Kelty and I skirted past the master's grave in a churchyard because it too had a sign in English and French to keep dogs out.

My thoughts ran like this. Certainly, Monet was an interesting character and a skilled painter and he did some fine work. But what was it about him and other artists and writers that immortalized them, that kept their memory alive, their spirit alive and worthy of interest to thousands if not millions of international visitors after they were gone? I had some famous authors in my sights for this trip myself: Wordsworth and Coleridge, to name two. My guess is that there are many, many creative types of the past who created wonderful works and, at their death or well before, were brushed aside and cast into the dustbin of history. I, of course, began to stew and ponder my own literary mortality at this point, which always makes Kelty nervous, I think. As if to lift me out of my sombre reverie, he took his first poop of the day perfectly in the middle of the narrow Giverny lane just as a tour group of bicyclists were peddling our way. I dutifully scooped it into a poop bag and, with our heads high, we marched on toward Rue Claude Monet with as much dignity as we could muster.

Linda was suitably impressed with Monsieur Monet's paintings and his flower garden, and I had walked up and down a fair number of streets until I felt at home here in this little oasis of the past. Only a couple of tourists from Nebraska stopped to talk to me about our Westie and, in their conversation, they were the first of many on our trek who would stop to pet Kelty, ask his name and then find themselves reminiscing about their own beloved mutt who had died just recently or distantly in the past. It may be true that some of the greatest of our painters and authors are easily and quickly forgotten even before their demise, but the memory and love of a family pet lives on long after they are gone ... or at least until the owners join them in the grave.

Our next night was in Calais at a typical beach motel — Hotel de la Plaige — whose interior walls were painted ungodly colours. I think orange and purple predominated. Monet would not have approved. However, the room had a small refrigerator, which is always a blessing on any pilgrimage no matter how sacred or blasphemous. There is a big wide sandy beach at Calais and the wind was gusty and grand, allowing kite surfers to skip through the water and then make that bold leap against gravity and sail up into the blue sky above the English Channel. We couldn't see the farther shore, but we'd be there tomorrow. Our two days in France were a fine prelude to our return to the English-speaking world and a country where a hungry man might find a meal at 4:00 or 5:00 p.m. if he so desired.

We watched the giant ferry sail toward an invisible Dover across the Channel, and I felt a sudden case of nerves about putting us on a train — wife, dog, car and me— and rocketing beneath millions of gallons of water and megatons of chalky rock. Everything I knew about the Eurotunnel was based on multiple viewings of the *Mission Impossible* movie where spies and helicopters were involved. I tried to put the worries out of my head.

But history was creeping up upon us here as we walked this often troubled shore. My grandfather on my mother's side had come ashore not far south and west of here at the port of Le Havre during the First World War. He told me the story once when I was a young boy, but it is most convoluted in my memory. It seemed he arrived on a troop ship from New York after a stormy and hellish crossing only to get sick and end up in a French hospital for an extended stay before being shipped back to the US. It seemed that he received some kind of medal for his illness, although that doesn't seem right. I'm sure I'm missing chunks of his story and wish I had paid more attention to his telling of his war years.

Indeed, centuries of warfare on land and on water had taken place along this patch of coast. Dieppe still conjures up black and white images of horror and no man's land. Farther to the east lay Dunkirk, whose very name reverberates with the memory of the brave and desperate English retreat in the Second World War and recently reimagined in film.

On the road to Calais, I realized my father had been on the ground here himself in the Second World War, six months after the D-Day Invasion. In his journal he wrote:

> Dec. 13, 1944 — Our truck Co. has been on detach. Service to France for 20 days. We are now back at base. We crossed the Channel on a Liberty Ship with our trucks loaded. Went up the Seine River to town of Rouen & unloaded from the ship. Seen a lot of damage done to towns & harbors. We went to the town of Denain. We went through the town of Amiens — totally destroyed. Saw a lot of German equipment destroyed all along the roads. Returned to England on L.S.T. from La Havre. We could drive right off of them. Saw a lot of interesting things while in France. Was my first trip there.

We had bypassed both Rouen and Amiens on our way to Calais and the Eurotunnel. It was hard to believe this corner of France had seen so much horror and destruction in both my grandfather's and father's day. But given their time here, perhaps it was appropriate that I was entering England from this side of the Channel, even if it was by a means hardly imagined in their days.

Calais itself was much as I expected — a port city with considerable industry, traffic and Calaisians rushing home near five o'clock. Oh no, five o'clock. We had failed to eat a restaurant meal at the proper time yet again and had to settle for ham and cheese sandwiches from the downtown Lidl supermarket.

Refugees from several nations had struggled to get to Calais in recent years hoping to make their way to England. Many had languished in camps and had been poorly treated. It seemed that Calais had always been at the centre of people coming and going, fleeing disaster and hoping for something better. Down at the Hotel de la Plaige we saw no trace of refugees, but an early evening foray to the beach with Kelty revealed more than one fellow dog walker shouting at his or her mutt to do this or that (in French, of course) with dogs that seemed to have a mind of their own.

Linda had been missing out on her daily exercise routines, so she was up early waiting for the daylight to grace us and then she ran the beach and into the town. "Very few people out," she wrote in her journal, "and those who were out were male and scary. Got lost and had to use the Navigon to get back." Yes, we had support from technology to help us find our way hither and yon, but I usually preferred using my maps when possible. Even then, the combination sometimes failed us and arguments ensued. But at least Linda's Navigon app led her safely back to me and away from those menacing 6:00 a.m. sailors, thieves and villains who must haunt the early morning streets of this infamous harbour city.

And so it was sandwiches again for breakfast. I would assert that France was a complete gastronomical failure for us except for Giverny's moules and frites. Of course, you have every right to say that I never really gave French cuisine a chance. 'Tis true, we did not. Perhaps on the next trip — Around France with a Dog (and a cooler of backup food), it will be different.

As we drove inland to make our way to the tunnel entrance, I tallied some final thoughts, both good and bad, about France. The motorways are most excellent, but they are toll roads and quite expensive, yet when you pull into the rest stops, the *aires* that are small picnic parks, the toilets have no seats, as if the owners of the toll road are too cheap to buy them or possibly travelling thieves have stolen all of them to recoup financial losses from driving the toll roads. And if, in fact, they were stolen, would they be taken home or would they be sold for cash? On Kijiji in Rouen, perhaps?

I need also report for the wary traveller that the coffee at the Autogrills, of which there are many, is good but the cups are small — miniature really, Lilliputian. The women who work in such places are friendly, but the men seem to have a slight whiff of, dare I say, arrogance. But only slight. Nonetheless, how can you not like the French? They do everything with charm and a degree of intensity. They have great art and literature and allow Canadians with dogs to fly into their country and go (nearly) wherever they want to without harassment.

We arrived at the pet office at the Eurotunnel with our whack of papers to find the staff there friendly, courteous and efficient. There was a great black and white photo of a young Paul McCartney with his beloved English sheep dog, Martha, the inspiration behind the song "Martha, My Dear." Later that day, fooling around on the internet, I'd discover there were hundreds of photos floating around of Paul and Martha. Of his famous dog he once said, "She was a dear pet of mine. I remember John being amazed to see me being so loving to an animal. He said, 'I've never seen you like that before.'"

We proceeded rather seamlessly through British immigration here in France with our stack of dog papers in order. I was queried about my job, as was Linda. When she said she was a retired high school principal, she was asked if she would remain retired or would she be looking for work in the UK. "No," she said. "I'm retired for good." "Okay then," was the reply as we were waved on. It made us wonder if there were a lot of retired Canadian high school principals trying to sneak into England to steal the jobs of British citizens. It was around this time that Britain was pulling out of the European Union and we'd hear far more than our share of stories about Brexit, so maybe education administrators from all over were heading this way, pretending to be on vacation and zeroing in on headmaster jobs from south to north before Britain began closing down its doors to foreign job seekers.

With that moment behind us, an hour later I was driving our rented Fiat up and into what looked like a boxcar. Soon the train gently began to move and we were about to leave France behind. At first I thought that it felt a little like travelling through space. Almost at once, there was nothing to see but the wall of the train and the concrete wall beyond. We each ate an orange as we listened to the safety instructions on what to do if we had to leave the particular coach that held us.

Plans for some sort of tunnel under the English Channel date back to 1802, with some serious thought about the possibility again in 1834. Digging actually began in 1880, and some of that original tunnel still exists today, but it is a tunnel to nowhere. It wasn't until 1987 that successful digging began — and a massive job of boring it must have been (as opposed to a really boring massive job). Queen Elizabeth and French President Mitterrand opened the tunnel for travel in 1994. More importantly, dogs, cats and ferrets were approved for crossings in the tunnel in 2000 to celebrate the millennium and, by 2017, the year before our own pooch bravely slept through the excursion beneath the sea, two million cats and dogs had crossed, as the authorities were keeping close count of the data. I couldn't determine how many ferrets had crossed but wondered about why ferrets had become so popular that lobby groups mounted significant campaigns for pet equality when it came to travelling privileges.

I emailed someone high up in the pet department of the Le Shuttle organization to find out exactly what number Kelty was but, as of this writing, no one has had the courtesy to answer this important question. I'll not pursue the point, but I'm betting the ferret travel lobby would chew away at such a thing until they got a decent (and proper) answer.

Just for the record, and to prove to my higher-ups that there was at least some honest research going on during my sabbatical, I can inform you that the tunnel is 31.4 miles long with 23.5 of that underwater and much of it a full 120 feet below the seabed. Thirteen thousand workers were involved in getting the job done, but not without tragedy as ten men died in the construction work. Since its inception, nearly 60 million people have crossed, not to mention all those dogs, cats and ferrets.

Of the crossing itself, I have little to report. We did finish those oranges and I tried to pretend to Linda that this was like taking a strange Jules Verne sort of voyage to the centre

of the earth or even into deep space. She seemed to be not listening and, instead, asked me if I could remember the name
of an ABBA song she said was repeating itself over and over
in her head: "You can dance, you can jive, having the time of
your life."

"That's just too easy," I said, adding the next quite obvious
line that gave away the title of ABBA's third most popular
song of its career: "See that girl, watch that scene, digging
the Dancing Queen." I then said how much I regretted the loss
of the colloquial use of the verb "digging," as in liking something very much versus ordinary underground excavation. I
wondered aloud if the two married couples who had created
the Swedish pop band had ever travelled like us through the
tunnel, and everyone in the car agreed that they must have
at one time or another in the process of selling 390 million
records. And, while I am not a diehard ABBA fan, I must say
I thought that naming the band by using the first letters of
the first names of each performer was somewhat shoddy and
the backwards second B reminded me of the backwards R in
Toys "R" Us, but clearly they knew much more about mar-
keting music than I did, and before that thought had reached
my vocal cords, we had crossed the channel from underneath
and arrived in England.

It had seemed to take almost no time at all — officially 35
minutes but really only about 20 minutes of actual travel. It
was the strangest little cocktail of boredom and anticipation
and all at once it was over. We were in England, driving out
of our train car with little fanfare and onto the motorway
in Folkestone.

CHAPTER THREE

BEXHILL, BOB MARLEY AND THE BARLEY FIELDS OF EAST SUSSEX

So now I was driving on the left with the steering wheel on the left. Linda noticed right away I drove a bit too close to or over the centre line of the roads once we were off the motorway, a habit I never could quite break during our journey. The A259 took us to Hythe, the birthplace of Mackeson Stout in case you were curious, and also home of St Leonard's Church, which has a rather large human bone collection in the basement. Housed here are 1,200 skulls and 8,000 thigh bones from medieval times, all neatly arranged on shelves. Some of the skulls had holes drilled into them, and the drilling, it is said, was done while the owners of said skulls were still alive, a practice called trepanning, which was said to cure various ailments. I reckoned that after the Black Death hit Hythe in 1348 and again in 1400, folks were anxious to try most any cure, even a rather painful one, to avoid dying of the scourge.

Not wanting to muse too long on death and drilling, we motored on to Dymchurch and New Romney. I apologize for saying this, but it was not a particularly pretty shoreline. The sea here was held at bay by a high stone wall for much of the stretch, and when we peered over the wall, I saw a steep beach with no sand, all stones. Whereas France had wide, white sandy beaches just across the Channel, here was a most unappealing beach, as if England had been cheated out of a fair distribution of the accommodating sand along these shores, yet another reason for the island people of England to historically hold grudges against their continental neighbour.

As if the walled-out sea and the grumbling stones of the shoreline were not enough to send us on, we noted several caravan parks to our right. I've often tried to convince myself that city people deserved to be able to have an inexpensive *pied-à-terre* along the coast, but the parks still appeared as a blight on the landscape to me. And I couldn't help thinking about the head of a hopeful middle-class family from some industrial suburb of London saying to his wife and family, "I think we should save all our quid and purchase a rectangular metal box among other metal boxes, close to a steep, stony shoreline where we can escape from it all and really enjoy life."

As we drove on, we ignored the side trip to Dungeness, whose name is lent to a species of crab found off the coast of Washington state, but also the home of two nuclear power plants, one now closed. Both had been constructed in a critically important wildlife sanctuary. Does that seem odd to anyone out there?

Pondering those power plants and the seemingly imminent threat of nuclear war back in 1982, Paul Theroux wrote in *The Kingdom by the Sea*, "There were places around Dungeness where it looked as though the catastrophe had already happened. The Denge Marsh had a bombed, broken look. It was craters and quarries and gravel pits; no trees, only scrub and weeds; much barbed wire and miles and miles of gray pebbles."

Although I found that Theroux could sometimes be a rather depressing writer to use as a guide to anywhere, I had taken him at his word on this and we had little trouble in deciding a side trip to jolly ole Dungeness was probably not worth the price of admission.

More to our liking was Rye, which the local tourism board flaunts as "a Medieval Gem! Perched on a hill, the medieval town of Rye is the sort of place you thought existed only in your imagination. Almost suspended in time, Rye's unhurried atmosphere and enchanting streets draw visitors with their warm welcome. It's small enough to make you feel at home almost straight away but holds enough secret treasures to entice you to stay much longer."

We found a delightful patch of grass in Rye to walk our dog and made good use of the free public washrooms handily equipped with toilet seats and Dyson hand driers that puckered the skin on your hands. Still a bit jet-laggy, we were anxious to get off the road and did not give Rye its due but hope to return there to explore what one other touristy source calls "England's best kept secret." That phrase cropped up several times on our trip concerning well-marked and well-visited towns and historic sites. Clearly, we all are curious about such secrets and flock to such locales when we think it is a special find just for us, only to discover the secret is out thanks to colourful tourist websites and reckless bloggers promoting "secret" sites.

I must have made a wrong turn not long after that because we went inland all the way to Cock Marling, so I had to turn down a small country road to get us back toward Winchelsea and Icklesham, then on to Guestling Thorn and Hastings. I've been a bit harsh so far about this patch of English coast and certainly didn't intend to be mean. Hastings was a bit larger than I expected. Sometimes places in the UK that I expected to be towns turned out to be cities. Hastings was like that. Busy and crowded, but a place packed with the curious and the historical. Lewis Carroll had gone to school here and it had been home to the brilliant man we never heard of who pioneered television. John Logie Baird had transmitted the first visual images way back in 1923 and without him we'd never have had *Happy Days* or *Star Trek*, but there are no monuments commemorating this inventor. If inventing TV was not enough to grant him a smidgen of immortality, it should also be noted he invented "damp-proof socks," primarily for soldiers, and I think he deserves our respect for that as well.

Alan Turing, the legendary wartime English codebreaker and subject of the biopic *The Imitation Game*, had grown up and was educated here in Hastings before going to Cambridge. Oddly enough, Archibald Belaney, later in life known as Grey Owl, was born here as well and made his way to Canada, where he pretended to be Indigenous, became famous as a champion of the wilderness and raised several families of famous beavers with an Iroquois woman.

We had almost booked a house in Hastings, but I instead chose a little cottage in Bexhill-on-Sea, which I thought was less commercial. In our planning for this venture, I had gone looking for small, obscure villages with rental homes or cottages in rural areas, while my wife lobbied for accommodations right in towns with proximity to shops, restaurants and pubs. Often we made compromises that suited us both. For some reason, I had convinced myself Bexhill was a sleepy little hamlet by the English Channel, nothing like Brighton or Hastings. But it turned out to be a rather standard British seacoast resort with a lot of traffic, a pier, endless fish and chips shops and a wall of hotels and apartment buildings blocking a good view of the shore.

I had first noticed the name of Bexhill when editing a manuscript for a book called *Where Duty Lies* by John Cunningham about a Canadian First World War soldier named Frank Grimmer. Frank had been shipped to a training camp here in preparation to go into battle. Cunningham wrote this of the completion of the program: "March 21, 1918, was graduation day. The celebratory dinner was at the magnificent, old-world-style Metropole Hotel, at Bexhill-On-Sea. Toasts were proposed to the King, the commandant, the officers and guests. Steaming bowls of cream of oyster soup were brought to the tables. There was a serving of fried plaice — a large European flounder. The main entree was roast beef with gravy, served with potatoes and Brussels sprouts, a far cry from the beans and stale bread of the trenches."

I thought of my grandfather's connection to France, my own father's connection of various postings in England. I also noted that March 21 was my birthday, although I certainly was not alive in 1918. Back in Canada I had decided that Bexhill was right for our first night in England and I looked up pictures of the Metropole Hotel, which indeed looked grand enough for our first dinner in the UK, and perhaps they'd allow Kelty at least into the pub.

And then, that night while watching a documentary about Bob Marley on Netflix, I learned that he gave his first ever concert in the UK in none other than Bexhill-on-Sea. According to *The Guardian*, it was a fundraiser for the local Lions Club hoping to raise enough money to build a community swimming pool. Somehow I never envisioned Bob Marley having any association with the Lions Club, yet I discovered part of their mission statement was "to promote peace and encourage international understanding." So maybe it seemed most righteous that Bob was bringing a little Trenchtown to East Sussex. It was clear we were destined to spend at least a few days there.

Unfortunately, the Metropole Hotel, which had survived a fire in 1920 and a German bombing in 1941, had been torn down in 1955. There would be no oyster soup or Brussels sprouts for us. But I did locate a tiny house for rent on the outskirts of Bexhill — perfectly rural but ten minutes from the Tesco, tea rooms and touristy shops. Once we were in Bexhill, the rental cottage was nearly impossible to find as the laneway had no markings whatsoever. The gravel single-track road was full of potholes and the house itself smaller than we'd hoped for, although what would one expect for an abode whose name is "Little House"? Many houses in the UK, I was discovering, had names instead of addresses, and the names were either dead-on accurate or blatant lies. One never knew. I think Linda was disappointed with the accommodation as she declared it was "very modest." But aside from the massive deposit of fresh cow shit in the driveway, I thought it was just fine and so did Kelty.

Once we'd unloaded, we retraced our route to the Tesco back on the highway and bought our first round of supplies. I had been told by an Englishman that dogs were welcome most anywhere in the UK, but that was a bit of an exaggeration. We went into the supermarket with our little white beast and no one said a word at first until Kelty started getting a bit excited near the seafood section. It was then that I was approached by a young man in an apron who asked ever so politely, "Excuse me but is that a service dog?" Kelty was wearing a harness attached to the leash I was holding and I was wearing sunglasses so I was tempted to lie and say yes. But this seemed bad form for my first day on English soil.

As a result of speaking the truth, we were asked to leave at once and escorted to the front of the store by a security guard while other patrons viewed us with their British scowls as if we were the lowliest of shoplifters. Linda continued to shop, and when she emerged from the belly of Tesco, it was my turn to go in without the dog and select a few more items, as well as refreshments. So our routine was now established as follows: Linda would go into a supermarket first with a list while I walked around the parking lot with the dog. Kelty and I became quite familiar with sidewalks and parking lots around Tesco, Morrison's, Marks & Spencer's and the odd Aldi store. Linda would then take the dog and I'd go into the market to buy things she might have forgotten.

When I returned inside dogless, no one seemed to remember that I had been booted out earlier and I was free to shop unmolested. Linda told me she had forgotten to buy crackers, cauliflower and broccoli and I was to select the beer and wine. At the checkout, yet another young aproned man looked curiously at my selected items, perhaps because there was such an ample supply of adult refreshments and not much food, so I felt some sort of explanation was in order. "It's a special diet I'm on," I told him.

He lifted an eyebrow and asked, "And how's that working out for you?"

"Just grand," I said.

"Hmm," he replied as I slid my Visa card into the little machine. "Maybe I should try it."

Back at Little House, there was a yard for Kelty to play in, free internet and a salmon dinner with new potatoes and Brussels sprouts. I took the dog for a solo hike on a footpath through a nearby ripening barley field. God bless the British for preserving those million-odd footpaths across private property throughout the country. We stopped in the middle of the field and I engorged myself on the smell of the field, the panorama of the blue sky and the sheer joy of moving along on our journey to everywhere and nowhere. The lyrics to Sting's song "Fields of Gold" came into my head.

At that moment I fully understood why someone would write a song about a barley field. I harkened back to the field of rye my father would plant at the end of the growing season for vegetables. It would ripen into the cold weather of early winter, go dormant and begin growing again in early spring. Then my father, driving the old 1949 red Allis-Chalmers tractor, plowed under the rye grass to rejuvenate the soil. Plant life is a wonderful thing.

On our walk back home, it was obvious to the dog and me that a farmer had just recently walked a few of his cows down the laneway while we were hiking in the field. The road was heavily mined with large, wet cow paddies, not the dry, fibre-laden ones like you see in the Prairies in western Canada, but sloppy, black, smelly deposits that made me think of a term used by Jonathan Swift in *Gulliver's Travels*, an onomatopoetic word that seemed to fit perfectly here: *splackmuck*. Steering Kelty this way and that around all the poop, it made me think that raising cows was a truly messy business that not all of us would aspire to.

That evening, I read *1066 and All That*, a classic satirical account of British history first published in book form in 1930. I suppose every British schoolboy knows that date and what it stands for. It was on October 14 of that year when William, the Duke of Normandy, stepped ashore with 10,000 soldiers to defeat an English army led by King Harold. Thus began the Frenchification of England. Although it is usually referred to as the Battle of Hastings, the actual fighting mostly took place inland near a town that was later appropriately named Battle. On a rainy day foray to Battle, we actually failed to find the battleground due to some vandalized signs and the heavy downpour that greatly diminished our interest in England's history that day.

In the morning we drove by the De La Warr Pavilion, where Bob Marley had once wailed, and saw the famous art deco curves of the façade. I noticed that one of the upcoming acts advertised was called the Kooks, a Britpop indie rock band from Brighton. I later discovered that all manner of famous bands had performed here. Not every band was so lucky as the Kooks to show their stuff in the De La Warr, however. *The Independent* reported that the "extreme metal grindcore" band Napalm Death were turned away in 2016 out of fear that their extremely loud, pounding grindcoring would damage the structure of the place, this despite the fact that it had withstood the attack of a German bomber during the Second World War.

While De La Warr was hosting original pop bands and solo artists, back down the road at Hastings, the White Rock Theatre had stuffed its lineup with tribute bands with names like Think Floyd, Rumours of Fleetwood Mac, The Illegal Eagles, Material Girl, Totally Tina and, for the even older crowd, Frankly Sinatra. I was somewhat shocked to realize that fans would pay £25 (C$42) to see fake versions of their favourite performers, but probably it's a way for musicians to cash in on another's success while putting their own creative efforts on the back burner.

CHAPTER FOUR

BEACHY HEAD, THE SEVEN SISTERS AND THE LONG MAN OF WILMINGTON

Like many English beach resort towns, Bexhill has plenty of those funny little buildings called beach huts parked along the pebbly shoreline. They seemed unnatural to me and I hoped that there might be some kind of movement afoot to remove them so that the view of the Channel would be unobstructed. And if so, I was willing to join it. But I soon learned that these little buildings were fondly loved by the English. In my research I would discover there are over 20,000 beach huts in the UK.

What do people actually do in their colourful beach huts? I wondered. Well, according to one old gent sitting on a park bench, they change into bathing costumes (yes, he used that term), they store floating devices, they take naps and they make tea. It hadn't occurred to me that the beach huts had electricity. But yes, some did. The owners of those who didn't settle for Coleman stoves or propane burners. You bloody well wouldn't want to have to go without tea if you were spending a day at the beach.

According to Millie's Beach Huts, "Choosing a name for your beach hut will be one of the hardest decisions you make. It feels as if the choice of name reflects you and your beach hut's personality and so taking some time to choose a name is key." Some of the more interesting beach hut names in the UK include After Dune Delight, Barefoot Bungalow, Beachy Keen, Baydream Believer and — in honour of Jimmy Buffett — Changes in Attitude. Rental of a beach hut in this part of East Sussex would cost you £200 or more per week, which seemed like a fairly stiff fee for a shack on the sand (or pebbles in many cases) that you could only sleep in during the day. But then, maybe your own private After Dune Delight was meant to be a place for mum and dad to sneak off for a bit of private nookie during the day while the kids were left to play shoot-'em-up video games at the local arcade.

I'd read about the fact that the oldest known spider web in the world, conveniently preserved in amber, was found on a beach in or near Bexhill, a spot also famous for dinosaur tracks pressed into rocks. No one locally seemed to know which beach it was, though, and it clearly didn't seem to be the one downtown, where I'm sure there would have been a bylaw preventing the construction of a beach hut on old dinosaur footprints. So we hiked along various chunks of Bexhillian shoreline looking but ultimately found no fossils or amber.

There's a fair stretch of open beach west of Bexhill near Pevensey, however, where the little beach huts do not prevail, and it suited us just fine. Kelty could run free and we could breathe fresh salty air and stretch our legs. I squinted into the sea mist hoping to see France on the other shore but could see nothing. Again there was no amber or dinosaur evidence to be found. Back in the car, I turned on the radio for the first time in England and tuned in a station called Heart that seemed to have transmitters throughout the UK, I would later learn. The music was contemporary, mostly something resembling hip hop by my estimation. The DJ spoke extremely fast and in the commercials the men and women spoke even faster. But what struck me most were the lyrics to the songs. In order to have your song played on Heart, I surmised, you had to have a considerable amount of repetition of a lyric and that lyric had to be banal, slightly offensive or positively absurd. If you haven't kept up with current music trends, you may think I've made this up, but one line in a hit tune was "My sexy shiny ass is from another dimension." I know I take things too literally, but I couldn't help but wonder exactly what dimension that was. I told Linda we should listen to Heart anytime things got dull and take note of the lyrics we heard. She rolled her eyes but dutifully took a few notes in her trusty notebook. On our way to Eastbourne, for example, we heard some doozies, but the song that took the cake was pure throwback to the disco days, with the endlessly repeated chorus line, "I'm horny, really horny. Horny, horny, horny." I am not lying.

We'd abandoned the radio by the time we arrived at the foot of Beachy Head and savoured the silence and sun as we ascended the trail going up the hill with the dog. Here was a spectacular place with green grass, blue skies, giant chestnut trees and happy hikers of all ages. My leg muscles got a good stretch and the dog could run free again until we arrived at the summit, which immediately dropped off 531 feet into the sea. Beachy Head has a great chalk cliff and, for my money, rivals the White Cliffs of Dover, even though I don't think anyone has written a lyric about it. Or I could be wrong. Perhaps there is a tune on Heart whereby a late night partier croons, "I woke up the next day with a Beachy head."

Having walked a good mile or two on a fairly steep grade, we felt slightly miffed at the top to discover there was a road that ascended the hill from another direction. Here were cars, tour buses, throngs of people wearing identification badges, a gift shop and tea room. Despite the fact that the hiking had been good, I felt somewhat cheated. I thought that the view from the top of Beachy Head was the reward for the labour of hiking up here. So, in my mind, those others had not earned it as they'd merely driven or were driven here. As Linda and I discussed this, with Kelty curled at our feet beneath a wooden bench, we began to feel smug and ultimately concluded we were better than all those people who had driven here. And that was that.

But then, of course, Beachy Head has been on the traveller's radar for many years. More than 35,000 people visit the cliffs each year. Not all of them are happy campers. It is a favourite suicide destination, sadly, with at least 20 deaths annually, although it can't rival the Sea of Trees "suicide forest" at the base of Mount Fuji, where hundreds of Japanese attempt suicide every year.

I was a bit shocked when I came across a reference to Eastbourne as "God's waiting room" but discovered it wasn't a reference to the suicides but to the age of so many of the city's citizens. According to the ever-insightful BBC, "The Meads district of Eastbourne has the oldest average age in England and Wales, the Office for National Statistics (ONS) said. The average age in the district is 71.1 years compared to the national average of 39.7 years."

On a lighter note, scenes from Harry Potter films take place atop Beachy Head with its exquisite backdrop. Karl Marx and Friedrich Engels both took a fancy to Eastbourne when they weren't pondering the fate of the masses. Engels even ordered that his ashes be scattered from Beachy Head after his demise. Lewis Carroll visited Eastbourne so many times during his life that the townsfolk put up a plaque about it on Lushington Road. Prime Minister Theresa May was born here and possibly got her first notion of distancing England politically from the rest of Europe by staring at the smudge of France across the water.

We hiked back down Beachy Head past a group of young men carrying out some sort of military exercise. They wore uniforms and carried what looked like extremely heavy packs. There was a considerable amount of yelling and falling to the ground going on but no guns were present. They were either some kind of official military cadet organization or role-playing pretend-terrorists, we weren't sure. But as we approached them with our dog barking, they stopped what they were doing and smiled benignly. A young man with a tattoo on his shaved head that said simply "hammer" told us we had a cute dog and the one who appeared to be the leader of the terrorist cell (or cadet cadre) said, "Have a nice day." That's something it takes a while to get used to when you are in England — just how polite everyone is, even the paramilitary types.

If you like Beachy Head, and how could you not, you'd also like the Seven Sisters. *Who are the Seven Sisters?* you might ask. Well, they're a series of chalk cliffs near Seaford just up the coast from Beachy Head. Sometimes they act as stand-ins for the Dover cliffs in movies — presumably when the Dover Whites have other contractual obligations. They are quite gorgeous, all seven of the sisters and, apparently, an eighth is coming into its own as a result of continued erosion.

When we reached the end of the road near these chalk cliffs, we parked by an ice cream truck in a field at the bottom of the hill and walked up an easy slope to the south. The grass was closely cropped by sheep that rambled about and the ground was littered with (what else?) pieces of chalk. I picked up some of the white rocks and studied them, wondering if this was the same chalk my teachers used on the slate blackboard back in elementary school. Of course, it was not. That chalk was made from gypsum, which is softer and less likely to scratch up Miss Smith's old blackboard. The chalk beneath our feet here was hardened calcium carbonate created underwater by the compression of seashells and other creature casings, and it was what made the sisters so white.

On the chalky plains near here once lived the Beaker people. Around 2000 BC, they arrived from mainland Europe and were later named for the unique drinking vessels from which they sipped their beer and mead. They made tools and artifacts of copper, gold and flint and buried their dead tied up into a fetal position. They had flocks of sheep and domesticated plants and eventually blended in with the other people living on this coast.

As we walked toward the top of one of the sisters, children were running about, with their parents urging them not to fall off the cliff. None of the sisters is as high as Beachy, but from the top of one of them along the South Downs Way, the rest looked stunningly bright and beautiful. These shores were known as the Sussex Heritage Coast and the whole of this coastal area was part of the South Downs National Park. Many homeowners hereabouts must curse the authorities for what they can do and can't do on their property thanks to this designation. But I for one am thankful for the preservation of this Edenic part of the world. If the English are good at anything, it's preserving things. And some things are certainly worth preserving.

Alfriston, just inland from nearby Seaford, is a great example of a well-preserved little village, but it was jammed with cars and weekend tourists having tea in outdoor sun-shaded tables so we didn't stop to give it a proper look-see. Linda had spied something called "The Long Man of Wilmington" on our map, however, and used her trusty Navigon to guide us there down some impossibly narrow roads with thorny blackberry vines reaching out from both sides threatening to scratch up the paint on our Fiat.

The Long Man of Wilmington is a massive chalk outline of human form on a green hill. He's holding onto two long poles. According to the Sussex Historical Society he is the "mysterious guardian of the South Downs, who has baffled archaeologists and historians for hundreds of years." The society goes on to say, "Many Sussex people are convinced that he is prehistoric; others believe that he is the work of an artistic monk from the nearby Priory between the 11th and 15th centuries." During the Second World War, the chalk was painted green to prevent German pilots from using it as a landmark. According to the Reverend A.A. Evans, "The Giant keeps his secret and from his hillside flings out a per-petual challenge." I'm not exactly sure what that challenge is, but he was said to be inspiration for ancient pagan rituals involving dancing and singing. Locals were more than a little peeved at national media when the *Undress the Nation* TV series portrayed the Long Man as a Long Woman for reasons that eluded both Wilmingtonians and visiting Canadians.

The Long Man of Wilmington was kind enough to lend his name and image to the Long Man of Wilmington Pub, not far from where he stands, and also to the Long Man Brewery in Litlington, which offers up Old Man Old Ale, declared as the "World's Best Dark Mild Beer" at the 2017 World Beer Awards. I myself haven't tasted all of the other entrants, but I have to say Old Man Old Ale is a mighty fine brew.

CHAPTER FIVE

OH, THOSE POLITE CANADIANS

Since there was a certain random element to our travels, I got it in my head that we should go to towns small or large that had funny names. To a North American, so many British towns sounded idiosyncratic, and this corner of England had its share of beauties. Just inland from Eastbourne and Bexhill were Lower Dicker and Upper Dicker, and I wondered if the universal nature of prejudice influenced citizens of Upper to look down upon Lower and vice versa. Reading in the local newspaper about a petty theft in Upper D., a Lower D. reader would undoubtedly grunt over his morning tea and toast and then say to his wife that he was not at all surprised, given the lowly nature of those idiots in his neighbouring town.

Horsebridge, Cowbeech and Ripe were nearby as were Chiddingly, East Hoathly, Muddles Green and Three Cups Corner. I realized there were just too many odd and interesting towns nearby to visit so I settled on driving us to Wartling, Hooe and Catsfield for starters. In Wartling I noticed a classic-looking pub called the Lamb Inn. I thought of taking us back there the next day but was shocked when I read a reviewer on Tripadvisor who wrote, "I was served soggy fishcakes, frozen peas & frozen chips. They had put lots of salt on the chips without asking. The puddings were horrible. My mother's crumble had no juice & resembled a flapjack!" However, not far from the Lamb Inn was a place of interest to me, one of those many abandoned air bases from the Second World War where uniformed men in brick bunkers once guided British fighter pilots toward incoming German bombers. It is also said that the vigilant soldiers at RAF Wartling were responsible for detecting and laying waste to 380 V-1 rockets. So we drove back that way the next day to see what remained of it, which turned out to be very little.

As we cruised along the A259, I noticed that someone had artfully enhanced the roadside signage pointing to Hooe by putting eyebrows over the two Os and adding a mouth below to create a rather charming smiley face. Like the road cone situated on the head of the statue of Lord Wellington in downtown Glasgow, this seemed to be one of those artistic acts of vandalism that was left intact, causing even seasoned travellers to smile a bit at the joke. Hooe simply means "ridge" in old Saxon and, as with so many truly interesting town names, if you sort out the origins, the meaning is often fairly dull — things like "place where you can walk across the stream" or "the bridge where horses pass over." When we arrived in downtown Hooe, there was roadwork underway and we followed the detour signs out of town a fair distance, one after the next, until there were no more signs and we were thoroughly lost. We finally returned to civilization at a place called Ninfield — meaning "nine and three quarter fields." A display of iron stocks, the kind you put prisoners in, gave the town an unfriendly feel. I later learned that the legendary Spike Milligan wrote a skit for *The Goon Show* about sixteenth-century Ninfield residents who were haunted by a plague that caused the seats of their trousers to catch fire.

The day had turned drizzly, but we soldiered on, me having promised Linda at least one castle that day, and I had spotted Herstmonceux on the map. Here was a finely preserved castle and home to classes for Canadian university students from Dalhousie (my school) and Queen's University whereby young people could spend a semester taking courses in England and bunk in a real castle. As we drove down an unpopulated back road and farther down a long and well-maintained driveway, I wondered where all those homesick Canadian students would go on a Friday night if they wanted to party. I believe it would have been the poorly reviewed Lamb Inn back in Wartling, where I trust the ale was at least better than the crumble.

I immediately liked the gatekeeper at Herstmonceux. He was about my age and looked lonely and wanted to talk. There were classes in session, he said, so we could only walk around in the gardens, which was fine by me. The entrance fee was only £5 and there was even a seniors' discount — unlike at the National Trust, which denies any age privileges whatsoever. I told him we were Canadians and he waxed on about how polite the Canadian students were to the point that I felt proud. Then he added, "Not like some of the young louts around here." He wished us a fine day and we drove onto the grounds through the drizzle.

Walking around the beautiful estate of Herstmonceux with Linda and Kelty, I imagined myself coming over here for a semester to teach creative writing but knew it would never happen. My thoughts drifted to larger subjects and settled on what stereotypes people travelling abroad have about people of different nationalities. For me, Americans were arrogant and opinionated (but not all of them, of course). The British were tidy, orderly, prompt and opinionated. The French were snobbish, sometimes arrogant, opinionated but fun loving. And we Canadians, in the eyes of the gatekeeper and others, well, we were polite. A little dull, but polite. I ask you, which of the above would you most want visiting your neck of the woods?

The castle itself dates back to the fifteenth century. In

the garden was a larger than life-size stone bust of John Flamsteed, an eighteenth-century astronomer who had discovered Uranus (no jokes, please, Canadian undergraduates), although he mistakenly thought it was a star, not a planet. He was big on comets and solar eclipses, among other things, and spent a goodly part of his scientific career predicting them. His stone likeness was here because he helped found the Greenwich Observatory, which was also on the grounds of the estate.

Kelty enjoyed himself immensely trotting around the well-trimmed lawn, peeing on bench legs and sniffing exotic flowers. Sensing that we were not giving our dog enough attention on this trip and realizing the book was to be called ... well, you know ... the next place I chose to drive to upon leaving lovely Herstmonceux was the village of Catsfield. "We're driving our dog to Catsfield," I said out loud for no particular reason.

I had planned for the day to be more literary, with forays to the nearby homes of Henry James, Virginia Woolf and Rudyard Kipling. Kipling's home in Burwash, called Bateman's, sounded interesting, and we could have even taken a peek at his Rolls-Royce. James's home was called Lamb House. (Do I see a theme emerging? Places we would or should not go to: anything with the word Lamb in it.) It was all the way back to Rye and we'd already been there, done that. Virginia Woolf's home, Monk's House, was in Rodmell, and it was here she had entertained contemporaries like T.S. Eliot and E.M. Forster and also written some of her most famous novels. I had never quite warmed up to *Mrs. Dalloway* or *To the Lighthouse* in graduate school and still sometimes fret if I see my female creative writing students carrying around copies of books by suicidal authors like Woolf or Sylvia Plath. I was tempted, however, to trek west to Rodmell to the place

on the River Ouse where Woolf had drowned herself —
purely out of curiosity, mind you, since I really like rivers —
but it seemed just too far out of our way and a bit morbid.
So it seemed I was failing at yet another of my goals on this
journey — that is, making as many literary connections as
humanly possible.

So, instead, we drove the dog to Catsfield. The town
coat of arms had illustrations of six birds of some sort on it,
possibly birds killed by the village's namesake cat hundreds
of years ago. I saw geese and a few ducks and the image of
a cat on the sign for the Catsfield Inn. There was an image
of a lion-like cat at the Catsfield Cricket Club and a cuddly
tail-curling cat on the sign for the Catsfield Primary School,
whose motto was "Achieve Excellence — Inspire Dreams."

But neither Kelty, Linda nor I spied one live cat roaming
about. Such had been this fool's errand. I pulled off into a
church parking lot and studied the map as we ate some leftover chicken, crackers with hummus, baby carrots and cherry
tomatoes from Spain. There were Pucklechurch, Netherfield,
Four Throws, Flimwell, Peasmarsh and Sissinghurst all beckoning me. But it had been a day of too much driving and not
enough inspiration. I decreed that Bodiam Castle would be
our last stop. It was Linda's idea and she promised it was a
ruin, not a walk-through-the-drawing-room type castle. She
knew I preferred ruins to buildings that were still intact. So,
we drove a dozen or so squiggly B class roads until we arrived
at Bodiam. Unfortunately, it was a National Trust Property so
I emptied my wallet to get us in. I walked only the perimeter
of the moat around the castle, since dogs were not allowed
inside. "Inside" seemed like a funny term, since it was a
ruin that had no roof. But Kelty and I enjoyed looking at the
giant carp in the moat and watching young mothers trying
to prevent their children from falling in and drowning there.

I sat down on a bench and read in Bodiam's promotional literature that the castle was once owned by a Lord Curzon. The National Trust said, "Join us for a light-hearted debate between Lord Curzon (aka actor Geoff Hutchinson) and a group of local suffragists. Hear the arguments for and against the case for women's vote and join in yourself if you feel so moved." Apparently, the man who once owned this grand medieval palace had been a most vocal opponent of women's rights right down to the end of the debate, and perhaps that explains why there is no roof left on his castle.

As Kelty sniffed at the base of a chestnut tree and I pondered the fate of lords who denounced equality, Linda waved down from the top of a fourteenth-century turret and I waved back. I read more about who owned this castle over the centuries and noted that the moat was there for a reason: to keep enemies away. Warfare had taken place here over many centuries and there had been winners and losers; that was my sixth grade synopsis of the lengthy description of territorial squabbling and violent overthrows, along with general and nearly continuous warfare, in this corner of the world.

In Linda's final notebook entry of the day, she added, "Back to Tesco for more fish and beer and finally, I had a big run — lots of traffic!"

CHAPTER SIX

IN SEARCH OF THE CANTIACI, CHAUCER, A CASTLE AND A CATHEDRAL (APRIL, 2016)

In a few days we would relinquish our tenancy on Little House and find a motorway to our next destination on the far side of England. I reminisced about a trip Linda and I had taken a few years back to many of the neighbourhoods in nearby Kent that we would not see on this pilgrimage. As I was then doing some research for an article for *Celtic Life International*, it was that region's Celtic connection that prompted me to explore this "Garden of England."

I hadn't given Kent much thought as being Celtic, but it turns out that back in the so-called Iron Ages, a loosely knit Celtic tribe known as the Cantiaci or the Cantii called this corner of Southeast England their home. Their lives were rudely interrupted by the Romans in 43 AD and things were never quite the same after that. Thus it was that on a mild April day my wife Linda and I (without the dog) found ourselves driving the M20 away from London to a green and generous land well suited for some good hiking, cultural exploration, literary inspiration and authentic British ale. As we arrived at our destination, a tiny village named Stelling Minnis, I envisioned the Cantiaci of ancient times living a good life in such a paradise, where this fertile land could certainly provide all you ever needed for quiet rural existence.

Mistletoe Cottage was located down a narrow, single-track road through horse pastures and horse chestnut trees. It was smaller than expected but inviting in every other way. It seemed that every plant on the premises had decided to bloom that week, so that made up for the cramped quarters. It was somewhat chilly that first night and the primary source of warmth in the place seemed to be a heated towel rack in the bathroom, although the place had the most effective on-command propane hot water heater I'd ever seen. It was perhaps the first time in the UK I'd ever taken a shower without it ending in a cold drizzle.

Canterbury was just 20 minutes away and we soon made our first foray into that legendary city. I had read the full *Canterbury Tales* in the original Middle English in graduate school and found the author, Geoffrey Chaucer, most entertaining, mischievous and insightful. The stories in the work were told by fictitious pilgrims on their way to Canterbury in the fourteenth century. So ours was a pilgrimage to ascertain what those pilgrims were seeking.

Somewhere along the way I discovered that Geoffrey Chaucer himself probably never once set foot in the town. On our drive into the city, however, I noted that a housing development, a regional hospital and a skateboard park bore his name in his honour. And, in my reading of the tales during an academic year burdened with tedious British texts obsessed with manner and custom, I had much appreciated Chaucer's wit, his wacky characters and his emphasis on love, sex and general good cheer. So I was pleased to see him properly immortalized.

And so why exactly were those good folk on their way to Canterbury in those days of old? Well, Saint Augustine came here in 597 to bring Christianity to England. In 1170, the highly revered Thomas à Becket was murdered here after a conflict with the Crown over the rights of the church. According to EyeWitness to History, "A sword's crushing blow extinguished the life of Thomas Becket, Archbishop of Canterbury, on a cold December evening as he struggled on the steps of his altar. The brutal event sent a tremor through Medieval Europe." And so, years later, the pilgrims began arriving for spiritual renewal.

About 44,000 people live in Canterbury today, but upon our arrival the old part of town was mostly overburdened with tourists as it was a weekend. So we cantered away in our Ford Fiesta rental car and decided to visit the cathedral later that week. I chose the verb "canter" because the locals had once upon a time used the phrase "Canterbury trot" to describe the way the pilgrims would ride upon their horses as they headed to town. This phrase was later shortened to "canter" and horsey people still use it to this day.

Far from the madding crowds the next day, we sought out the backest of back roads exploring tiny villages like Stouting Common, Whatsole Street and West Brabourne on our way to Wye. Along the way we stumbled upon a hiking trail above Hastingleigh Downs and found ourselves at a look-off where the sign modestly boasted that it was "Possibly the Best View in Kent." Below us was the England of my dreams, and for the most part the view would have been much the same as viewed from here in the eighteenth century. Hills, farms, stone houses, tiny villages, endless trees and rolling hills. The only anomaly seemed to be an array of gleaming white buildings that looked like a space station on the westerly horizon. They seemed alarmingly out of place and we determined to find out what it was later that week.

Wye was one of those little rural English towns that make you want to abandon North America and settle here into a quiet tranquil life of porridge breakfasts, morning tea, crossword puzzles, crustless sandwich lunches, afternoon tea with scones and an early evening pruning of your prize roses. Alas, I would not survive a day of it. But such thoughts do run through my mind. Linda and I made a familiar tour of a church graveyard. The older gravestones had been "polished by time" and the names and dates were worn off by the years. I surmised that the towering chestnut trees in full blossom were not as old as most of the souls planted in the soil here. I like old graveyards immensely and grieve slightly that I'll eventually be interred in a country so (technically) young as 150 years.

On another fine day, we made a beeline for the Channel coast to hike the trails above the cliffs of Dover. My father sometimes played cassette tapes with wartime music and I remember listening to Vera Lynn sing,

> There'll be bluebirds over
> The white cliffs of Dover
> Tomorrow
> Just you wait and see
>
> I'll never forget the people I met
> Braving those angry skies
> I remember well as the shadows fell
> The light of hope in their eyes.

He'd planted images in my head of Allied bomber pilots, their planes riddled with bullets and their engines smoking, struggling to keep their planes aloft over the English Channel. They were praying out loud that the next second those stark white and oh-so-hopeful cliffs would appear in sight.

I've never been disappointed by any form of coastal hiking in the UK, and the Dover cliffs were as good as it gets. (We skipped both the castle and the town — probably my doing.) The views were magnificent, although it was not clear enough to see the French shore. Once you're past the parking lot and the gift shop, the grassy fields and trails are more or less untainted despite the thousands who visit here each year. The wind was high and the hikers were mostly elderly, with walking sticks that made them look like skiers without skis. We all had runny noses and reddish cheeks from the cold, salty breeze, which made it easy for us to look like locals rather than tourists from abroad.

I don't know exactly how we got somewhat lost, but we did as there were several different levels for walking. I asked some directions from another pair of hikers who turned out to be German, and they sent us in the perfectly wrong direction. It could have been they misunderstood my question, but nonetheless it added an extra couple of kilometres to our jaunt so I reckon it was good for our health.

After we finally found our way back to our car, we headed to the seaside town of Deal, but it reminded us too much of those British coastal towns like Bridlington and Brighton where inland city dwellers flock in the summer to stake out territory on crowded pebbly beaches before turning their skin beet-red in the sun. Sandwich was a fair bit more quaint and interesting. And, yes, it really is the place of origin of the ubiquitous word we use today for anything involving two slices of bread. Thanks go to John Montagu, fourth Earl of Sandwich. We wandered around the shops and twisty streets until we were lost yet again. Truth is, getting lost somewhere is usually the most fun to be had in many situations. We ended up on a path beside a small river or canal (I couldn't decide which). My wife doesn't like me to ask for directions from anyone. Her belief seems to be that we should be able to find our way with our own wits. And hadn't the Germans sent us hoofing on the wrong path? But my legs were giving out, so I asked for help from one of those know-it-all old British coots who must have been dragging himself home from an afternoon at the pub.

He looked me up and down as if he thought I was a terrorist or at least a Russian spy. "Where are you trying to go?" he asked.

I explained we were trying to get to the car park near the quay. Although I had pronounced quay as "kay." His response was that the word was "key" not "kay" and that we were walking in the wrong direction. Then he added, "You couldn't possibly be further away from your destination." This made it sound like I was a buffoon and hopelessly lost. He pointed in three possible directions we could take to the "key" as Linda elbowed me, so I thanked him and we just kept walking in the direction we had been going in only to discover the car park was a mere eight-minute walk away.

My wife has a device on her cell phone that tells you how many steps you've walked in a day, what the total distance is and how high up or down you've gone. By the time we'd finished with Dover and Sandwich, we had logged many thousands of steps, ten and a half kilometres and gone up (and down) 30 storeys. We slept soundly back at Mistletoe Cottage that night and woke to sunlight and singing birds the next morning, something straight out of a Romantic poet's sonnet.

Our landlady had given us free tickets to Leeds Castle so I decided to drive the back roads there rather than the M20. This, however, took us first through Ashford, where my wife purposely conspired to lead us to the Ashford Designer Outlet shopping centre. This turned out to be that very strange and otherworldly set of buildings I'd spotted from the look-off over the Downs. It is a somewhat hideous North American-style collection of, well, outlet stores for every brand name of fashion or gobbledegook you've ever heard of. Ashford is probably the poster-child city for why someone would NOT want to go to England.

However, we were here and we made the rounds. The place was mobbed with what I assumed to be British families whose dream it was to live in places like Teaneck, New Jersey, or Columbus, Ohio. The Gap was doing a brisk business as was Tommy Huffinger or whatever his name is. People were almost frantically grabbing for goods. I checked the price tags of various items while my wife inspected some rather torturous-looking shoes. As far as I could tell, the sales game worked this way: first print a price tag with a sum three times what the item is worth. Then take a marker and mark it down not once but twice until the "sale" price (40 to 50 per cent off) is only 10 to 20 per cent more than what the item could possibly be worth. And then wait for the hordes to descend and purchase.

The *London Daily Express* states that England has been invaded 73 times since 1066. Many of those invasions took place here in Kent. Clearly, the Outlet Store Invasion was the most recent. We had a not-so-bad lunch at a Chinese restaurant and I drove as fast as the back roads would allow on toward Shadoxhurst, Woodchurch, past the South of England Rare Breeds Centre and on to bucolic Tenterden, known for its steam railway. I should note that it also made national news in August 2013 when it announced that it was the first town in the UK that year to put up its Christmas lights.

There was a crisis underway in the car park and I walked right into it as I went to get my ticket at the pay station. Two gentlemen were cursing the machine and a woman was wringing her hands. It appeared that the machine was not working. I wondered how I could help.

The most elderly of us suggested it was "bloody awful" and that we should all just leave angry notes on our windscreens about the faulty machine and the blight of politicians. But no one seemed to have a pen. No one but me, that is. I am a writer, after all, and dread the times when inspiration will burst upon my cranium like a solar flare and I find myself with no writing instrument. Now I'd saved the day. We all wrote our notes, although mine had no political commentary. And that was bloody that.

I don't remember much else about the town except for a very lovely church called St Mildred's. Saint Mildred, in case you didn't know, was an eighth-century abbess from Kent whose remains ended up in Canterbury.

Then it was on to Leeds Castle, which was once the home of Catherine of Aragon, the first wife, later divorced, of Henry VIII in the sixteenth century. The grounds were exquisite and the castle was opulent, a reminder of what people might do if they have a prodigious amount of wealth and unlimited manpower. The two things I found most interesting, however, were the maze and the dog collar museum.

The maze was a series of high hedges. The man outside said it would take us 20 minutes. After 20 minutes of taking all the wrong paths, however, we were no closer to finding our way out. I had mistakenly thought we could leave the way we came in, but I couldn't locate our entrance. Finally, I asked some visiting Belgian students if they could help us and they led us to a small Disney-like cave underground that was the key to freedom.

And, yes, there really was a dog collar museum on the property at Leeds Castle. It had never occurred to me that nearly everything under the sun, even dog collars, probably has a museum somewhere on the planet. Suffice it to say, the collars were fascinating and bizarre, all of them far more elaborate and complex than the one we use on our little Westie at home.

On our final outing, we headed to the coast to the north, the wide mouth of the Thames. We hit Herne Bay and Whitstable, both a bit too Brighton-like for our liking, and then retreated south for our final pilgrimage to Canterbury on a sunny afternoon. There were Belgian and French students milling about as we entered the cathedral and lit a candle to our much-loved deceased parents. Whatever your religion, a cathedral invokes a feeling of spiritual depth, and this one certainly did the job.

It was built between 1070 and 1180 and more construction happened from 1379 to 1503. Obviously, it was an intergenerational project. An earlier version of the cathedral was "burned and rebuilt" on a number of occasions. There are tombs inside with the remains of Henry IV and someone known as the Black Prince (possibly a Harry Potter character?). The Germans used the cathedral for target practice several times in the Second World War. The bombing of historically significant buildings later became known as the Baedeker Bombings. It would appear that, at more than one point in the war, both sides started bombing monuments, as well as historical and sacred buildings. How that can help win any war is beyond my scope of understanding. But then so is much of history.

Search as I did, I couldn't find a significant remnant of Cantiaci culture in rural or urban Kent. These people who had this wonderful patch of earth to themselves for so many ancient years were invaded, conquered and beaten, but eventually melded into the ethnic fabric of Kent and mostly lost to the proverbial mists of time. But I'm fairly certain I could feel the spirit of these ancient ones, as I shared the vision looking out over the Downs and sitting in pews above the stone floor of Canterbury Cathedral.

And since Chaucer had drawn us here, perhaps he should have the final say (translated to modern English). As a surfer,

I've quoted him many times: "Time and tide wait for no man." I'm sure you've heard that before as well. But he also wrote, "Women desire six things: they want their husbands to be brave, wise, rich, generous, obedient to wife, and lively in bed." Listen up, gents, it's the wisdom of the ages.

CHAPTER SEVEN

ENGLAND AND CANADA –
SOME RANDOM OBSERVATIONS

So here we were in 2018 back in Southeast England again and this time the whole family was here: Linda, Kelty and me. Linda was out for a final run through the bustling streets of Bexhill and I found myself contemplating a number of pressing issues on my curious mind. I was sitting by the window with the dog curled up at my feet and for some reason I found myself wanting to compare current-day England with Canada, and Nova Scotia in particular. So much of our heritage is shared in common, but in other ways, small and large, we are worlds as well as an ocean apart.

The month was June and it was still cold and clammy back in Nova Scotia, where winter gives up grudgingly each spring with last-minute snowstorms and endlessly damp, windy, cold days. Here in Bexhill, however, the weather was balmy, everything was as green as a Wordsworth poem and it was hard to find a plant of any sort that was not in blossom. Question my loyalty to Nova Scotia and my patriotism if you must, but I'd take June in the south of England over June in Nova Scotia most any year.

But weather isn't everything. Just to be fair, let's talk about central heating. Back in Nova Scotia, I could always kindle a good blaze in the woodstove or throw a bag of pellets in the pellet stove and make the house toasty any time I wanted. Here in the UK I've braved more than a few frosty winters and spring mornings trying to coax warmth out of a wimpy electric heater designed much like a hot water bottle made out of metal and screwed onto the wall. It provides little heat and barely has the means to warm your hands. But I suppose the most discouraging of wintertime accommodations here was a converted cowshed we stayed in once that was exceptionally chilly by North American standards. It did have one of those shiny electric towel racks, however. You could wash your socks in the sink and hang them to dry there, but it was not up to the task of driving the cold from the house.

On the other hand, Brits are smarter than us when it comes to hot water. Our last rental home here had on-demand hot water. It heated water only when you wanted it and, finally after decades if not centuries of cold showers, they got it right. Back home we waste money and vast amounts of energy heating the water and keeping it hot whether we use it or not. Time to take a hint and wise up.

But let's get even more serious for a minute. England, one of the most densely populated countries on the planet, has performed the magical task of preserving its magnificent rural countryside. It's nothing short of a miracle. There are large tracts of farmland, green and lovely, well-preserved forests that are not harvested for anything, grazing fields aplenty and endless footpaths to allow hikers to enjoy all the splendour.

This is certainly a sharp contrast to Nova Scotia, where we have allowed big pulp companies to ravage our once healthy Acadian forests, clear-cutting untold hectares of woodlands and destroying our natural heritage. Provincial governments for decades have allowed the pulp companies to call the shots, devise their own "environmental" regulations and reap for profit the forests that we should be protecting for our grandchildren.

Shame on us.

But now, return to Kent with me for a brief hiatus from all that plundering and look at the vista I once found on the hiking trail called the North Downs Way. From a grassy country hilltop you can look out over hundreds of hectares of fields, forests and farms, perhaps as much as 20 kilometres hence, and the view is almost exactly the same as it would have been during Jonathan Swift's day back in the eighteenth century. God bless the tree huggers and rural enthusiasts who conjured that.

Perhaps even more interesting is that sign above Hastingleigh Downs that modestly proclaims it a beautiful spot. It was the word "possibly" that caught my attention. No point in boasting or pontificating, no need to stir up opinions or debates. It's just "possibly" the best.

In North America, and even in Nova Scotia, announcements are made endlessly that something — some place, some product, some person or some thing — is "the best" or some other form of superlative. Nova Scotians are more modest than the rest, but I've still seen signage in our province bragging about "The Best Pizza in New Glasgow" or "The Highest Tides in the World." I mean, maybe they technically are the highest, but let's follow the Brits on this and just put up a sign saying "Possibly the Highest Tides in the World." It would sound so much less boastful.

And those hiking trails I mentioned — those footpaths — are everywhere, intersecting each other and taking you through kissing gates across private property, eyeball to eyeball with sheep and cows and allowing you to ponder the endless green magnificent land. Just take an internet peek at the South West Coastal Path that rounds Devon and Cornwall. It's an incredibly long (a whopping 1014 kilometres) and exciting hiking trail, and any guidebook will tell you where the pubs are located along its peripheral path for needed rest and refreshment.

Enough about footpaths, you might say. But what about roads? What about those bloody English narrow country roadways, not much wider than the hallway leading to your bathroom back home?

True, we in North America, for the most part, have better roads, almost all of them wide enough for a car to pass each way without having to wheel your Nissan into a muddy ditch off to the side to let the other vehicle pass.

I've smacked off a couple of side mirrors, I admit, driving in Britain and Ireland. But no pain no gain, or something like that. However, I've improved my backing-up skills immensely, driving in reverse for at least a kilometre on occasion in order to allow an elderly gent in an aging Lancia to pass. And there is an art to the gentle negotiation that occurs on those rural single-track back roads of places with names like East Hoathly, Witherenden Hill, West Grimstead and Nackington. I'm half convinced that if properly applied to differences between nations, these subtle diplomatic skills of give and take could one day lead to world peace.

And being here abroad has given me some leisure to ponder what was not long ago touted back home as Canada's 150th birthday. We were prompted by our government to believe that 150 years is somehow significant as a record of how old Canada is. By British standards, 150 years is a mere blink of an eye. I think there are dry cleaners here that have been around for at least 150 years. I'm not sure we should even mention to anyone from Europe that Canada is now over 150 years old. I'm just not sure it matters all that much. We're just way too young a country to advertise our age.

I wouldn't want to set off a debate as to how old England is, but suffice it to say that the Romans left this part of England where I sit in the year 410. The Celts had the place to themselves again until overrun and diminished by what Bill Bryson refers to as a "slow pagan onslaught."

On the other hand, in Canada, and particularly in Nova Scotia, we didn't need to worry so much about invaders, since we were the ones who invaded the land, wreaking hell and havoc on the Mi'kmaq who had lived here for thousands of years.

This, of course, reminds me that Halifax, with its less than diplomatic governor, Edward Cornwallis, was founded in 1749, a respectably "old" year, I admit. I too considered that "historical" until I found myself eating lunch one sunny day at a country pub in Cornwall that had served its first meal in 1348. It did have a true antiquated feel to it and was pleasantly comfortable at that, even though the washroom was an outside privy, also apparently dating back to the fourteenth century. The best part of that was having to shoo goats and chickens out of the way to make it to the loo.

When I see plumbers' trucks in Halifax festooned with the message "In business since 1987," I am again reminded of what a young country we really are compared to England, where you can read beer can labels suggesting the company has been brewing ales since the Dark Ages.

As a writer, I've observed that roads and institutions in the UK are often named after famous poets. Over in Canterbury, of course, Chaucer was one of the most famous of them all. Not only does he have streets named after him but a hospital as well.

Once again, Canada could take a lesson. Does Montreal yet have a Leonard Cohen Street? And shouldn't Nova Scotia perhaps have a Lesley Choyce Memorial Hospital?

Politically, I guess, the Brits are as mixed up as we are back home. What with Brexit and all. There's a good chance Scotland could leave the UK after this snub of the continent. Rumblings of Quebec separation have been with us in Canada for many years. Maritime Union and the idea of forming our own country has never fully died off, since most Nova Scotians were opposed to Confederation to begin with.

Yet Britons drive on what we think is the wrong side of the road. And they have different names for things. Potato chips are called crisps, a stove is a hob, a car trunk is a boot and a windshield a windscreen. These are minor differences. They don't obfuscate a washroom in any manner at all but simply refer to it as the toilet. This is, after all, the homeland of our mother tongue and they have every right to use words as they see fit.

I think the class system is still a problem here. The aristocracy, as far as I can tell, still has certain unfair advantages, although they can't really afford anymore to live in those big houses, so they charge money to people like me to see how the other half lives. I think new money is probably more a problem here than old, mimicking North American ways for profiting from the rest of us.

I may be myopic, but I don't see much classism among the Bluenose folk. Even if you are a multi-millionaire in Nova Scotia, you need to stay humble and connected to us, the great unwashed, if you want to get on without your neighbours thinking poorly of you.

So, yes, Canada is a relatively new kid on the block on the world stage and I rather like many of our youthful ways as we accept a multitude of refugees and embrace a broad ethnic mix.

But as I prepared to leave Bexhill and drive the three of us on toward Bradford-on-Avon and Bath, I was reminded of the lessons that England and its history has taught me so far:

1. We are all descended from immigrants;
2. Don't forget the past;
3. Small is better than big;
4. Green (space) is better than gold (profit);
5. Don't jump the queue; and
6. Mind the gap.

CHAPTER EIGHT

"FRESH CHERRIES NEXT LAYBY"

The original plan was to follow the coastline more or less — head north from here, skirt along the North Sea and then west, following Hadrian's Wall to the Irish Sea, then south and east again to the Eurotunnel. But housing availability where pets were allowed prompted us to change our itinerary. And we'd already spent considerable time in places like Cornwall, Kent, Yorkshire and Scotland. I knew we'd never see all of England, but by the time our month-long excursion with Kelty was over, we'd have covered more cumulative territory than most English citizens did in a lifetime.

And so it was that, upon Linda's return from her morning run dodging the commuters of Bexhill, it was time to zig across England to our next home in Bradford-on-Avon, not far from Bath. Kelty was restless and whined from the back seat as we passed a sign outside Whatlington that read, "Fresh Cherries Next Layby." I liked the sound of that so I stopped at the next layby and indeed the ripe dark cherries were fresh and delicious. It was like summer singing on my tongue.

As we drove north eating cherries, there was another song on Heart radio where the female singer informed us, "I'm horny all night long." In the brief news that followed, it was reported that parliamentarians were debating a new law against "upskirting" whereby convicted perpetrators would receive a two-year prison sentence. Neither one of us knew what upskirting was so Linda looked it up on her phone using up precious and expensive data time. Apparently, it is when someone, presumably a horny pervert of some sort, uses a phone or camera device to take photographs up a woman's skirt. This led me to realize that, despite coming a long way in their social evolution, the British were still a little funny about some things when it came to sex.

Later on our journey, the BBC reported that one parliamentarian in the House of Commons was vocal in his opposition to the law. It wasn't that Christchurch MP Christopher Chope was exactly in favour of the new voyeuristic fad of upskirting, but he was trying to uphold some other democratic principle — one that he failed to explain clearly.

It was a long drive north through Royal Tunbridge Wells ("a large affluent town in western Kent") and past Sevenoaks ("a popular tourist area with lots of things to do"), then connecting to the heavy traffic lanes of the M26, part of the massive ring road around London. There was far too much driving and considerable BBC discussion of the upskirting issue but also the sad news that Stephen Hawking was to be interred on this day in Westminster Cathedral. I had thought he had wanted his remains shot up into space. News about his death was followed by news about birth, as it was recently determined by researchers that the majority of spontaneous births in England occurred at 4:00 a.m.

I found that to be an interesting detail. Even though I've never given birth, I do find that I wake up (spontaneously) quite often right at 4:00 a.m. And I remembered spiritual author Wayne Dyer once stating in an audiobook that 4:00 a.m. is when you should wake up to meditate, while yet another spiritually minded individual told me that it was precisely at 4:00 a.m. that I should communicate with angels if I believed in them. If you are open-minded about angels, you should definitely give them a shout. My point is that 4:00 a.m. is, for some strange reason, a very important time for us humans and we should pay more attention to whatever happens then.

After the M26 merged with the M25, we made a nostalgic stop at the Clacket Lane service plaza, for it was here that on a previous trip we had reversed directions illegally, having passed our intended turn on the M3 toward Southampton and the Isle of Wight by about 50 miles. We had flown overnight to Heathrow and I was yet again jet-lagged and bleary-eyed. At this very service plaza we had our first-ever argument on British soil. Linda had been reading the map and I had been driving so the blame lay clearly on her side of the car. However, the heated discussion that followed quickly reminded me that in most marital arguments being right does not necessarily win the argument or gain you any bonus points. In fact, in such situations, it's actually best not to attempt victory at all, but to just let things go or admit you are wrong even if you are not.

Today, however, we were in good form — on the right road headed in the right direction and just taking a break to buy a coffee and walk the dog. Walking the dog in so many service areas in England, I got to know a lot about litter. A close reading of expendable items in the far reaches of the parking lot revealed a plethora of candy bar wrappers, McDonald's coffee cups, plastic forks and knives, discarded butane cigarette lighters, plastic cup lids, plastic straws, gum wrappers, shiny crisp bags and cigarette butts. I even found a crumpled-up metal "No Littering" sign warning of a possible £100 fine. American comic writer David Sedaris claims that UK litter is the "worst in the world," but I haven't travelled enough to know and, in general, I think of most Brits as being tidy, sometimes even too tidy. However, a mere year before our trip, when Environment Minister Thérèse Coffey announced new, higher fines, she had especially harsh words for drivers who littered, saying, "Throwing rubbish from a vehicle is just as unacceptable as dropping it in the street and we will tackle this antisocial behaviour by hitting litter louts in the pocket."

Inside the service area hub was much like a shopping centre, with a McDonald's, WHSmith and Costa establishments. In order to get to the washroom, you are strategically directed through the eating and shopping area in hopes that you get distracted enough on your foray for a pee to buy a Big Mac, a pre-made cheese sandwich or several extra-large cans of Foster's. I actually find these service plazas nowadays to be rather cheerful and friendly — even dog-friendly for the most part. Roadchef runs the place, and though I do recall their coffee and food to have been quite hateful at one time, now it's as if someone has fired all the old school employees who ran the business and hired some young smart alecs who came along with the radical idea of actually giving people a half decent cup of coffee and the option to buy a vegetarian rice bowl if they were so inclined. Three cheers for Roadchef.

Well, what else is there to report about the drive onward toward Leatherhead, Downside, Byfleet and Addleston and beyond? There was considerable traffic and several slow-downs, the kind where, when the slowdown is over, it appears that there was no observable reason for it at all — just a whole hell of a lot of cars and people slipping from lane to lane greedily trying to get ahead of one another.

We took a turn onto a road that we hoped would steer us away from the even heavier traffic near Heathrow, but it led to even more traffic tie-ups due to construction and several dozen roundabouts, one after the next, placed strategically in our way to give me white knuckles and a bad feeling in the pit of my stomach. Eventually, the blessed M4 presented itself and we fled west, leaving Slough, Maidenhead and Little Marlow thankfully behind.

It seemed like we veritably blasted our way past Swindon until we turned south toward Chippenham, then west on some minor road to Box and ultimately to our townhouse rental named "Lilac Cottage" in Bradford-on-Avon. I saw no lilacs, and it was a row house not a cottage, but it was clean and comfortable and immediately felt like home. Kelty, I soon observed, felt the same way. He immediately jumped up onto the sofa, tucked his tail, curled up in a ball and fell asleep. We would break many of the rules printed out for us at our rental houses, I confess, especially the one reading, "No pets allowed on the furniture." Wasn't it Pablo Picasso who said, "Learn the rules like a pro, so you can break them like an artist?"

Lo and behold, we remembered it was Father's Day as we settled in. This earned me a much-deserved roast dinner late that afternoon at the Castle Inn ("A Flatcapper Freehouse") just next door. We could sit outside with our dog and watch well-mannered Bradford children running and falling on the grass and scuffing up their Sunday clothes. The Castle Inn boasted "proper pub food" and, as I cut up my Yorkshire pudding into edible parcels, I asked Linda why the word "proper" seemed to crop up so much in this country. She thought it had something to do with respect for authority — more so in England than in, say, America. But I thought the word was a bit of a cop-out. What is proper to me is not necessarily proper to you, etc. She advised me to change the subject and I did, although throughout our journey I kept track of pubs and restaurants that use the word "proper" in their promotions, as well as phrases like "an honest meal" or "honest real food" to complement the "real ale" on tap. I kept hoping to actually see a really tacky modern-style bar or pub proclaiming it had fake beer on tap and "dishonest" or "improper" food. But such an establishment never presented itself to us on our travels.

CHAPTER NINE

A MAGPIE AT MORNING
ON A BATH DAY

In the morning, a magpie fell down the chimney and into the coal fireplace of our little dwelling while Linda ran up and down the hill that led into the downtown. Kelty and I were sitting quietly in the little living room at the time. The dog was asleep and I was reading up on the history of the city of Bath.

I had heard some strange noises coming from the roof and it must have been two magpies fighting over who had the right to be perched on the chimney cap. The magpie who lost the battle was the one who apparently had fallen down the chimney, and it was his good luck that it was a warm day and there was no coal fire to singe his feathers. It took me a split second to make sense of this odd event, but my first instinct was to grab the dog so he didn't attack the bird. Kelty seemed more baffled than me and was stunned enough to allow me to drag him into the kitchen and close the door.

The magpie, for his part, looked around and then flew to the window and started bashing at it frantically with his wings. This near automatic move led me to believe he'd fallen down this chimney before, and I wondered how many citizens of Bradford-on-Avon had their breakfast or lunch interrupted by a big bird like this dropping into their home. Back in Canada, I'd seen birds accidentally fly into the windows of our house and the occasional sparrow find its way into the airport or the shopping mall, but we rarely had large birds coming down the chimney like a winged Santa Claus.

In fact, we don't have magpies in the part of Canada where I live. We have crows, of course, and I even had a pet raven that I trained to fly after an injury. But magpies were a novelty. And now I had one up close. I thought I'd better grab the big-beaked bird before he injured himself against the glass, so I got a good grip on him with two hands — firm but gentle. He flapped and pecked at me and had a look that was both arrogant and guilty at the same time. All I could compare it to was the look on Donald Trump's face when he was caught in one of his many public lies.

I rather wanted to hang onto the magpie and see if he would calm down and let us be friends but, having spent considerable time around wild creatures winged and otherwise, I knew that first on the magpie's personal agenda was to get the hell out of the house and back up into the sky or at least back up on the roof. So I gingerly walked to the door, holding him to my chest with one hand while I opened the front door with the other.

With a dramatic flair, I used both hands to launch him up into the bright morning West Wiltshire sky and he rocketed toward the clouds. I watched until he was gone from sight and then turned left to see that one of my new neighbours, a middle-aged woman in a housecoat, had been watching. I would have tipped my hat to her, a flat cap that is, if I'd had one, but I had none, so I gave her a small wave and my best Canadian smile and retreated back into Lilac Cottage, where the dog still seemed somewhat stunned at the morning's events.

I couldn't help but wonder what my Bradford neighbour thought about seeing me and the magpie. Either it was a common event around here — big birds falling down your chimney and having to usher them back to the sky — or it was a rarity. If the latter, I could picture her returning to her husband sitting perhaps at the kitchen table with his cup of Earl Grey and saying to him, "Edward, I just saw a man, a foreigner I believe, walk out his front door and throw a large magpie up into the air. What do you suppose that was about?" Edward would put down his newspaper and clear his throat and say something like, "We don't really want to know, do we, love?" and leave it at that.

Back inside, Kelty curled up on the chair with me as if nothing had happened, and I wondered if it was a good or bad omen if a magpie drops down your chimney into your living room. I looked around for a bird book to discover what I might about magpies and quickly learned that seeing a lone magpie is decidedly bad luck. If I can believe the bird-loving folks at the British Bird Lovers organization, "In most parts of the UK people will salute a single magpie and say 'Good morning Mr. Magpie. How is your lady wife today?' By acknowledging the magpie in this way you are showing him proper respect in the hope that he will not pass bad fortune on to you. By referring to the magpie's wife you are also implying that there are two magpies, which bring joy rather than sorrow according to the popular rhyme." So I guess I blew it. Since the magpie failed to query me about the health of my own wife, who was out jogging about the hilly town, I didn't think to inquire about the health of his spouse if he had one. And how, indeed, was I to know if this was even a male or female magpie?

The more I read about magpie lore, the worse it got. That damn sole magpie was associated with death, witchcraft and any manner of impending doom. Things I could have done to offset the malevolence included "doffing my hat" had, I worn one, spitting on the ground three times or flapping my wings like a bird. What would my neighbour have thought of me if I had done any of those deeds? Or maybe she would have understood. I decided to ignore what I had just learned about superstitions, but then I also read that magpies would raid nests if they were hungry and eat eggs or even baby birds.

The British Bird Lovers also warned, "They have also been known to kill small pets such as guinea pigs." Thank God that my magpie didn't take a fancy to our small white dog. Yes — that might have been difficult to explain to Linda upon her return. And how, I wondered, did those British Bird Lovers still find it in their avian-loving hearts to maintain fond feelings for pet-ravishing creatures like this? And exactly who were the careless pet owners who allowed their guinea pigs to fall victim to magpies, unless the magpie suddenly flew down the chimney one morning while their little rodent was running around the living room? These questions would go unanswered like so many other mysteries that the English countryside had in store for me. But I did my best to console myself that the bird's appearance was not a dark omen cautioning me about our upcoming foray into Bath, where we would possibly confront mobs of elbowing tourists and hordes of contriving trinket salesmen.

After that I took Kelty for a walk in the nearby churchyard, where I studied the gravestones and the words written on them. On one small monument there was this statement: "In death there is life and in life there is death." Certainly, this was a quote by somebody, but I never could track down the source and the message seemed more negative than positive. In the morning mist of the graveyard, it set me troubling over yet another dark message.

I noticed that there were soldiers who had died in both world wars buried here. One soldier who was buried in 1940 "died defending England." Another from 1914 died from "wounds suffered in France." Yet another "died bravely for the cause of freedom." There also seemed to be a large number who had died in childhood. An infant of 2 was "asleep in the arms of Jesus." One double tombstone recorded the husband had lived from 1895 to 1935, but the only date given for his wife was her birth in 1898, making me wonder if she were perhaps still alive or possibly remarried and dead and not wanting to be interred with husband number one. The graveyard had a number of tilting and toppled stones and was not at all well maintained, but then there were no recent burials at all. I reckoned that, after a certain amount of time, the living get a bit weary of mowing the grass above the dead and righting the stones that have toppled. But at least here in England, many, many old graveyards still remain.

Back in New Jersey, where I was born, old graveyards often get turned over to the municipality, which then sells the property to a Walmart or a Lowes for a big box store that might generate some revenue from taxes. This is what happened to the cemetery where my ancestors from Leicestershire were buried in Hunterdon County, New Jersey. Some distant relatives of mine back there sent me a letter saying that the town was going to lease the land to Kmart for a new store and a parking lot. The letter stated that I should send money for a legal battle, but I knew that legal battle would most certainly be lost. I felt guilty, however, for not doing so but ended up writing out a cheque to Doctors Without Borders and mailing it off to assuage my guilt, believing it's always better to help the living rather than the dead. And thus, I am sure, my ancestors were most certainly paved over and I expect there is a shopping cart corral precisely where my great-great-great-great-grand-father James Choyce was buried.

By the time Kelty and I returned from communing with the dead, Linda had finished her run and I told her of the bird event. She had found a dog sitter for the day on the internet and soon, Laura, with her boyfriend Tom, arrived promptly at 9:00 a.m. They were a nice young couple who had good references and would walk Kelty around town here while Linda and I took in Bath, a city that was high on her list of places to see. Tom, curiously enough, had gone to a folk music conference in Prince Edward Island, back near our home in Nova Scotia. There he had met Lennie Gallant, a well-known folk singer from the Island. Lennie had written a song recorded by none other than Jimmy Buffett and had brought Jimmy out to my house once so I could take him surfing. Jimmy and I surfed and then we had a little party at my old farmhouse and he slept in the back bedroom. In the morning, he left quite early and, gathering up his board and wetsuit from the yard, he made his getaway, taking my own wetsuit boots with him.

It seemed incredible that Jimmy Buffett had stolen my wetsuit boots, and perhaps it was accidental, but they were my favourite wetsuit boots and now they were gone. To commemorate my loss, I wrote a song called "Jimmy Buffett Stole My Wetsuit Boots" and hoped to make a lot of money from its success (or at least recoup my losses and buy a new pair of neoprene booties) but, as of this writing, I've been unable to convince Garth Brooks, Keith Urban or Rascal Flatts to purchase the song rights.

I'd probably do a poor job trying to capture the history of a city like Bath in a book like this but, just for the record, the town is rightly named: the pesky, ambitious Romans built the famous spa and temple here around 60 AD. Before that, the property of the hot, healing waters was known by the Anglo-Saxons who called the place *Acemannesceastre,* which means something like "aching men's city." Presumably, after a hard day in the Anglo-Saxon world you could go to the spring for a good soak and all would be well.

The traffic in Bath proved particularly challenging and I accidentally drove past two car parks without finding their entrance. Passing the Hospital for Rheumatic Diseases, I was fairly certain we were headed out of town, so I doubled back as best I could and found a metered parking spot not far from some lively activity at Kingsmead Square. I had several pound coins left over from previous trips and dutifully put them in the meter that would issue the little ticket for our windscreen, but it rejected my coins. I had a flashback to the previous encounter with a faulty parking machine in Tenterden where locals sharing my frustration cursed quietly but intently about city councils and parking enforcement.

Fortunately, Linda now spotted a parking enforcer with a bright yellow and orange safety vest. We explained our dilemma and he examined my coins only to tell me those coins had gone out of circulation quite a few years ago. They wouldn't work in the new defiantly digital meters. He was a hefty young man with five earrings in one ear and none in the other and I couldn't help but wonder what that signified. It turned out he had compassion for our plight and said this was his territory so we should just leave our car and he wouldn't issue a fine. I think Linda kissed him on the cheek, which seemed to be a tad overdoing it for this act of kindness, but at least we could get on with our exploration of this ancient city.

Some sort of fair or market was happening at Kingsmead Square and, even though it was still morning, it seemed like the party was in full swing. There was a plethora of ethnic food — the culinary salvation of the British Isles — and we partook of samosas and pad Thai for an early lunch. A bowls tournament was underway and the crowds were cheering their favourite bowlers. I was not familiar with the game and it seemed quite odd indeed. The "bowl" or ball the player uses is not quite spherical and he or she aims at a smaller ball known as a jack. The game dates far back to the thirteenth century and has a checkered career, at various points having been banned by Edward III, Henry VIII and Richard II. I think it had something to do with soldiers rolling their bowls rather than practising archery. But today the activity appeared to be all about fun and games, shouting encouragement to your favourite bowler and drinking plentiful pints of beer.

Bath was, as expected, a touristy city full of gaggles of visitors of various nationalities following raincoated guides holding up little flags. There were street performers about in legion and I was really impressed by one electric guitar player with a battery-powered amp playing some gob-smacking good echo delay riffs à la Mark Knopfler. Several generic folksingers performed Bob Dylan and Neil Young tunes and an accomplished cello player played classical music to a large audience just outside Bath Abbey.

We were headed to (where else?) the Roman Baths, and I was persuaded to stand with my wife in the long lineup outside. I paid £14.50 for a seniors' ticket and Linda a whopping £16.50 for the privilege of entering. Once inside, we queued up with the masses, were given our audio guides and set loose to wander amidst the throngs of humanity who had come here to see where long ago Romans did their washing up. Linda was a bit squeamish about the idea of actually bathing with other people in the same water, but I reminded her this was long ago and it seemed like the thing to do at the time. I still couldn't quite get my head around how those invaders from the Italian peninsula made their way to England and why they stayed. One more place to conquer, I suppose, but they not only conquered but brought their customs, including bathing habits, with them. Sure, an outdoor bath in Amalfi might make sense, but in England in winter? Wouldn't it seem more sensible to heat some water at home and have your servants or slaves pour it into your own personal marble tub?

According to *The Guardian*, the hot water comes up to the surface through the delightful-sounding Pennyquick Fault. And it was here, "in 863 BC legend says the exiled Prince Bladud took a hot mud bath with his pigs and found himself cured of leprosy." Mud baths with pigs indeed. Oh, those quirky ancient ones.

Certainly, the whole place was impressive, if a bit confounding. And oddly enough, along with the usual BBC-sounding narrator on the audio guide, it turned out that none other than Bill Bryson had added his own commentary. Given the fact that Mr. Bryson had denied my request for an interview, this rubbed me the wrong way. Maybe, in fact, he lived hereabouts and had some personal affinity to these Roman baths. I was irked, though, that he'd lend his words and wisdom to this ancient bathhouse but had succinctly and quite sourly refused help to a fellow author writing a dog book about his own beloved England. Still feeling the sting of that slap in the face, I concluded Bill Bryson must be a sad and bitter man. That petty thought comforted me enormously. I vowed, however, that should he ever turn to me for assistance in a literary project, I would be gracious and kind and help out. Polite, considerate Canadian that I am.

Like me, *The Guardian* was a bit miffed with Bryson's snarky audio additions to the tour. Although its writers had glowing reports about the mineral water, they were "less impressed" by some of Bill Bryson's commentary on the audio guide. Standing before a stone mask of a woman, Bryson comments, "This is the face of Minerva. I've never really liked the look of Roman women." Well, hey, Bill, maybe the Roman women wouldn't have thought much of you, either.

I couldn't help but think there must have been a dark side to whatever shenanigans went on in these Roman baths. There were, after all, naked men and women and slaves who served them. I suppose we were expected to be impressed with the architecture and not dwell on such things. Aside from that, the Bath baths were unique, if a bit Disneyfied for my blood.

It was raining when we emerged from the bathhouse and walked over to the Abbey, where more than 8,000 bodies were buried over the years under the stone floor. I couldn't help but think about the mingling of all those many bones and the logistics of so many centuries of indoor burial. I learned that the windows of the great abbey had been bombed out in the Second World War. This was a reminder of the wholesale destruction the Nazis visited upon this small island. I guess most of us don't need a reminder of those horrors, except for neo-Nazis perhaps, who somehow think we'd all be better off if Hitler had been allowed to rule the world. So, of course, he had to be stopped and all sides proceeded to bomb the hell out of one another, laying waste to churches, homes, pubs — well, everything really. There were strikes, reprisals and then more strikes and reprisals. And so it goes, as Kurt Vonnegut Jr. would say.

Back outside, Linda shopped while I stood on the sidewalk and proved myself to be an annoyance to women walking by with large umbrellas. One lady shopper nearly put my eye out and instead of apologizing said, "Well, you were just standing there, weren't you? Why didn't you move and get out of the way?" So I moved myself off to the wall in front of the Marks & Spencer and leaned there beside someone with an empty coffee cup begging for change.

The few coins in his cup reminded me of my own defunct coins, and when Linda emerged from a scarf shop, I guided her through a maze of umbrellas toward a branch of Lloyd's of London. At the wicket, I explained to the teller I was hoping to cash in some old pounds for new ones and she asked me to put all my change on the counter, where she picked out the outdated pound coins and proceeded to give me new shiny ones that would work in present-day coin-operated machines. It was my first-ever transaction with Lloyd's of London and, while it was a small one (I wasn't, after all, trying to collect insurance money for a sunken oil tanker), I found it a pleasant and rewarding experience.

Not far from the bank, I noticed a sign that read "Jane Austen's House." I hadn't known that Ms. Austen had spent time here, but then I'd spent a good share of my academic career avoiding writers like Jane Austen and the Brontë sisters. Having missed several literary homes already, we should probably have toured the house, but a colleague of mine, a scholar of Jane Austen back at the English Department, had said it was too commercial and crass so we didn't bother.

Bath, however, has a strong literary past that would have been worth exploring if I'd felt inclined to give it more time. Jane Austen lived here from 1801 to 1806. She had been inspired by the town and it was described in glowing words in *Northanger Abbey* and *Persuasion*. This, I suppose, for a Jane Austen fan, would be like getting a dazzling review on Tripadvisor. I did later peek into the online shop to discover we missed out on a chance to buy *Pride and Prejudice* throw pillows, a Jane Austen tea strainer, a *Persuasion* mug and a "Blue Rose Cake Slice and Knife Set."

Jane's aunt was arrested while staying with her in Bath and accused of shoplifting. I don't know what we should make of that except that sense and sensibility did not always rule in the Austen clan. And it made me ever so curious to learn what items were most often shoplifted from the JAH gift shop. But there's only so much research a writer can do on a single-term sabbatical.

Mary Shelley had parked her creative self here in Bath as well to work on *Frankenstein,* but it was a troubled time for her with her sister Claire pregnant with a baby fathered by Lord Byron and several people in her sphere of friends committing suicide. Charles Dickens spent some time here as a young reporter and after, finding some inspiration to satirize the social norms of Bath citizens in *The Pickwick Papers,* but later in life, he maintained a grudge against Bath for some bad reviews that appeared concerning a play he was involved with. Nonetheless, he too inspired a plaque in his honour at 35 St James's Square, where he had once lodged.

The plaque reads simply,

HERE DWELT
CHARLES DICKENS
1840

We wandered some more about town, checking out the buskers and watching an ironsmith hammer away at a red-hot piece of metal that he was presumably shaping into a sword. Next we returned to Kingsmead Square to buy some Indian food to take home for supper. Linda was beginning to convince me that food trucks were the way to go for really tasty grub.

After that we left town in search of Solsbury Hill near Batheaston. I had always had a high respect for the song

"Solsbury Hill" by Peter Gabriel wherein he described some kind of epiphanic experience while standing atop this ancient mound. There was something about the structure of the song, the lyric, the unusual time signature and the authentic spiritual nature of the tune that resonated with me. So I wanted us to hike to the top of this hill (which was indeed Solsbury, not Salisbury as so many people thought) and see if we had any great revelations.

After several wrong turns down country lanes, a narrow, potholed road — yet another on our quest — led us to a dead end high up in a sheep field above Batheaston. The drizzle had stopped as we parked the car precariously near a rock wall and hiked up among the sheep to the top of the hill where there was a solitary concrete monument with a commanding view. Beneath the grey roof of the sky we could see all the way back to Bath and the spire of the abbey that housed those 8,000 dead souls.

As we explored the hill beneath an ominous dark cloud, we realized there were cows about, as well as sheep, which seemed curious to me as I thought they were usually kept separate. You had to keep a sharp eye on where you stepped here, probably much like the ancient people who once tended animals on these slopes. It was a wild and windy place this day and, like Peter Gabriel, I waited for some kind of message telling me to change jobs or become a pilgrim or a Hare Krishna supplicant. But time was running out. We were due back in Bradford-on-Avon to retrieve our dog and settle in for the night.

Bradford had grown on us as we walked around town in our short stay. The Avon River, the same one that flowed through Stratford-on-Avon farther upstream, was picturesque and the shops were friendly. The town had an old honest feel to it, as if to say, "We really are just an old market town and like to keep it that way. We're not here just for the tourists and hope you like us, but we're not going to do anything special to impress you." My own research indicated that this was probably not a bad place to live, but the only famous person of interest to me that I could locate was Jesus Jones, who had once had a hit with the song "Right Here, Right Now."

However, it turned out that Jesus Jones was a band, not a person, and I'm not sure how Bradford-on-Avon might have inspired them. Their heyday seems to have been the late 1980s and 1990s as they fused electronic and techno with other elements of indie rock. They must have made a pile of money because the "Right Here, Right Now" song ended up on TV commercials for TechTV, Toyota and in Canada for Molson beer (which is why it probably stuck in my head) and even as a theme song for Joe Clark's successful bid to become leader of the Progressive Conservatives in 1998. I would guess all that might tarnish a band if they wanted the label "alternative" to stick, but I'm sure the money was welcome. And if that commercial success was not enough, Alvin and the Chipmunks recorded a mock version in 2017.

Seriously, though, Bradford-on-Avon mostly prides itself as a good old market town with a Saxon church dating back to the eleventh century and a semi-famous downtown café called the Dog House that is also a pet store and pet grooming establishment. The chapel by the town bridge once served to incarcerate drunkards and non-criminal low-lifes for the night to keep the town quiet.

The mornings at Lilac Cottage were noisy, with big trucks taking the turns too fast in front of the pub, but across the street the soldiers slept on peacefully through the grey light in their unattended graves.

CHAPTER TEN

THREE CHEERS FOR CHEDDAR

South of Bristol and Bath is the amazing Cheddar Gorge in the Mendip Hills. We'd hiked the circuit — both sides of the gorge, with trips to the bottom of the canyon on both ends — twice before but never with the dog. Linda had a special fondness for this hike and for the town of Cheddar — yes the very place famous for its cheese.

Driving there on the back roads from Bradford-on-Avon we got lost. I was navigating by way of quick glances at the AA map book and attempting to follow road signs from one village to the next. I had learned in Ireland that hooligans occasionally steal or redirect signage just to send tourists like us off in wrong directions. Somewhere around Gurney Slade a sign was missing and we ended up going south to Binegar and West Horrington and ultimately Dinder instead of farther west to Cheddar. Admitting my defeat, I turned navigation over to Linda and the Navigon, but my wrong turns meant we had to suffer the traffic of Wells and were forced to drive past the hoopla of the Wookey Hole with its Edwardian fairground, old-style amusement games and maze of mirrors before we could find our way to the gorge.

According to my *Lonely Planet* guidebook, "Cheddar Gorge cuts a mile-long swathe through the landscape, exposing great sections of 138 metre-high grey stone cliff." We had first walked it one frosty morning in December 2011 with blades of grass enclosed in jackets of ice. It started out cloudy, but while we were atop the southerly ridge the winter sun blasted through the clouds and lit up the plains beneath us with a spectacular view of the perfectly round man-made Cheddar Reservoir. We slept that night in a rented cottage in nearby Drayton without central heating and the north wind blew so cold and hard against the house that we were forced to huddle before a wood fire where we burned every possible scrap of firewood we could lay our hands on, eventually sleeping on the floor before it with a pile of blankets from all three bedrooms of the house.

After we left, the landlord emailed Linda to ask if, in fact, we had slept in all three of those bedrooms the night of our stay, hinting that we'd had some kind of wild party or something even more bizarre in his imagination.

But Cheddar turned out to be not far off our beaten path on this our third trip to Southwest England, and so we had the privilege this time of walking Kelty up and down the steep trails of the gorgeous Mendip rift. The road that cuts through the centre of the gorge is itself quite breathtaking, so if the hike seems a bit much, the drive is still worthwhile. It follows the ancient path of travellers, pilgrims, peddlers and soldiers, probably dating back to the Bronze Age or before.

We parked in downtown Cheddar and wrestled with the parking meter for an appropriate amount of time and then walked east past pastry shops, ice cream parlours and gem and fossil stores until we found the path going up. As you begin the path, you are almost instantly transported into another world, first a steep trail beneath massive oak trees that shut out the sky and then into open fields of sheep and cows, passing through kissing gates and dodging the spikey bull thistles of the kind that once warned Scottish soldiers of the invading English.

We passed dozens of cheerful hikers as we kept Kelty leashed and well back from the dangerous cliff edges where teenage boys cavorted and kicked stones onto unaware hikers below. It was an altogether invigorating if familiar hike.

Britain's oldest preserved human skeleton was found in a cave in the gorge and determined to be 9,000 years old and promptly, unimaginatively, named Cheddar Man. The TV show *Seven Natural Wonders* pegged the gorge as the second most wonderful wonder of the country, which helped to boost the tourism traffic to half a million people a year. But we encountered only small clusters of panting hikers on either side of the gorge. Yes, there's cheese to buy if you prefer to linger in town. Be sure to check out the cost of parking first, as it is rather dear and requires at least a master's degree to figure out the digital meters. And if your pockets are feeling weighted down with cash, do pay to visit the caves, home of Cheddar Man and the site of the photo shoot for an album cover by the Troggs. In 1966, the Troggs had a smash hit with their catchy song, "Wild Thing."

Soon the hike was over. We were back on the road for our final night in Bradford before moving on to our next leg — our dogleg — north and east, skirting above the melee of London suburbs and back to the other side of England.

On the way back we detoured to go through Glastonbury, where we had once hiked to the top of the 60-metre high Tor and shopped at the Glastonbury Morrison's on a journey through town. Home to the famous music festival, Glastonbury is also known as a uniquely spiritual place, popular with the New Age crowd (now mostly old age and in their sixties or seventies). Legend suggests King Arthur and Queen Guinevere were buried here, but no one in the Morrison's parking lot could tell me where that might be. I wondered if, in fact, this was also the town where Lady

Guinevere had paraded about naked on horseback. With nothing better to do, I asked this question to a classic old duffer with a flat cap (a flat capper??) returning his shopping cart to retrieve his £1 deposit. He gave me one of those curious British looks that immediately implied I was a nincompoop American tourist but had the courtesy to say he'd not heard of any naked women on horseback riding through town, not in his time anyway, and if such an event had happened, he was sad to have missed it.

Well, it turned out I was a nincompoop on this issue, although a Canuck one, not a Yankee one. My limited education on all things European had led me to mix up Guinevere with Lady Godiva. Ms. Godiva, if she even existed, was Countess of Mercia, the eleventh-century wife of Leofric, Lord of Coventry. She was a compassionate soul who tried to persuade her greedy husband to lower the taxes that were crippling the townsfolk. He refused over and over until he said he would only do so if she rode naked on horseback through town. Which she did — according to legend at least. Townsfolk were asked to stay indoors and not look. Which they did. All except for Tom, and he became known as "Peeping Tom" who looked, after which, legend has it, he was struck blind. Taxes were lowered nonetheless and Lady G gained her place in legend if not in history.

Fantasy authors and movie makers have made much of Guinevere, but not much is really known about her, particularly by old men buying their weekly groceries in Glastonbury or probably anywhere else.

But legends abound in a place like Glastonbury. There is one suggesting that Jesus and Joseph of Arimathea had once visited here and that later Joseph returned with the Holy Grail and it was still hidden somewhere here. I noticed several locations on our travels where there were stories extant of Jesus or other Biblical figures visiting England. I would always wonder how on earth Jesus (or the Holy Grail for that matter) could have found a way to England in those long-gone days.

Logic aside, I could see why stories of Arthur and Jesus and a holy icon were enough reason to stage a yearly rock festival hosting the likes of the Who, Neil Young, Lady Gaga, David Bowie, Johnny Cash, the Pixies, the Rolling Stones and Leonard Cohen.

No further magpies or other avian creatures visited us in Bradford, and in the morning we packed up and bid adieu to the town here on the southerly edge of the Cotswolds that we had called home for a short time. We had a fair bit of driving ahead of us. After a repeat stretch of the M4 we were back into the sluggish congestion of the M25 that would loop us around London again, this time to the north, and set us on our way toward Saffron-Walden just south of Cambridge. Near there was the tiny village of Little Walden, where we had rented "The Little Barn." Along the way, we learned from the BBC that the upskirting bill had been defeated and that the whole Brexit thing was stirring up a real hornet's nest among the population.

We seemed to have selected yet another house that was quite difficult to locate and we ended up on a dead-end road at the gate of what appeared to be some sort of secret research facility with a sign warning all visitors to keep out. I had the feeling that behind those gates were scientists cloning sheep, monkeys, owls or possibly humans. I don't know why.

It just had that sort of feel to it. I rang up the gatekeeper on the speaker phone and asked about our place known as The Little Barn at Burntwood and he said that he had never heard of it, but when I said it was on the property of "The Family Farm," he explained we had passed it on the way and sent us packing. At the converted barn that had once been home to chickens, sheep, horses and possibly pigs, there was a giant willow tree in the driveway and a gaggle of noisy but entertaining geese in the backyard.

Inside was airy, sunlit and comfortable and I studied the titles of the many books on the shelves. You can often tell a lot about the owners of a rental house by studying the DVDs, games and especially the books. Here on the shelves were books about the plague, stomach disorders, epidemics, cancer and ear infections. Some were medical textbooks, I assumed, with titles like *A Short History of Tuberculosis*, *Essential Malariology*, *Handbook of Bacteriology* and *The Syphilis Story*. They sat beside a complete collection of Beatrix Potter books about rabbits, dogs, squirrels and talking chickens.

Later that day, I learned by email that my pregnant daughter Pamela had been suffering from a bad tooth and had been unable to find a dentist or oral surgeon willing to extract it. Her husband was away in Fiji of all places, training Fijian soldiers to build huts. This was not good. I had a sleepless night worrying about her and the twins she was carrying and wondered if we had made a mistake to be so far away when she might be in need of our help.

In the morning, I learned she was soon to get treatment for her tooth. But this was followed by reports of premature contractions. More wringing of hands on my part and concerned emails back and forth. The contractions soon proved to be false labour and we all breathed a small sigh of relief, but still, a father worries.

CHAPTER ELEVEN

KELTY GOES TO CAMBRIDGE

What can I say? I've always been a bit gaga over Cambridge. My father had been stationed near here during the war. One of his jobs was driving truckloads of American soldiers into the pubs at night on narrow roads with no headlights. This, of course, was because of the German air raids. He drove airplane parts and various other freight during the day and had been stationed at several air bases nearby.

On one memorable excursion in 1944 he wrote, "I hauled a part for a B-17 to Land's End.... We stayed in a lodge in the country one nite & had fresh trout for breakfast. Never will forget that trip." And soon after that he added matter-of-factly, "Planes sure are flying every day — bombing Germany." And, as if to add another note of equal significance, two days after that the entry read, "May 12, 1944 — Mother's Day — Sunday — Had the whole day off. Had a good chicken dinner." My father always did like a good chicken dinner on Sunday.

As a graduate student I had dreamed one day of teaching at Cambridge University, but it was, naturally, just a pipe dream — marijuana, probably, not tobacco. But the place had always called to me. A lot of brilliant and important people had lived, studied and worked here. Isaac Newton and Ernest Rutherford come to mind. And here lived Stephen Hawking, so recently deceased, whose famous book *A Brief History of Time* sat unread on my shelf back home. John Milton had written here, as had Bertrand Russell, Charles Darwin and Ludwig Wittgenstein. Cambridge was my kind of place. Oddly enough, a cheeky British website suggests that the most famous person *born* here was Olivia Newton-John. I had always thought she was Australian, but I guess I had been wrong and, given the middle name and the Cambridge connection, perhaps she is the great-great-great-granddaughter of Sir Isaac Newton. Stranger things have happened in history, you know.

We parked not far from Jesus Green in a parking garage and, happy to be on our feet and not in a car, I directed us to the River Cam, where I rented a punt for an hour. I had punted once before and found it difficult. To my surprise, this time round, it was still difficult. As a veteran surfer, I have no trouble paddling a ten-foot surfboard and then standing upright cruising across the face of a six-foot North Atlantic wave. But standing on the stern of a small punt with only my wife and dog on board, I found punting to be at once arduous, clumsy and frustrating. Nonetheless, with my chin up and my knees buckled, I shoved us forward with my pole as we headed to the region behind several of the colleges known as the Backs. Along the way, I discovered that I was particularly good at bumping into stone bridges and getting us tangled in overhanging weeping willow branches. If it hadn't all been so embarrassing, it would have been great fun.

Other wiser, mostly Asian, tourists had hired strapping young university students to pole them along as they sat placidly in their seats listening to the poler relate the history of this storied place. The Asians thought we looked funny, I suppose, because I was fumbling with the process and because we had a small white dog on board looking at me with worry in his face, fearing that we all might soon end up in the dirty river. They smiled, those Asian tourists, laughed, pointed and took photos of us that would, by nightfall, appear on Facebook around the world, no doubt.

We punted a fair distance, nonetheless, down behind St John's and Trinity colleges until I bumped us into the Bridge of Sighs, named not for the famous Venice bridge by that name but for the sighs of students crossing it to take their exams. University students worldwide are known for their pranks and Cambridge undergraduates are no different. It was here that on two occasions students had tied a car to the bridge and dangled it above the water, once in 1928 and again in 1968 as a kind of fortieth anniversary gesture to the original pranksters. The logistics of such a joke leave me speechless, but then this was Cambridge and these lads (and ladies?) were walking in the footsteps of Newton, Darwin and Russell. Maybe even Stephen Hawking had something to do with the second dangling.

I succeeded in getting our punt somewhat stuck sideways beneath that very bridge before coaxing it to the side, where I crashed — at ultra-low speed fortunately — into the wall of the Wren Library with its horde of priceless manuscripts and books. It housed 1,250 medieval documents, autographed poems by John Milton, the original *The Vision of Piers Plowman* and A.A. Milne's manuscript of *Winnie the Pooh*. As I backpaddled and nearly lost my punt pole in the soft muck at the bottom of the Cam, I noticed a small flotilla of empty cider bottles, their caps still on, floating downstream, the remnants, I supposed, of a philosophy club party where contemporary Cambridge students had shared personal accounts of their existential angst while drinking Scrumpy Jack.

The trip back to the boat rental was as difficult as the trip out, and I chalked it up as a "humbling experience." More tourists took our photo as I tried to look like I knew what I was doing. Kelty had settled a bit and obligingly posed for the Chinese families on a rather large punt snapping images with their cell phones. We had obviously distracted the young man controlling their craft and he smashed hard into us as I was approaching the dock. Kelty started barking loudly at the doofus, who deserved a good dressing down. I got a simple "Sorry, mate" from him but wondered if it was intentional.

We were all happy to be back on land as we walked Magdalene Street to Bridge Street and turned right at the Round Church down Trinity past Caius and King's colleges. The streets were much more crowded than I expected and most of the colleges were closed to anyone but students.

Cambridge was, of course, a famous city, centre of international attention, and now it had become a mecca of international tourists. "My" Cambridge and the one my father had known were long gone. If you are looking for Cambridge University hoodies, T-shirts or drinking mugs, however, this is definitely the place to be.

I stared in awe at the architecture, breathed in the same air that brilliant intellectuals, ancient and modern, had breathed, while we looked for a dog-friendly pub to have lunch. We had wandered as far as Silver Street and I took a picture of the Mathematical Bridge. Legend has it that Isaac Newton designed and built the bridge; that has been proven to be untrue like so many legends, but I felt obliged to report it here nonetheless. The original bridge was built in the eighteenth century but by someone else, and it's been rebuilt twice since then, holding to the original design. *Why is it mathematical?* you might well ask. It has something to do with straight lines and tangents, which I am sure could be very interesting if you'd care to look into it. As for me, I just rather like the sound of it and regret that we were not allowed to walk over it, nor had I come this far in my punt to have the opportunity to bump into it.

When it was time for lunch, I consulted my list of dog-friendly pubs but none seemed nearby so we settled again for some Indian food at an outside market square. After that Linda wandered off to shop and I sat in reverie with the pooch, who seemed quite content to hang out with me and drift off into thought despite the hundreds of people walking by. I don't know what was on Kelty's mind, but my thoughts carried me back to graduate school in New York City and the many silly things I had learned there. During a course on the Romantic poets, the lecturer, a man I recall who spoke primarily in multi-syllabic words, told us that Lord Byron somehow had a bear for a pet in his room at Cambridge and he was allowed to keep it since, technically, the college had no rules about keeping bears in rooms.

I wondered at how this might have worked out. I could see why he would want to do it; of course, the likes of Byron and Shelley were always dedicated to pissing off authority, especially when they were young. But I was having my fair share of cleaning up after Kelty in urban settings on this trip. We'd gone through a whole pack of poop bags already — doing the right thing, of course, since no one on the planet has a right to allow their dog to shit on the street and then walk away. But what, then, did George Gordon, the Lord B himself, do when it came to dealing with his bear's business? Maybe this is in part why he was once labelled "mad, bad, and dangerous to know."

My graduate instructor had also revealed that Byron soon preferred dogs to more difficult pets and is best known as the owner of a Newfoundland dog named Boatswain. Boatswain is immortalized in the poem "Epitaph for a Dog." Sadly, Boatswain died of rabies but was remembered by the poet for his "Strength without Insolence," "Courage without Ferocity," and my personal favourite, "Beauty without Vanity." Good dog.

When Linda returned, we headed toward our car, this time on Sidney Street, which in a number of ways contrasted to Trinity Street and the colleges. A Christian of some stripe was standing on a platform holding a Bible aloft. He had a most impressive sound system and a microphone with a helper beside him holding up a placard that said, "Atheism is a Lie." The speaker thumped his Bible and in a loud voice proclaimed, "The only salvation, the only way out of your struggles and your sins is belief in Jesus!" He quoted what seemed to me to be a completely unrelated bit of scripture and added, "Darwin was a liar. Evolution is a lie." It was as if he was debating someone who wasn't really there. Although, I guess if you are going to trash atheism and evolution, what better place than the streets of Cambridge, which are likely rife with atheists and Darwin-lovers.

Most pedestrians made a wide arc around the man, although I was under the impression that this was a common everyday occurrence and I bet that Christian fundamentalists had been right here at this spot preaching their views for hundreds of years. A few in the crowd were listening, the Asians were taking pictures and I found the whole scene fascinating. Then, out of the blue, a young woman who looked like she was a university student walked up to the speaker, who was now sweating profusely, it being a hot day in the middle of an English heat wave. She confronted him, saying, "Who are you to say only your way is right?" Her accent was Spanish by my estimation and I wondered what prompted her to take on a rigid-minded soldier of Christ on this hot, sunny day. To that, he quoted another irrelevant line of scripture and then accused her of being an atheist.

"What if I am an atheist?" she countered, much to the audience's delight.

"Then you need to repent and be saved."

"Saved from what?" she now shouted.

He held the Bible higher and seemed for a split second to be at a loss for words, but then it came to him. "Saved from yourself!" he bellowed.

Most folks had stopped walking at that instant, realizing that some real drama was unfolding here on Sidney Street.

The young woman did not look at all flustered and the anger that had been mounting in her seemed to subside. She took a deep breath, looked the man in the eye and said, "Bullshit." And then she walked away. A few people applauded but most just went back to whatever they had been doing — eating ice cream from a cone, sipping cappuccinos or heading down Sidney Street to buy an official Cambridge teacup.

I had been told that Oliver Cromwell's skull was stored or buried somewhere in Cambridge and I'd been meaning to try to understand just where Ollie C. fit into English history. I had read various articles with titles like "Oliver Cromwell, Hero or Villain?" and found them intriguing. It seemed to me that you could probably be both in the same life and even at the same time, so I determined to keep my ear to the ground when it came to this historical figure. I would later learn that there was quite a collection of famous skulls pocketed away at the university for quasi-scientific purposes around this old scholastic institution.

As if to outdo Cambridge, however (and that often is a mighty task), according to online magazine *Atlas Obscura*,

Jeremy Bentham has been sitting in a corridor at University College London since 1850. The moral philosopher, whose advocacy of animal welfare, prison reform, universal suffrage, and gay rights was far ahead of his time, left a will with specific instructions on the treatment of his corpse. In it, he decreed that his skeleton and mummified head be assembled, clad in a black suit and seated upright on a chair in a wooden cabinet, under a placard reading 'Auto Icon.' He also suggested that his corpse could preside over regular meetings of his utilitarian followers.

Well, we did not have London on our agenda for this trip, but I made a mental note to visit Mr. Bentham the next time I was in the city. Perhaps there would be a sequel: *Around London with a Dog*. And what exactly would Kelty make of the mummified utilitarian philosopher, I wondered.

Walking farther along, I was more than a little shocked to see so many homeless begging people of all shapes and sizes along Sidney Street. I'd seen none on Trinity. Somehow this part of town, a few mere blocks from the prestigious colleges, seemed more real to me, with shops selling great slabs of bacon, used books and wheels of cheese instead of trinkets and selfie-sticks.

Walking up the stairway in our car park, we came upon a 20-something young man with long dreadlocks and a backpack. He politely asked me for change and I ignored him. I've tried to analyze why I do often ignore poor souls begging for money. I purport to be a socially conscious, humanitarian type wanting to do nothing but good for my fellow man. I am aware that they are not homeless and/or begging for spare quid because this is what they want to do. I know they have somehow fallen through the cracks in the system and, above all, they have fallen on hard times. Whether society has dumped on them or if this is from their own doing, it doesn't really matter, does it? If you are down and out, you need people to be kind to you.

And I wasn't. Why? I think because there is something about it that embarrasses me and, like so many others, I'd prefer *not* to make personal contact. Bloody hell on me.

But when we got to the car on the third floor of the car park, Linda asked me if I had any cash. I showed her a handful of coins and she shook her head. "No bills?" I grumbled but held out my wallet. A £20 note and a fiver. She grabbed the £5 note and walked back on her own down the stairway. "Be careful," I admonished, standing there like an idiot by my rental Fiat with Kelty, wanting nothing more than to escape to the bucolic realm of Little Walden. A few minutes slipped by and then she returned. "That could have been my son back there. Or yours," she said, slightly displeased with me for good reason. I didn't have a son, of course, but I got the point. Five pounds lighter and a little bit more embarrassed, I drove us down the dark sloping pavement of the car park and back out onto the sunny streets. I got the point. I was an old skinflint while Linda had taken the higher moral ground. Kelty, wisely, had nothing to add to this little interlude.

What to make of Cambridge? As always, there is a price to pay for being world-famous if you are a movie star or a university town. Once away from the city core, I noticed a lot of trees and open green spaces, like the one called Christ's Pieces where uniformed lads were playing rugby.

John Milton had been a student at nearby Christ's College and walked through that field right here where the young men ran about in short pants and knee-high socks. There were now towering trees here and ornamental flowerbeds and, for some reason, I craved for it to be winter with a real snowstorm so I could walk the dog all alone across the great expanse. Summer looked a little too tame, too pretty, too civilized here in Cambridge, and I vowed to return when the summer visitors were gone, when the weather was more properly miserably English and the students were sneaking off to the steamy pubs to complain about their arrogant, stuffy professors.

CHAPTER TWELVE

HEROES AND/OR VILLAINS

After a brief rest in our converted barn, we drove the few miles south from Little Walden to the larger market town of Saffron Walden. Walden refers to this being a valley of Britons, and the Saffron part was tagged on because the fields around here once produced great quantities of saffron-crocus. Today we think of saffron as a spice that is the product of the stigmas of the crocus flower. A gram of it sells for more than £75 ($126 Canadian), making it more expensive than gold, and since each flower produces only a miniscule amount it would take considerable labour to harvest it.

Yet over a number centuries it was grown here and harvested and used for dying, flavouring, medicines and aphrodisiacs. It faded away during industrialization when it was more profitable to send workers to factories instead of fields, and today most saffron comes from Iran, Morocco and Spain. In recent years, a few farmers around Saffron Walden have been trying to bring saffron crops back into production, and I wish them good luck.

Kelty was much enamoured with Saffron Walden's 14-acre town commons, which was appropriately grand and green. Long ago, the Saxons had communally grazed their cows here and, in essence, the commons belonged to all the landowners hereabouts. Tournaments were also held on the grounds and I wondered if there was jousting involved, a thoroughly ridiculous contest of manliness that made for good scenes in movies about medieval times but wreaked havoc on large numbers of aristocratic families.

I understood these parcels of common land were disappearing in many parts of the world, especially in North America, where they get leased out by municipalities for shopping malls, movie theatres and Ikea stores. Halifax, in Nova Scotia, still has a wide-open commons used for sports, skateboarding and ice skating. Paul McCartney played a concert there, as have the Rolling Stones. Long live the Halifax Common.

I don't know if the Rolling Stones had ever played Saffron Walden Commons, but it was a good place to walk our Westie on this pleasant summer afternoon, with families ambling about and little kids rolling around on the grass. We made our way to the famous landmark I had read about: "the largest turf maze of its type in Europe." I'm not sure exactly what purpose a maze serves. I remembered that Linda and I had once attempted to negotiate a maze of hedges at Leeds Castle and were unable to find our way to the centre or even backtrack and find our way out without those rambunctious but helpful school kids from Belgium. The turf maze was not like the maze at Leeds Castle, where freedom was achieved through an underground cave.

It wasn't like that at all. There was turf and there was a brick path through it — one mile of it to be exact — crammed within a 100-foot diameter. Once upon a time, the path had been chalk. Linda and I both tried separately to find our way to the centre of the maze, with our dog trying to figure out why we were walking around in such odd ways forwards and backwards. Growing ever more frustrated as I hit dead ends and tried to retrace my steps, I kept wondering who had originally constructed this thing and why. I expect there were some who had become locally famous for knowing their way around the maze in years past and it was clear the town was mighty proud of it, but by modern standards it was a little tame and downright frustrating as far as a game or entertainment goes.

But the great thing about a turf maze is that it's easy to cheat and just cut right across the grass and the bricks and walk away from it to the nearby outdoor market, where yet another proud concessioner will sell you delicious ethnic food that you can take home and feast upon. There were also more fresh cherries to be had and, since the market was about to close, we were given two pounds for the price of one.

Saffron Walden had been mainly Puritan in the seventeenth century and the Quakers had flourished here as well. The town seems to also have some claim to fame in the world of cheese, according to one bit of historical information on a brass plaque, but I was too anxious to get home and eat to hang about and study it.

In the middle of the seventeenth century, the town was home to Cromwell's New Model Army as well, and he had slept at the Sun Inn, which we passed on Church Street on our way back to Burntwood.

That evening I looked through all the tourist brochures at our rental house and spied one colourful little item trying to lure visitors to the Oliver Cromwell House in nearby Ely. Apparently, there were quite a few lodgings in this part of England where he had lived or at least slept overnight and that earned a few quid for whoever owned them now. This particular house in Ely was proclaimed to be fun for the whole family although I wasn't convinced that applied to my family.

The brochure had hired a most excellent public relations person to come up with intriguing questions that might make you want to go there and pay admission to answer the following:

1. Why did he order the execution of King Charles?

2. Why was he king in all but name?

3. Why did he ban Christmas? [Well, now this was getting interesting.]

4. Why is he a hero to some, a villain to others? [There it was again.]

These questions and many more are answered in an audio tour of the house. At the end of the tour you can decide.

But there was more. At the Ely house, you would also learn that Mr. Cromwell (hero or villain?) was also a family man. "Hear about Mrs. Cromwell's love of cooking and find out why eel pie was her favourite recipe." And if that didn't make you drop everything and drive to Ely to visit the house, you could also "Dress up in the clothes, play with the toys and write your name in Cromwellian Style."

It seemed that here was fun for the whole family at a historical place that had done a grand job of tidying up a man who had also done a countless number of cruel and heartless things while revolutionizing a nation.

It was only after we had vacated Little Walden altogether that it was brought to my attention that the legendary scoundrel and highwayman Dick Turpin was born here. (Well, he had to be born somewhere, didn't he?)

Dick Turpin was an eighteenth-century criminal who somehow became a Robin Hood–style legend after his death. According to the *Encyclopedia Britannica*, "Son of an alehouse keeper, Turpin was apprenticed to a butcher, but, having been detected at cattle stealing, he joined a notorious gang of deer stealers and smugglers in Essex." He racked up a long list of decidedly cruel and nasty crimes along with his thievery and was eventually hanged for horse stealing in York in April 1739. Oddly enough, there had been a pub named Dick Turpin's in Halifax, Nova Scotia, in the 1980s and '90s. How curious that such a lowlife would be immortalized internationally as a symbol of good cheer and fun. If I recall correctly, the lovable Irish Rovers had even performed there as far back as 1978. Wasn't that a party?

CHAPTER THIRTEEN

DOGGY DAYCARE AND
LUNCH ALONG THE THAMES

Well, it was turning out that the only real problem we were encountering when travelling about the isle of England with a dog was that sometimes we wanted to do a thing or two without the dog. We'd found dog sitters in Bradford-on-Avon and now Linda had tracked down a doggy daycare in Southend-on-Sea where Kelty might cavort for a few hours while we met up with a girl I'd had as a pen pal when I was 12. Rest assured we researched the credentials of K9 Corner, and when we arrived the young woman in charge fell immediately in love with Kelty. Before the day was over, images of Kelty with his new friends were posted globally and it was my hope that his fan base was rising, as it seemed that J.K. Rowling's West Highland White Terrier, Brontë, was getting way too much press coverage these days, with shameless photos on Twitter and gratuitous follow-up by the British tabloids.

K9 Corner was located right next to a Papa John's Pizza in a strip mall, and I wasn't terribly impressed with Southend, which I guess is really somewhat of a suburb of London way out here near the mouth of the Thames on the North Sea. But Kelty was happy and we were away for a few hours to meet up with Kim Olah, whom I had not seen since 1972 when I had temporarily dropped out of university to "find myself" by hitchhiking around Europe.

Kim was the daughter of a woman my father had palled around with when he was stationed at airbases in England during the Second World War. This was before my mother came into the picture as his one and only, I might add. He and Kim's mother, Pat, had kept in touch over the years after the war ended. Pat had even travelled to New Jersey to visit my parents once. She had since died and so had my father, and I can't say that I had done a good job of keeping in touch with Kim. But here we were on our English sojourn, and part of the plan was to connect not just with places but with people, especially one who had a connection to my father's days in England.

We were to meet Kim at the railway station in nearby Leigh-on-Sea, and indeed there she was standing by the roadway, although I would not have recognized her. Many years had slipped between us since we met last. My hair was no longer down to my waist and hers was cropped shorter than mine, but Linda recognized her from her Facebook photo and, as we pulled to a stop, much to the chagrin of a bus driver, she hopped in the car and directed us to a parking lot near the oldest part of this coastal community.

Leigh-on-Sea was a fishing village a thousand or more years ago and fishermen have been harvesting whitebait, cockles, mussels and anything else from these waters ever since. *The Domesday Book* reports there were merely "five smallholders above the water who do not hold land." So, for a long time, it was a fairly marginal place. Today, however, it attracts its fair share of Londoners who choose to live there and commute to the city in the popular little c2c train.

As we walked around the cobbled streets through old fishing shacks and newer tourist shops, Kim pointed out the

Mayflower pub, where her father had somewhat grudgingly taken me for my first pint of British ale back in 1972 when I was but 21 years old. I had more or less shown up on their doorstep after flying in from Reykjavik in January after my flight to Luxembourg on Icelandic Air had been interrupted by a strike. I needed a place to crash and took the train from London to Southend, hoping Kim would persuade her parents to allow me to sleep in their living room.

Her father no doubt saw me for what I was: an American hippie with long hair and bell-bottomed jeans who had just dropped out of university to get up to no good in Europe. Nonetheless, he introduced me to my first pint of bitter and allowed me to sleep on the aforementioned sofa for a couple of nights. After that I caught an early morning flight to Brussels to get on with my plan of hitchhiking south across Europe to Cadiz, Spain. I'd cross to Morocco and then travel by thumb (or camel) across the north shore of Africa to Egypt and beyond. (Well, it seemed like the thing to do at the time.)

The "On-Sea" part of Southend and Leigh was a bit puzzling to me. The wide but mostly shallow river mouth of the Thames hardly seemed like a sea to me at all. Joseph Conrad, who once lived not far from here, observed that "the estuaries of rivers appeal strongly to an adventurous imagination. This appeal is not always a charm." If I get his drift, he suggests the beauty of such places is often in the mind of the beholder. But it was coastal and it was in its own way captivating. We sat down outdoors at the Peterboat Restaurant along the shores and had a magnificent view of the Thames estuary. It was low tide and dozens of boats were sitting on grass and mud. It reminded me of Nova Scotia's own Bay of Fundy, where fishermen's boats sit on the bottom of the bay twice each day, several metres below the dock, awaiting the rising tide before their owners can motor them out into the channel.

I admit that living on the outer ocean as I do — Lawrencetown Beach in Nova Scotia — I'm a bit of a snob when it comes to references to oceans and seas. Was this really the sea or merely the mouth of a river? I reckoned it was the latter but felt constrained to keep my opinions about bodies of water to myself.

Kim was a charming, chatty woman and she and Linda hit it off nicely. I noticed that cockles were on the menu and I remembered them from nursery rhymes my mother had read to me long ago when I was still just a squirmy armful. There were no cockles on any menus in New Jersey where I grew up, and I thought perhaps they were some tasty exotic (in a British nursery rhyme sort of way) seafood. Kim warned me they were not. Later, when I examined the little shelled buggers at a fish market down by the wharves, I agreed. Good thing I passed on the cockle pie or whatever it was on special that day.

So now was my time to pick Kim's brain as to what she remembered about her mother's stories involving my father.

"Were they dating? Like boyfriend and girlfriend?" I asked.

She looked a little puzzled. "I think they were just friends," she said. "They were both interested in swimming and got involved with a project to build a swimming pool." This was when he was stationed near Bedford, north of London, and Kim's mother-to-be Pat was living in the vicinity. It was commonplace during those times for American servicemen to go out with young British women. I'd seen photos of my dad at the time and he looked quite confident and handsome, the young smiling man in uniform who drove other soldiers to the pubs in St Neots and Cambridge. In my mind's eye I can still see him driving at night down those narrow laneways without the use of headlights.

Kim didn't know anything else about this pool business, but I reflected that both Bob Marley and my father, under rather different circumstances, had come to England and helped in the creation of a public swimming facility. I admit, it was the first time in my life that I had ever considered even the most remote connection between George Howard Choyce Jr. (better known as Sonny) and Robert Nesta Marley (better known as Bob Marley). But there it was.

I recalled that Kim's mother was legendary for swimming in the "sea" year round, presumably when the tide was in. Unlike me, she never wore a wetsuit, and I do admire someone who can jump into the incoming waves of the North Sea in winter without an ounce of neoprene on their body. Kim's mother and father had first lived together in the upstairs of an old, old fisherman's house just across the street from where we were dining, and she pointed it out. Kim's father had once built a rope ladder so that Pat and a friend could sneak into the local public seawater swimming pool on cold December days. An ambitious photographer from the local newspaper had taken note and snapped a photo of the two women in bathing suits swimming on one such cold January day, and it was splashed across the town paper for all to see, bringing a certain degree of fame to Kim's mum.

Kim had only recently sent me a military hat that had probably belonged to my father — one of those little caps like old ice cream vendors wore. It had been kicking around at her house and used as part of Halloween costumes on various occasions through the years and she had determined it should recross the Atlantic and reside with me. It was much appreciated.

Kim, like many UK citizens by this point, said she was weary of all the talk about Brexit and there was some brief discussion about how upskirting had so become such a national disgrace, but then it was on to more important issues.

Kim told us she worked at a store called Sally's Out of Curiosity, and every day on the job she had an assortment of the most interesting customers. That is due to the fact, no doubt, that they sell the most fascinating and unusual retro and antique clothing, furniture and all kinds of quirky goods from the near and distant past. If you are interested in purchasing life-size Betty Boop mannequins, stools and tables from old diners, pub paraphernalia, pink and blue wigs, 1950s slot machines or lamps shaped like women's legs, this is definitely the place to go when you are in Southend.

Kim's husband Mick worked as a railway driver on a train that went up and down the famous Southend Pier. If I craned my neck, I could get a good look at it from where we sat on the outdoor shoreside terrace.

According the Royal Geographical Society's Discovering Britain website, "1.3 miles, 2.2 kilometres, 2,158 metres, 7,080 feet — however you measure it, Southend's pleasure pier is the longest in the world. On hot days walking to the end can feel like making a pilgrimage to the sun. No wonder most of the pier's 200,000 annual visitors hop aboard one of the special trains. From this proud symbol of Britain's seaside you can enjoy sweeping views across the Essex Estuary, sample various amusements and send a postcard from the pier's own letterbox."

I could see that it was indeed one heck of a long pier. Because of the shallow water and the persistence of tides going up and down, ships traditionally docked miles from shore and goods were sent by rail car on to the mainland. Mick drove the current day trains for the tourists who wanted to travel the length of the pier without having to hoof it, and he had plenty of stories about the foolishness of passengers.

Picking up one bloke at the sea end of the pier, the gent asked if this was the train to London and would it take him to Pancras Station. Mick also had overheard an evening conversation of a mother to her son whereby the boy asked his mother what the light was on the farther shore across the wide river mouth. The mother told her son, "That's the Eiffel Tower," when in fact it was the lighthouse in Margate.

But Mick's favourite story involved a couple of young men who had been drinking up their quota of bitter one night and, finding late night Southend quite dull for their spirit, were walking out the pier toward the sea. Mick saw their wobbly procession and stopped to ask what was up. "We're walking over there," one of them said, pointing to the lights of Margate, over 30 miles across the water. "We seen those lights," the other one said, "and it looks a bit more lively than back where we just come from."

Mick dutifully explained that the pier would come to an end, another mile or so out, and they would be sorely disappointed, wrecking the fun they were hoping for that evening but at least sending them safely back to the mainland.

We said our goodbyes to Kim after lunch, promised to stay in touch and headed back to pick up our pooch at K9 Corner, with Linda already noticing Facebook postings of Kelty on her phone.

CHAPTER FOURTEEN

STUD HORSES, PACK HORSES AND THE MEAN STREETS OF BURY ST EDMUNDS

Our next major destination was Leicestershire, home of my Choyce ancestors, but while back in Canada, poring over my *AA Concise Atlas of Britain* (AA stands for Automobile Association, not Alcoholics Anonymous in this case), my eyes drifted across a bulging chunk of England that jutted out into the North Sea. This, I discovered, was known as the Fens, and I knew virtually nothing about it. North of Southend and stretching all the way to a bay simply called "The Wash" — 15,500 square miles of low-lying and reclaimed marshland. It is mostly what the citizens out there like to call "low country — good flat arable land." In the heart of this bump of low country is Norfolk.

H.V. Morton in *In Search of England* had this to say about the local inhabitants in 1927:

> Norfolk is the most suspicious county in England. In Devon and Dorset men hit you on the back cordially; in Norfolk they look like they would like to hit you over the head — till they size you up. You see, for centuries the north folk of East Anglia were accustomed to meet stray Vikings on lonely roads who had just waded ashore from the long boats.

Morton gives us an odd impression of the population out that way. It seemed to me that the Vikings had stopped coming ashore long before 1927, but perhaps the wariness pervaded through many generations. I thought we should definitely head out there on our tour and find out.

There, east of Cambridge, were the cities of Colchester and Ipswich, Newmarket, Bury St Edmunds and Norwich, as well as Great Yarmouth and King's Lynn. Early on it was decided we should do at least one overnight somewhere in this neighbourhood, mostly because we knew so little of this side of England.

Somewhere near Merton in Norfolk was "possibly the largest glacial erratic in the UK." The so-called father of modern geology, Charles Lyall, who had also spent a fair bit of time digging around the rocks of Nova Scotia, had visited the Merton Stone on many occasions and written about it in his textbooks. As noted earlier, we had visited the Madison Stone in New Hampshire and found it most entertaining so, as a fan of big unusual rocks, I had this on my list of places to visit. Unfortunately, I would soon discover it was quite difficult to find, sitting in the middle of an untended field and not far from a military artillery range.

On our way east and north from Little Walden, we drove past the zoological gardens of Linton. On their website, they encourage face to face encounters with very big cats. "At Linton Zoo we have African Lions, Amur Tigers and Snow Leopards," the park promises. "Viewing windows in some of the enclosures make it possible to get as close as a whisker." Then it was on to Newmarket, driving past the 500-acre National Stud Farm. I admit I know next to nothing about horse breeding, but when I read that the facility keeps only eight stallions and up to 200 "broodmares," I was a little taken aback. The gender odds seem more than a little imbalanced in these times of equality. The stallions must get a bit weary of it all, do they not? I'm sure there is a society in Britain looking out for their rights and welfare, however. The British Society for the Proper Care and Protection of Stallions, perhaps. Alas, we were headed farther afield and did not make a stop there to inspect on behalf of stallion rights.

Needless to say, nearby Newmarket is an upscale town obsessed with horses. There are at least 3,500 horses in Newmarket at any given time, which means one horse for every six citizens living there. Horse culture rules the town and has for a long time. Three royal palaces have been located here and a lot of money goes in (and out) of horse racing. It is said that 75 per cent of the money won by English-bred horses racing in the UK results from the offspring of stallions in or near the town.

Linda needed to go into a rather busy downtown mall to look for a connector cord for her MacBook so we could hook it up to TV sets, so we had the privilege of sitting in several traffic jams of those horse people in their cars. Kelty and I wandered around the downtown parking lot, as was our routine, studying the methodology of drivers attempting to wedge their vehicles into those rather tight parking spaces that the British are so fond of. When Linda emerged from the shopping mall, a £90 adapter cord in hand, she said that she would love to stay and shop in a place like Newmarket, but we took a vote and Kelty sided with me so it was two to one that we move on as quickly as possible.

I selected a back road to a little place called Moulton because I had seen something on the map called Packhorse Bridge. We passed fields of properly dressed horsemen exercising their horses. They were trotting, galloping, cantering and whatever else it is you do with a horse when wearing the appropriate attire and trying to look like you are a snob who knows what you are doing.

With minimal difficulty we found the historical site we were looking for, a nicely preserved medieval bridge that once spanned the River Kennet. I say "once" because it seemed the river had dried up, leaving a bridge that spanned a low-lying parcel of grass. According to English Heritage, "The river has shrunk in size since the bridge was built in the fifteenth century. While a single arch would have been suitable to span a narrow stream, if used over a wider stretch this design would have created an inconveniently steep slope at both sides." And let's face it, no one wants an inconveniently steep slope for your trusty but overburdened pack horse.

England is fairly littered with wonderful old leftover structures like this that no longer serve practical purposes, and I am thankful that groups like English Heritage preserve them, come up with clever classification systems and then, well, just leave them be for folks like us to come along and wonder why someone has built a bridge over a small patch of lawn. I studied the chunks of flint embedded in the bridge. Flint seemed to be ubiquitous in the parts of England we had been in so far. Houses, barns and bridges were built partially of flint, the same variety of stone I had once used as a Boy Scout while learning to start a fire without matches.

We ran Kelty around a fine community football field nearby and soon were on our way to Bury St Edmunds, where I'd once driven with my daughter Sunyata many years ago while we were staying in Bedford. I recall being stopped by a policeman on our way there at 9:30 on a Friday morning. He put his face in the window to smell my breath and asked if I had been drinking. I was a little surprised by the question and assured him I had not and if he didn't mind me asking, why was he checking all the cars on the road for alcohol on a Friday morning?

"Well, it's a bank holiday, you know?" was his response. At the time, this meant nothing to me. I didn't understand the British term "bank holiday" and tried to sort out the logic. If the bank was closed, did that mean one might be prone to wake up Friday morning, down a pint or three and then take a drive to Bury St Edmunds? Perhaps it did.

There was no roadblock this time on the way to BSE and, instead, by noon Linda and I found our way to the old part of downtown and I sought out a parking machine that would accept my coins. A good singer was busking some Cat Stevens and James Taylor tunes in front of the Starbucks, which offered me a free sample of watermelon iced tea that led me to ask Kelty why anyone would want to mix watermelon with tea. I blamed Starbucks for that and admitted it was probably an American idea gone bad like the other flavours they had been known to defile both tea and coffee with. Kelty yawned as I watched another man nearby sip his watermelon tea sample. He made a face and discreetly poured the offending libation onto the sidewalk and walked rapidly away.

Linda went shopping yet again for yet another electronic adaptor we needed to interface with British technology. For us Canadians, it took a fair bit of adapting to make our gadgets work with the power supply and the TV fittings in the UK. I listened to the Starbucks busker sing "Country Roads" by John Denver and then Dylan's "All Along the Watchtower" before the dog and I strolled over to a shaded park bench where a woman and two men were passing around a bottle of something in a paper bag. They were a bit boisterous and commented about my dog but not in a kind way. I smiled and led my insulted pet onward.

Sometimes called "Suffolk's Floral Town," Bury St Edmunds probably deserves a handle more interesting than that since it seemed lively and full of animated interactions on the street. For one thing, it is very, very old. For another, there are tunnels beneath the ground where men used to dig out chalk, which makes me wonder what all that chalk was used for if not for teachers scratching sums and cursive writing on slate boards. Mary Tudor, Henry VIII's sister who became Queen of France, was reburied here in the old church and Queen Victoria had a stained glass window created there to commemorate her passing.

If none of that sets you drinking in celebration on a bank holiday morn, then you might also want to know that the country's first "internally illuminated street sign" was constructed here, the town is home to the Greene King brewing company and actor Bob Hoskins came by his Limey accent honestly by growing up here. (And I had thought he too was Australian. I was sure of it.) And Saint Edmund, by the way, has his hands full as the saint of kings but also wolves, pandemics and torture victims.

Sadly, Kelty and I had to pass by the Nutshell, purported to be the country's smallest pub, because it looked too crowded for a man to enter without his dog being stepped on.

Bury St Edmunds has some grand old architecture and a good feel to it. There was an old clock and some well-preserved houses and a lot of elderly people about on very slow motorized wheelchairs. On our walk back to the car, the town police had stopped to talk to the drinking bench mates we had passed. I hovered nearby thinking there might be an event that would add a little drama to my day. But, to everyone's credit, the police were cheerful enough as they chatted up the drinkers with questions about the FIFA World Cup and the chances of England to win. In the end, one of the two cops laughed and said something like, "Well, be cool and don't cause any trouble," although I can't remember the exact phrasing he used. Nonetheless, I was impressed by both the

Bobbies and the drunks and was sure the scene had played out many times before. Or maybe it was just because this Saturday had come right after (or before) a bank holiday and a little toast to the Queen was all in order on a day like this.

Later that summer, on August 3, back home safely in Canada, I came across this headline in the *East Anglian Daily Times*: "Teens arrested after Suffolk flour and egg attack 'not placed under police protection.'" The article went on to say,

> The teenagers arrested in connection with an attack on a vulnerable woman in west Suffolk last week have not been placed in police protection, officers have clarified.
>
> The victim, a woman aged in her 40s, was reported to have been assaulted by a group of teenagers who threw flour and eggs over her after a row in St Olaves Road, Bury St Edmunds.
>
> The woman was said to have been "severely distressed" but unharmed.
>
> The assault, which happened at around 5.30 pm on Friday, July 27, sparked nationwide outrage after a picture of the incident was shared on social media.
>
> Suffolk police have warned the public not to take the law into their own hands saying we do "not support vigilantism in any way, shape or form."

I also noticed, however, that some national newspapers were quite critical of the Suffolk Constabulary after claiming the suspects had been placed in police protection for their own safety.

I saw the photo and do feel sorry for the woman, and maybe police protection for the louts was in order, but I remained most curious about the combination of flour and eggs. Perhaps this is some sort of political statement I'm not familiar with, but it rather sounded like the ill-begotten youths were attempting to mix the ingredients that go into making a cake. And, yes, I admit to tossing at least three or four eggs from a full dozen in my own reckless youth, but it never occurred to me to add flour (or butter for that matter) and would love for someone to fully explain this new way that British teens have invented to harass adults.

If I had to guess, I would say you throw the eggs first to give the flour something to stick to, and the finely sifted flour would make the victim look white and ridiculous. Some may argue that there is no need to sift flour anymore. But I have fond memories of my own mother sifting away in the sunlight on a warm summer afternoon, so I prefer to envision a BSE teenage hooligan himself sifting some King Arthur All-Purpose Flour for the job and when his mother asks him why he has borrowed her sifter, saying something like, "'Tis okay, Mum, it's just a little practical joke me and me mates have cooked up." But, for the record, I will assert that, aside from a bad sample of watermelon tea, Kelty, Linda and I found Bury St Edmunds a perfectly fine little city.

CHAPTER FIFTEEN

FORESTS, FLINT AND ABANDONED AIRBASES OF YESTERYEAR

I noticed on our map that Thetford Forest was on our way to our one-night stay in the town of Brandon. I wasn't sure we'd ever visited a national forest in the UK and was feeling ready for a hike through a really big stand of trees after our urban spree in Bury. So we left behind the town drunks, the watermelon tea and the mean streets of Bury St Edmunds for a walk in the woods.

During the First World War, much of England's trees had been chopped down for wood used in the war effort. Thetford is a man-made forest with pines, larch, fir and a variety of hardwoods planted over nearly 20,000 hectares. This big patch of woods was just what we needed for a hike with Kelty and a chance to breathe in the scent of pine needles.

We entered the park at a place called the High Lodge where you paid a hefty sum to park, but it was, nonetheless, a very agreeable place. The pine trees were tall as advertised in the brochures and there were various contraptions set about the field with ropes and poles for school kids to climb on. The parking machines were not working, and when I tried to pay for parking at the main office, there were two women in front of me with small children complaining that something was not in operation that day. I'm not sure what — the Monster

House or Monkey Mania, something like that. There were a few signs promoting High Lodge that said simply, "Go Ape," but I couldn't quite make the connection with a vast man-made pine forest in Suffolk and the presence of any form of simians.

It was rather hot there, though, and it reminded me of the Pine Barrens of South Jersey near where I grew up. This part of the Garden State was made famous many years ago by the wonderful 1968 book *The Pine Barrens* by *New Yorker* writer John McPhee. Growing up in New Jersey and aspiring to be a writer like McPhee, I, too, thought that one day I should write for the *New Yorker,* but once I actually read the articles and pondered over the pseudo-intellectual cartoons, I realized I was more likely to write for *Surfer* magazine (which I did) and later a hippie New York weekly tabloid called *The Aquarian,* which paid me up to $25 per article to write about whatever I wanted. I did, however, once have a sketch of me and an article about my winter surfing in Nova Scotia on the front page of *The Wall Street Journal,* as unlikely as that sounds. At least some things worked out with my New York literary connections.

Once the mothers at Thetford with their tykes in strollers cooled down a bit, I paid my parking fee in cash and asked about hiking trails. Since it was so hot, we were looking for a short, shady one, please, and which one would that be?

The parking person steered me toward a young, bored-looking lad in another booth and I explained to him about looking for an easy short walk. "Just follow the purple path," he said. We did and it was quite nice, but it kept going and going and, according to my wife's smart phone — which could have told us ahead of time it would be a bloody long and wickedly hot hike, it was that smart — it turned out to be seven kilometres. The trees were straight and tall, however, and the floor of the forest was an appropriate carpet of pine needles, which is worthy of note. And Kelty liked it immensely.

There were rumours of a Bigfoot-type creature roaming around in the forest, but neither Linda, Kelty nor I gave it any credence. People don't trust big forests and are easily persuaded there are hairy monsters stalking about there. Back in the Jersey Pines, we had the Jersey Devil, so it only seemed natural that the woods of Suffolk would have a creature or two, be they real or imaginary.

Upon returning to the car park and studying the posted map there, I quickly determined that the purple route was by far one of the longer ones. We should have taken the yellow route. Had the young wanker been having a go at us or did he perhaps not understand my Canadian accent? At any length, I was proud of the forestry people who had determined those many years ago that replanting a forest that had been completely cut down by your countrymen was a really, really good idea.

I bought us an ice cream and determined it was time to leave. From more snooping around, I discovered that here at High Lodge many famous outdoor concerts took place in the summer, not the least of which was a recent one by a rock group named Kasabian, a Leicester-based band named after Charles Manson's getaway driver girlfriend. It turns out that the Forestry Commission, while not organizing young workers to plant trees, has a summer concert series in the woods here. We had missed Kasabian, however, a band "famed for their energetic and hedonistic live performances guaranteeing a set list of earth-shaking rock anthems," according to their Facebook page. I had not heard of them but vowed to listen to their earth-shaking tunes on albums with names like *West Ryder Pauper Lunatic Asylum*, *Velociraptor!* and *For Crying Out Loud*. While I was apparently snoozing on the pop music hedonistic scene, they had made it big with singles like "Eez-eh," "Club Foot," "You're in Love with a Psycho" and "Bless this Acid House." Somehow, I just couldn't envision them playing here, going ape, I would reckon, among the whispering pines and long, distant purple paths.

I daresay we were weary by the time we reached our backyard rental called Duke Lodge just down the street from Mr. G's Bowling Centre. It turned out to be yet another fairly miniscule cottage built to rent to travellers like us. The main house had once been a pub or inn called Duke of Wellington Pub that was no longer in business.

Brandon seemed like a terribly generic name for a town, and I kept mistakenly referring to it as Bradford, but it was pleasant enough for one night. Military jets zipped over at low altitudes as if we were in a war zone, reminding me of just how heavily militarized Britain still is today. Given how many foreigners have invaded or wanted to invade the little island, I can understand why. Thus you can be hiking in the Lake District or out for a stroll behind the little town school in Brandon and see a fighter jet screeching straight at you at any time of the day. It's a nice bit of an adrenalin rush to get the old heart pumping, eh?

As with almost anywhere else in England, ancient peoples once lived here. And there had been a heck of a lot of flint mining in the fields nearby, which rather surprised me. I hadn't thought of flint as actually being mined. I thought you just walked out into a farmer's field and picked it up, but once upon a time, outside Brandon, flint mining was a big thing.

As far back as 2600 BC, people were digging flint out of the chalky ground and using it for axe and tool blades. Much later, flint was used to create sparks to set off gunpowder. As a matter of fact, the gun flint used in the muskets at the Battle of Waterloo came from outside Brandon. Preparing the flint for use in firearms involved chunking it up in appropriate sizes and then "knapping" (shaping) it. If that was your profession, you were a flint knapper, a job that has mostly fallen by the wayside since the days of Napoleon's advances.

While sitting in my underwear trying to cool down in little Duke Lodge, I went searching for some "local colour" and found an old copy of the *Thetford & Brandon Times* from the previous March under the sink. On the front page (front page, mind you!) was this headline: "Football club launches poster competition to help with dog mess on playing fields."

There were two police officers, two parents and three young athletes in very bright running shoes holding up poop bags and smiling at the cameraman, who had told them to "say cheese" or perhaps something else that made them grin.

The *Times* informed its readers, "Young footballers have been handing out dog bags, donated by Jollyes Pet Superstore in Thetford, to walkers. They have been aided by Police Community Support Officers from Suffolk Constabulary." There was also to be a poster competition "for three categories, five and under, six to 10-years-old and over 10." I showed the article to Linda and Kelty, but they didn't find my research as illuminating as I did — but then, I'm the writer of the family.

Having completed all my necessary research in Brandon concerning flint mining and community spirit, we were off the next morning to seek out defunct military air bases and ultimately the region of England where my ancestors once lived.

Our next home for several days would be in Leicestershire,

near my ancestral roots in Sibson. We couldn't locate a rental house that accepted pets in Sibson so we were, instead, headed to yet another small town I had never heard of (and those are my favourites) — Osgathorpe. I had selected a route that would take us past several air bases where my father had served in the US military during the Second World War. It would be a long drive, but I truly wanted to touch down at Little Staughton, Alconbury and Abbots Ripton.

We looped around both Newmarket and Cambridge and sailed easily on our way to St Neots —another of those little towns where Dad carefully navigated dark country lanes so American bomber pilots in need of a de-stressing pint of warm English beer could visit the local pub. During his time here, he noted that he was, in March 1944, "Doing a lot of ration runs — start early in the morning."

Although we skirted the town itself to avoid traffic, we made a pit stop at the Tesco along the highway to stock up on food. Linda shopped as usual while I took Kelty for the traditional walk around the parking lot, making my custom-ary evaluation of the available grassy patches and the litter. I thought about putting on my sunglasses and testing the store itself to see if I could get away with walking my dog through the produce section but decided I should stick to more serious pursuits and abandon adolescent notions of causing trouble.

After a brief drive up the A1, we turned off to the west to find what was left of the airbase at Little Staughton. I stopped the car in Great Staughton and got out to speak to a man doing some landscaping. I asked him if he could direct us to the American airbase and he told me to head up past the Anglican Church of St Andrew and turn left down a single track road, then through the little village of Little Staughton and then turn left into an industrial estate to what was now a private airfield.

Suffice it to say, it wasn't that simple. The field where American bombers once raced down a paved runway was now converted into various industrial properties that were homes to welders, recyclers, heavy equipment repair shops and the like. We could see a Second World War hangar in the distance across a barley field, but when we arrived at the entrance there was a big "Keep Out" sign. I got a glimpse of an old runway with tall grasses growing up through cracked concrete, but that was about it.

Nothing in or around the town of Little Staughton suggested that there had ever been an American presence here or that this area had in any way been touched by the events of a global war. Something about that haunted me, maybe only because this little patch of English earth had once been so important to the man who was my father. I had rooted through his journal for some telling detail about the place but only found, "Still muddy here at Base — Little Staughton #127."

The next stop would be Alconbury, farther up the A1. On our retreat back toward Great Staughton, we pulled off the road across from that Anglican church because there was a bench conveniently located there on a shady patch of grass. The good folks of the Great Staughton Horticultural Society had the foresight to construct the bench in this ideal location just for those like us looking for a comfortable place to eat a baguette, ham and cheese lunch. It was not hard to envision the members of the society when the vote was taken on such an undertaking. Linda was even more curious than I about the group so a quick trip to their website on her phone revealed the following. "Established in 1965, the Horticultural Society is mainly involved with organizing horticultural events in the local community. This includes a plant sale in early spring, an annual show in late summer and a 'garden talk' in the autumn." I much liked the sound of that and, as Kelty sniffed some nearby marigolds and I chewed my baguette, I thought that maybe if I moved to a small village in England and got old, really, really old, say 90, I too would want to join such a group and organize "horticultural events."

"Darn," my wife suddenly said, interrupting my reverie.

"What is it?" I asked.

"We missed the Plant Sale and Cream Tea that was held on May 27."

"Shucks."

"And we won't be here for something called the Scarecrow Event in July."

I made the appropriate regretful sounds, more heart-felt than intended because I was actually really enjoying my sandwich of ham, Stilton cheese and Dijon mustard and wondering exactly what a cream tea entailed. Kelty, ambitiously sniffing around the base of the privet hedge, seemed unmoved by missing out on these events in the Great Staughton social calendar.

After that round of disappointing news, it was on to Alconbury, where it was not at all difficult to find the other old airfield where my dad had been stationed during the war. It had been swallowed up in what was now RAF Alconbury, a fully active military airbase. There was a high barbed-wire fence and some serious-looking uniformed personnel in the road as we approached the gate, but I had visited a number of army and air force bases in New Jersey with my parents while growing up so I figured they might yet allow us to just drive in and look around if I explained our purpose.

In fact, I had fond memories of my dad driving us to Fort Dix, McGuire Air Force Base and other active military sites to look at bombers, tanks and even underground bunkers with intercontinental ballistic missiles designed to carry nuclear warheads. Back in the 1960s, it was considered the height of family fun to take your kids to see war machinery and weapons capable of setting off a thermonuclear war that could destroy civilization.

Sadly, times have changed.

I boldly drove up to the tall Black soldier on guard at the main gate. He was kitted out in a well-starched khaki uniform, wielding an impressive rifle. I don't know what kind of rifle, but it looked like a really good one.

"Hi," I said, in what would have sounded to him like an American accent. "My father was sent here during the Second World War and I was hoping to just take a look around, just to get the feel of the place where he was once stationed." My father had been a particular fan of the British Alconbury base because the food was better there than at the American base. But I figured that detail would not impress the guard.

I don't quite know how to describe the look he gave me. It's that thing you do when you furrow your brow and crunch up your lower lip. From his point of view, he had probably already noticed we had a French licence plate and our steering wheel was on "the wrong side" of the car. Here was a 60-something man with shaggy hair, a pretty wife and a small white dog asking to have a quick drive through the base on this warm post-9/11 afternoon.

In the few seconds that it took him to consider my request, I wondered if, in fact, the rifle was loaded or just for show. I decided not to ask. All too soon, he responded to my simple polite request by saying, "I'm sorry, sir. I can't permit you to do that." It sounded like a line from a movie.

"We only want a quick look around," I countered.

"I'm sorry, sir. Now you'll have to follow me." Oddly enough, he ran forward and we drove on, following him past the gatehouse and onto the base, but he then stopped and pointed with his rifle for us to make a U-turn and leave. Linda suggested I should do as he was indicating. So I'm hoping the young man noted the extreme disappointment on my face as I turned the Fiat around and headed back to civilian territory. Kelty too seemed a bit put out. He'd been in the car for quite a while and, like me, he was probably hoping to stretch his legs and maybe find a quiet place to take a pee before driving on. A big noisy jet was taking off above us and the roar was deafening. So I supposed it was just military business as usual there on the old Alconbury tarmac and no nosey foreigners allowed.

But we had struck out for a second time.

Our last hope was the airbase at Abbots Ripton, the American one with the notoriously bad food that had so disappointed my ravenous father.

We had miles to go before our sleep and Linda was getting a bit tired of our military quest. When we arrived in Abbots Ripton, I stopped at an ice cream shop and asked about the old American airfield. The young woman serving a customer a banana split had never heard of it. She asked an older colleague, a woman who looked quite a bit like Judi Dench, if she knew of such a place, but she shook her head no. Then they both gave me a look that suggested I was up to something no good. At least that's how I interpreted it. So I left.

Outside, some men were drinking beer at a picnic table beside their motorcycles, making me realize the place was more than a mere ice cream parlour. I thought I'd give it one more go so I walked over and asked if they knew of the airbase.

They laughed, as you would expect beer-drinking motorcycle men to laugh on such occasions. "No," a bearded fellow said. "We're not from here. We're German."

By this time it was late afternoon. Linda was restless and so was Kelty and it was time to give up on the war and move on to Leicestershire. Which I did.

I pride myself on my map-reading abilities and, as you know, never fully trusted Linda's Navigon, but as we headed north I discovered we were farther from our destination than I thought, since I had mixed up the A1, highway with the M1. I was convinced we were on the M1 but it was its lesser cousin, the A road. Buggers.

So I have little to report about anything of great interest occurring as we drove past Sawtry, Wittering, Tinwell, Woolsthorpe-by-Colsterworth and Long Bennington. And I won't bore you with details about the longish drive west along A47 through places like Tugby and Skeffington, which no doubt are delightful towns to while away an afternoon if you had the inclination. We slipped around the big city of Leicester, where I am sure some of my ancestors visited when they wanted to go to a big city.

Not far from our destination, outside Loughborough, we passed a very large doggy establishment called Dogs Trust. It looked like a resort of some sort, so I asked Linda to look it up on her smart phone. We discovered that it was a national organization whose purpose is "to bring about the day when all dogs can enjoy a happy life, free from the threat of unnecessary destruction." Dating back to 1891, it is an enormous organization for helping dogs. It was originally called the National Canine Defence League, which I rather prefer, a name that sounds powerful and militant whose members campaigned against vivisection, muzzling and chaining and had a particular hate on for railway companies that mistreated dogs.

Back in the early days of the space race, they railed against the Russians for sending dogs up into space and even held a special vigil for Laika, who died while orbiting earth.

Dogs Trust claims they never "put down" an animal and they sponsor Dogmobiles that "rehome" as many tail waggers as possible. I'd never heard of them before, but probably everyone in the UK knows someone who supports them or received their family mutt from these dedicated dog devotees. Learning about them did my heart good. They don't like "docking" of tails either and do not have kind things to say about the fox hunting crowd. In 2016 they found proper homes for over 13,000 dogs. Way to go, Dogs Trust. Their slogan is "A Dog is for Life, not just for Christmas." Most recently, they've been campaigning against puppy smuggling, a crime I was heretofore unfamiliar with.

Clearly, the Dogs Trust members were our kind of folks. I gave them a silent but emphatic salute, patted our much-loved Westie and drove on.

CHAPTER SIXTEEN

FAMILY POETS AND OTHER PREDECESSORS

With great relief we pulled in the driveway of Number One, Church Lane, Osgathorpe, to find our no-name rental apartment above the garage alongside an opulent-looking home sitting on a small parcel of land adjacent to a magnificent large pasture with roaming horses. Way back in 1871, John Marius Wilson wrote, "OSGATHORPE, a village and a parish in Ashby-de-la-Zouch district, Leicester. The village stands on an affluent of the river Soar, 2 miles N N E of Swannington r. station, and 5 E N E of Ashby-de-la-Zouch; and is a pleasant place." Perhaps that is more than you need to know, but I am pleased to report that it is still a pleasant place. After trying to track down old American airfields, pleasant was what the weary travellers needed. That and a spaghetti dinner.

I took Kelty for a long walk down a country road that led out of the village and into unpopulated rolling hills that had not changed for several centuries. The birds were singing and I wanted to name them all but could only give names to the magpies and a large family of squabbling shitting crows that ruled one tall gnarly oak tree by a stream. Along with the birds, there were rabbits, cows, horses, green fields and blue skies straight out of a watercolour painting.

Later that evening, we watched a movie called *Identity* on our computer. The IMDB description of the film reads, "Stranded at a desolate Nevada motel during a nasty rain storm, ten strangers become acquainted with each other when they realize that they're being killed off one by one." It was just the thing to counter our bucolic location in the lush English countryside.

In the morning, we heard our host open up the garage door below and fire up what sounded like a fairly souped-up sports car with a modified Thrush muffler. When I peered out the window, I saw him and his wife driving out of Church Lane in an impossibly swanky space-age vehicle. The car in question turned out to be a McLaren, a vehicle whose base price tag is US$285,000, or £222,000. I had never heard of a McLaren, but it is a most impressive vehicle. I watched as the driver tooled off down the lovely country lane I had walked with Kelty yesterday and thought it would be a fine thing to drive around in with the top down and your scalp warmed by the gentle June sunlight. It's a two-seater so you couldn't take the whole family, but Linda and I could probably squeeze the dog in, although I doubt I'd find any place in the UK where I could give the car a full workout, as it is rated to go 196 mph if you push the pedal to the metal.

As we drove off in the morning in our humble Fiat, I kept wondering what prompted a person to buy such an expensive toy and, if you had so much money to burn, why would you be renting your flat above the McLaren to travellers like us?

Once we were up and about on this fine Saturday morning, we went looking for something old and ruined and found the perfect combination in the Grace Dieu Priory near Thringstone. A priory, in case you are wondering as I was, is a monastery for nuns or monks, and this one served as such until it went out of business, so to speak, and was taken over by a local scoundrel as his own personal estate. *The Spooky Isles* considers it the most haunted location in Leicestershire. There are considerable reports of spirits wandering around here, including one "white lady" who walked out to the road once and appeared so real that a bus driver stopped to pick her up.

The remains of the priory date back to the thirteenth century and I saw nothing spooky about it, although I do think we all put a little bit of our own spirit into our homes, our possessions, even our cars. So, although I didn't personally meet any ghosts or other spirits, I do think it's possible that those who have heard voices and seen apparitions here are tapping into something real. However, things must have gotten a bit out of control in recent years because the trust that owns the property states that enthusiasts "are no longer able to hold Paranormal events or Ghost walks, and Paranormal events organised by 3rd parties are Forbidden." Either the trust doesn't believe in ghostly spirits or they are hoping to protect their privacy from prodding ghost hunters and poltergeist chasers with their video cameras and "ghost boxes."

We walked through the forest behind the priory and poked around a very cool-looking abandoned railway arch bridge, bringing me to conclude that I like most all things that are ruined, abandoned, overgrown and otherwise half-forgotten. And England is a very good place for finding such attractions as long as the ever-greedy National Trust hasn't gotten their white-gloved paws on them. The only problem is you have to know where to look.

However, the true quest for the weekend involved me looking for more Choyce connections. Sibson, home of my ancestor James Choyce, was a ways to the south of here and I had decided to first seek out connections with Arthur Newberry Choyce, a First World War poet from these parts who had become famous enough to go on a tour of England and North America to read his poetry. He's mostly forgotten now but, as a poet myself, I felt a strong connection.

Arthur lived from 1893 to 1937 and had fought in the Great War with the Leicestershire "Tigers," which designated him as their official poet. It is curious to think that, in such a bloody mess of a conflict, the English remained civilized enough to appoint poets for their regiments. I don't think modern-day battalions of soldiers select honorary poets for wars in Afghanistan, Iraq, Syria or anywhere for that matter. Bigger bombs and high-tech weapons, I suppose, have bullied away the writers of sonnets and sestinas.

In 1917, Arthur published a book of poetry called *Crimson Stains* that portrayed trench warfare and the horror of the battlefield. In a short poem about the fallen men called "To the Leicestershires," he wrote,

> If in the next life or the next there be
> A starting of our quarrels all again,
> May Fate give task of leadership to me
> And let me find the souls of these dead men.

His poems were sentimental at times but not overly patriotic, and he was well liked enough to tour extensively reading his work to surprisingly large audiences. After declining in health, he died at age 43 as the result of wounds he had received in the war and, unlike war poets Wilfred Owen and Rupert Brooke, he was soon forgotten by the literary world.

Arthur had written longingly about Charnwood Forest and, as we drove through there, I could see why. If you'd romped around those giant trees and played in the streams of Charnwood, you could see why your mind and your pen would want to take you back there while trying to erase the nightmares you saw on the battlefields of France.

After the war, the poet was a headmaster of Snibston Primary School, so we went looking for it in Coalville. We didn't like Coalville (pronounced Coville for some reason). Linda kept asking me why we were there and I said I didn't know. I thought we might find a statue or a plaque for ANC or maybe locate someone who could tell us where his grave was, but Coalville wasn't giving up any secrets about its one-time war poet in residence. The Bitter and Twisted Micropub looked somewhat interesting, but it was too early in the day for a pint and I saw a sign for a paintball park that could have entertained us, but we never warmed up to the town.

A bit of digging after the fact revealed that Coalville has a bit of a miasma hanging over it. One particularly unkind anonymous writer on iLiveHere wrote, "The whole town seems to have a depressing feel to it, and most of the time the inhabitants seem to walk around in a zombie like state, probably from the sheer boredom and dismal atmosphere of the place.... If Coalville were to be summed up as a smell, that smell would be of urine, damp dog, and cheap cider."

Perhaps we would have had better luck in nearby Hugglescote, where the poet was born, but Linda felt we'd squandered our time among the Coalville zombies and were better off back with the quiet ghosts of Grace Dieu. So I steered us back into the beautiful countryside to the south toward Sibson, the tiny village where James Choyce had lived before emigrating to America.

I was having a tough time navigating the back roads that would take us there and mistakenly took us down narrow lanes into Odstone, Congerstone and Shackerstone. After yet another wrong turn, we ended up on a tiny pot-holed road with a narrow bridge and a sign indicating that it was a "Weak Bridge," which was not encouraging. Throwing caution to the wind, we drove over it and wound up in Sheepy Parva, which I knew to be a stone's throw from Sibson.

Again the question was posed to me by my soulmate: What is it we are looking for? And again, I wasn't sure. What was I looking for? Some kind of connection, I suppose. I wanted to stand somewhere and say to myself, *The man who set in motion my very existence came from this place.* Some of my ancestors were buried (and probably forgotten) here. I waited for a revelation that never fully gelled.

Sibson was a tidy little well-upholstered town with brick houses, flowery, well-maintained lawns and ducks snoozing here and there on the sidewalks. I walked Kelty into the graveyard behind the church and saw no tombstones with my family name, although it was cool and shaded and felt old and, well, proper.

Like so many small British towns, Sibson had one pub. The Cock Inn claimed to be one of the oldest drinking establishments in the UK, constructed in 1250. It played a role in the 1485 Battle of Bosworth Field, both before and after. That famous robber, Dick Turpin, hid out here from the authorities along with his loyal horse, Black Bess. Turpin is reported to have paid the locals to keep their mouths shut about him being in the neighbourhood. Quite possibly some of my ancestors took coins from the famous highwayman. And, if so, I don't think I should be proud of that.

Although Dick Turpin has been mythologized as a lovable rogue, the truth is quite the opposite. Frank McLynn of *The Independent* writes, "The historical Turpin was a rather nasty thug, a butcher's apprentice who graduated to highway robbery via burglary, robbery and murder." More myth than man, Turpin was a criminal who became a kind of folk hero. He's even had a sausage and a sex toy named after him. In real life, he was ultimately arrested for shooting someone's chicken in the street.

And speaking of chickens, the Cock Inn, owned down through the ages by the church, which kept it open six days a week (not the Sabbath, of course), had a pit in the back reserved for regular cock fights up until the 1870s. The pub today garners some most favourable reviews, including that of Brian F. of Nuneaton, who writes, "The battered fish was great but the chips were warmed up and a few chips were hard but the Banoffee Pie was fantastic. Staff friendly and helpful. The best thing is that the wife likes the Cock & the Willey on the A5." I'm assuming the Willey is the name of another pub thereabouts.

On the way home, I scored a few more wrong turns to add to my list of errors that day and we found ourselves in yet another micro-community with the novel name of Barton in the Beans. Historically, a considerable amount of broad beans were grown here. A common old quip was, "Shake a Leicestershire man by the collar and you may hear the beans rattle in his belly." A reference to the town shows up in the famous *Domesday Book*, but today it seems not much more than a scattering of farms and houses, a Baptist church and no pub to be found. There is a wonderful town sign as you enter should you ever want to post a thought-provoking Facebook image of yourself standing beside it. We did not, but in retrospect I wish we had.

CHAPTER SEVENTEEN

OF BIRDS, BEASTS
AND SHIRTLESS MEN
PLAYING PING-PONG

Back in our little apartment above the $285,000 McLaren, we relaxed on the small deck and I gazed off into the fine fields beyond Osgathorpe. The sky was again like a Renaissance painting. Linda went for a run and Kelty and I hiked down to the babbling brook and the treeful of complaining crows, then out into some pasture land where I let him run free among the cropped grass and tall spikey purple thistles until I spotted a bull with a red bandana around his neck waltzing our way. I tethered Kelty and we crept out through the makeshift gate, looping it shut with a piece of bailing wire hanging there.

When Linda returned, we opened a bottle of Malbec and watched the sun slowly sinking in the west over the horses in the field. We talked about how things were going so far on our adventure — this after a rather trying day of travel due to so many wrong turns and so relatively few enlightening experiences. It was just one of those times you get weary after days on the road and expect there are more to come.

Across the laneway outside an ivy-covered cottage, two sunburnt shirtless men were setting up a Ping-Pong table in the front yard. England often seems to me to be the Land that Sunscreen Forgot, but it's really just that a lot of pale-skinned, pasty-faced Brits forget they are fair-skinned, and when the outdoors call — or in this case, Ping-Pong in the yard — they forget all about solar protection.

We had a hole in our itinerary — our last four days in the UK — and Linda was itching to nail down some final accommodations. We studied the map of England again to find the proper shire where we had not yet visited. We figured it should be something south of Wales and a bit east if possible, two locations perhaps, and somewhat on our way back to the Eurotunnel and the toll roads to Paris.

I had stayed in touch with the one writer who was willing to give me an interview — Tony Hawks — and he had told me he lived somewhere on the edge of Dartmoor near the town of Moretonhampstead ... so that sealed the deal. There was a big green splotch on the South Devon page of my *AA Road Atlas* that was Dartmoor National Park and it looked pleasantly unpopulated and enticing. The truth is, it wasn't really on our path back to Folkestone. Nonetheless, we'd drive back to England after our next stop in Wales, then south past Bath and Cheddar again and then farther down into the boot. But we decided not to go all the way down to Cornwall where we had lived short-term in homes before on several occasions.

Finding a rural house near Moretonhampstead for a four-day rent, one that would accept dogs, proved to be difficult, but Linda eventually discovered a house in the village of Manaton, not many miles south from there. I was sure that if we parked ourselves there for a few days, Tony would give me directions to his home and I'd have my interview. Without consulting him, we booked our Manaton accommodation, which appeared to be blessedly out in the middle of the moor with fields and forests aplenty.

Linda also decreed that, after that, we'd spend our final night in England at an old estate, a fairly posh arrangement at Eastwell outside Folkestone, where we could celebrate our travels with our dog on a back patio, and then hire a dog sitter again so we could have a fancy meal in the dining room where the well-heeled once made small talk about the decline of the British Empire while sipping claret.

So we had sorted out our final travel plans and fell into a kind of reverie there on the Osgathorpe Nirvana balcony. Despite the idyllic surroundings and our fine adventures so far, I expressed some doubts about the book project that had brought us here. It was the very title that was bothering the literal part of me: *Around England with a Dog*. Well, our loop on this core part of our journey had so far been Bexhill to Bath (and Beyond), Bradford-on-Avon to Saffron-Walden and Cambridge, forays into the Thetford Forest and Brandon, a dash across those airfields north of Bedford and then north to Leicestershire and the land of ancestors, ghosts and McLarens.

Soon it would be off to Betws-y-Coed and Snowdonia for some hiking and surfing and then down to Devon before looping back to the tunnel for France and home. Some might argue we were zigzagging around England with a dog. What about the *around* part? The critics might also argue we missed much of northern England and that France and Wales, well, the last time they looked, weren't even part of England at all. And if we'd wandered far from the core of the kingdom by the sea, why not include Scotland, at least, as well?

The answer, I soon realized, was backstory. There *was* substantial backstory leading up to the book in question and it was worthy of the telling. In fact, the very first trip that Linda and I had ever taken in the early days of our midlife relationship was to the UK, and it remained a most special place to us.

On several more occasions during our time together, Linda and I (without our dog) had departed North America and immersed ourselves for a week to two weeks at a time on this side of the Atlantic and gotten to know the place fairly well. Our experience would always be that of outsiders — not mere tourists, I would argue, but pilgrims searching for bits and pieces of the past, the key elements of a grand culture that had bred geniuses and saints but also pillaged a fair part of the globe. I had a love for the place and I believed in my bones I had an eye for the less obvious truths that glued together the many cultures that lived in this united kingdom by the sea.

And, as the sun set over the Leicestershire fields, we reflected on that first time together in England. Shortly after Linda and I had first become "a couple" — she 50, me 60 — she was diagnosed with cancer. Non-Hodgkin's lymphoma to be exact. Cancer of the lymph nodes was something that could spread throughout the body and, as far as we knew, it might have already started doing that.

Linda had a serious sit-down talk with me about it one foggy afternoon back at Lawrencetown Beach early in our relationship where she had told me the news. Then she said she had no real sense of how things would go in the year ahead with the scheduled chemo and whatever side effects that might have.

We were sitting in the small office of my old farmhouse at the time and her dog was asleep in the corner. Murdo was also a West Highland Terrier, who upon first entering my house, the day Linda and I met, had staked out the territory by immediately peeing on two walls and the leg of a sofa. Murdo would last a few more years before he succumbed to cancer himself after a series of expensive experimental treatments to save his life. But alas, for most of us, we tend to outlive our dogs — a sad but elemental truth and one you need to get used to if you want to live with a shaggy pet.

On the day Linda told me her medical news, however, she wasn't even sure she would outlive Murdo. She'd done her homework on the disease, but she just didn't know how this would play out. The upside of the illness was a cliché that kept cropping up. "If you have to get cancer, this is the one you want to get." Which was no particular comfort to either of us. I had been falling in love with this woman, this high school principal who was both brilliant and beautiful, and I said that we shouldn't let a little thing like cancer deter us from any damn thing we wanted to do.

"When's the chemo?" I asked.

"It won't start for another two months."

"Let's go someplace, then," I said. "Let's get away. It won't matter. The chemo will be there when we get back and I'll coach you all the way through it."

"Where should we go?"

"Let me work on it," I said.

CHAPTER EIGHTEEN

KNOCKING ABOUT NORTHEAST ENGLAND (APRIL 2011)

I'm not sure, in the end, what prompted Linda and me to travel to North East England in 2011. I think I'd seen photographs of good waves along the beaches of Sandsend, Scarborough and Saltburn-by-the-Sea. I had never thought much about the North Sea as a surfing destination, but images of certain glassy walls of moving water can lure a surfer to unlikely places on this small planet of ours.

And so it was that in the spring of 2011 we found ourselves landing at Newcastle International Airport in Woolsington on a fine clear day with high hopes of some sort of adventure. We had rented a house in the tiny village of Boynton far to the south of there but decided to spend a couple of days exploring to the north for starters.

Here was yet another corner of the ancient Celtic world, one primarily populated by the Brigantes a long, long time ago. Brigantes refers to "high" or "elevated," and it may mean these ancient ones were noble or tall or simply that they lived high up in the hills. The Parisi occupied southerly parts of modern Yorkshire and the first record of them appears in Ptolemy's *Geographica*. Based on some cursory research, however, it was obvious that we'd be hard-pressed to find any physical evidence left anywhere of these ancient Celts.

Our route north took us through Gosforth, Wideopen, Dudley, Cramlington and Morpeth. Along the way we *almost* visited eleventh-century Alnwick Castle, made famous in the Harry Potter films. I say almost because, as we pulled into the parking lot, I spied nearly a dozen tour buses. The site of hundreds of tourists spilling out of those buses sent a shiver down my spine and, much to Linda's chagrin, I had us back on the road almost at once with me uttering yet again, "If you've seen one castle..." Sleep-deprived from the overnight flight from Nova Scotia to Heathrow, I failed to comprehend how much Linda really wanted to visit Alnwick. Gentlemen, I would advise you that if you find yourself in Yorkshire (or anywhere else on this spinning globe) and your wife wants to visit a certain castle, do pull off the road and oblige.

So, instead of Alnwick, we drove on to Bamburgh, home of another famous castle. The Normans built part of what is still standing, and it was improved or altered by various conquerors over the years. Here was the site of a previous fort known as *Din Guarie* built by Celts, and it was probably the capital of this region from AD 420 to 547. It went through several owners until the ever-nasty Vikings arrived in 993 to destroy it. The current castle remains most impressive and worthy of note and was used for the setting of at least two *Macbeth* movies but, sadly, no Harry Potter blockbusters.

Below the castle, we walked a long empty beach, noted the lack of any surf but began to get a sense of the big swaths of coastal landscape, which remained thankfully undisturbed by thousands of years of human habitation. The preservation of grand chunks of forests, coastland, estuaries, moors and mountains is a testament to the British love of all things natural.

After Bamburgh, we retraced our route, retreating south as the Romans once did in the fifth century. We lodged for the night at one of those cozy inns on the highway with a public house down below. In the pub, everything was old and crooked the way we liked it, and I'm sure there was roast beef and Yorkshire pudding involved.

Not far from our lodging was Hadrian's Wall, built in the second century AD to keep the "barbarians" to the north out of the Roman Empire. It stretches 117 kilometres from Solway in the west to the appropriately named Wallsend in the east.

In the morning we did a fair bit of driving on the A1. The trouble with driving on motorways is that you really don't get any sense of the life in the communities you zip past. I'm sure there were exciting dart tournaments in Kibblesworth and probably a great punk music scene in Great Lumley, and no doubt a great comedy club renaissance in a place called Shiney Row or Thorpe Thewles. But I will probably never know.

Passing over the River Tees, I grew despondent staring out at the great sprawling industrial areas of Middlesbrough, but things changed greatly by the time we entered the North York Moors, a vast, seemingly untamed wilderness for the most part, still a bit stark this early in the season but certainly a place to let loose a brooding literary imagination.

As we motored our way through the moors, I noticed on the map that the next large town was Scarborough, and I immediately began to hum that famous Simon and Garfunkel tune that had been resurrected from folklore and revamped as part of the soundtrack to *The Graduate*. Sadly, what I remember most about Scarborough were the dozen or so roundabouts with edgy aggressive drivers having little patience for a Canadian trying valiantly to get his rental car into the proper lane. So, no thank you, Mr. Art Garfunkel, I guess I am not going to Scarborough Fair.

But Boynton was everything we'd hoped it would be: a quaint cottage off on a tiny paved track of a road. Everything in bloom. Horses nearby eating grass. An old stone chapel next door and hiking paths leading off through fields of wildflowers. The next morning we set off walking a back road toward Grindale and found ourselves gazing across a near-endless canola field on a most pleasant morning. A fine spring morning in rural Yorkshire is worth celebrating and many a poet has done just that, I am sure.

Soon after that we paid respects to the Rudston Monolith, said to be the tallest prehistoric standing stone in Britain at eight metres in height. Strong, dedicated workers had once lugged the big rock here from Cayton Bay, 16 kilometres to the east. As I gazed at this ancient monument, I envisioned myself as a tribal leader from Yorkshire those many years ago, announcing to my fellow citizens, "C'mon, lads, let's find a really big rectangular stone and set it upright in this field so people hundreds of years from now can wonder what it may mean."

Well beyond Rudston, on our travels inland through Thwing, Bugthorpe and Skirpenbeck, we arrived at the city of York. We ditched the car, of course, and wandered the narrow, enchanting streets with their old storefronts of wood, brick and stone. It seemed that everyone was walking around eating something — hot dogs, ice cream cones, ham sandwiches or some kind of cake. York must certainly be a city that makes everyone hungry. We dodged endless processions of eaters, it seemed, on our quest for the cathedral. Once there, we took as many pictures as the other tourists. Inside those stone walls, I felt the sort of piety one is expected to feel in those sanctuaries designed to inspire spiritual moods. I always think I'll be disappointed when I join the mobs of sightseers and enter into famous places of worship. But I'm usually not. The smell of old stone, the sun streaming through stained glass, impossibly high ceilings, the arches, the statues of the once-famous and now-forgotten dead. They all add up to a true feeling of awe and produce a meditative mind. I am forever thankful to those dedicated souls who conceived and built and sacrificed to leave us such edifices to remind North Americans that once upon a time, people cared more about their deity than their dollars (or their quid).

In the days ahead, having fulfilled our desire for urban adventure, it was back to the coast to explore, first, Flamborough Head with its limestone cliffs and steep, stony trails down to exotic pocket beaches. To the north, we found Filey less inspiring, then braved the surly traffic of Scarborough once more to seek out Robin Hood's Bay. Here was a small seaport town tucked between two hills and a most happy place to tromp around on cobbled streets envisioning the life of fishermen and smugglers from days gone by. I walked by a building with a big sign announcing that here was the Robin Hood's Bay Men's Institute and wondered what on earth that could be. There seems to be scant evidence that Robin Hood ever spent much or any time here, but the village is nonetheless a place with many stories of danger and adventure dating back to 1538, when it was known as a "fisher hamlet of twenty boats."

The tide was out and we could hike the shoreline for many miles to the south toward a headland known as South Cheek. Again there was not the slightest sign of surf, but walking along on the ocean floor was a very satisfying experience. Along the way we passed a most impressive spot called Boggle Hole, well marked with a National Trust sign, but later

I read one Tripadvisor reviewer who regarded it as "the best kept secret in England" or something like that. Nonetheless, if you are ever in this corner of the world, I suggest Robin Hood's Bay and Boggle Hole are both worth a visit.

Whitby was a much larger coastal town and was once apparently scary enough to inspire Bram Stoker to use it as a location for part of *Dracula*. Captain James Cook had learned to be a sailor here before scouting off to far corners of the world and getting himself killed in Hawaii while trying to kidnap a local king.

I recall having an afternoon pint of ale sitting in a second-storey pub overlooking the beach at Whitby. The walls were covered in velour and the barkeep played endless tunes by yet another king, Elvis Presley, prompting me to yet again ponder what a curious and surprising island this England can be.

As the days went by, we continued to scour the coastline, looking for idyllic seaside communities. Scarborough was still a bit too frantic for my liking and is home to the rudest drivers in the United Kingdom, so I will thumb my nose at it should I come this way again. Filey, however, seemed like a much more pleasant coastal town on our second visit, with a sandy beach that stretched for many worthwhile kilometres. We made the mistake of driving south one day to Hornsea only to discover that it too has a fine beach but is home to a large caravan park. I reminded myself yet again that urbanites need to get out of the city and be able to afford some kind of *pied-à-terre* by the sea. It's just that those multitudes of aluminum boxes by the water can't help but detract from the natural beauty. Forgive me. I'll stop whining now.

While retreating to Boynton each night, we had never yet dared to drive deeper into the nearby city of Bridlington than necessary. This usually just meant a foray into the Morrison's to buy a pint of Hobgoblin and some freshly caught fish. (If York was good for the soul, then the Bridlington Morrison's was equally good for the sole.) But our time was slipping away so I finally announced that, yes, we would chance it and drive to the coast at Bridlington to walk the well-trod promenade by the sea.

The British don't tan well, as you may have noticed, and I am as pale as they, but the nation's health care system really should invest a bit more money in promoting sunscreen. It was a Saturday as we strode the planks in Bridlington, and a lively one at that with vendors and amusement rides and crowds of bustling people. I kept thinking that you could replace Bridlington with Brighton and probably no one would notice. Old seaside British resorts have a feel to them. I can't quite place it, but if you study the faces of vacationers, it's like they are all silently saying to you, "I'm here on a holiday and, despite the noise and the crowds and the cold sea wind, I'm going to bloody well enjoy myself and to hell with you."

Or something like that.

But, with the proper mindset, the Bridlington board-walk can be a grand place to stroll and take in the throngs of humanity eating fish and chips from cardboard plates. All that salt air eventually got to us, I guess, for we finally gave in and bought our own fishy plate from a crowded fish and chips shop. On a small floppy plate, we were delivered a battered slab of fish three times the size of the plate itself. Along with the greasiest chips I'd encountered outside South Philadelphia was a generous dollop of mushy peas. The fish and chips were extremely unhealthy but delicious. Yet, like all foreign travellers to England, we wondered, what could they possibly be thinking by adding the green mush?

After the fish was somewhat digested and the madding crowds put behind us, we aimed our rental car east and away from Bridlington. It's certainly not the Sodom and Gomorrah of this north coast, but we did not look back. Instead, we drove east to the Bempton Cliffs and the world-famous birds.

Once you leave the car park at Bempton, you enter another world. It is a realm ruled by vaulting sea mist, magnificent otherworldly vistas, birds and birders. Bempton Cliffs and the fields nearby are home to many exotic and ordinary species of birds. Along the cliffs you can spot razorbills, puffins, gannets, guillemots, fulmars, kittiwakes, shags and herring gulls. Just a few metres away from the coast in the fields you can watch tree sparrows, linnets, skylarks, meadow pipits and at least two kinds of buntings. Flying predators such as short-eared owls and peregrines are often about. If that's not enough for you, keep looking and you're likely to see whitethroats, willow warblers, chiffchaffs, reed warblers, sedge warblers, redstarts, goldcrests, stonechats, wheatears and whinchats.

Bempton is a place of raw natural splendour and should not be missed. Looking out over Thornwick Bay, as the mist cleared, I found myself soaring with the seabirds, catching spiralling updrafts of salty air and leaving all the frenzy of modern England behind.

The early settlers here, the Celts among them, would have lowered themselves down on ropes to rob eggs from the nests of these soaring seabirds. But today, these are protected areas, celebrated by the benign armies of bird watchers who come here from around the world. For our final day of travels in this corner of the Celtic world, the birds lifted our spirits high into the heavens, reminding us that we share this planet with some amazing creatures and need to do all we can to protect them while we support and celebrate all those who dedicate their lives to the preservation of living creatures and natural beauty.

CHAPTER NINETEEN

SWEET MEMORIES OF ABERDEENSHIRE (MAY 2015)

We returned from Yorkshire to Canada, cancer and chemo. I remember buying wigs for Linda at a wig store in New Jersey run by friendly young Puerto Rican women who let me try on several cheap and expensive wigs. I bought one of each.

Linda never needed them. I refused to allow her to take the advice of all the experts who told her to shave her head so she didn't have to live through the hair falling out, but hers never did. After that, the wigs sat forlornly on their ghost-like Styrofoam heads and I think we only brought them out at Halloween.

The chemo and, I like to think, my coaching worked, and soon the lymphoma had gone into remission. The brush with cancer prompted Linda to retire from her big-city high school principal job and we had more travels to plan. Murdo lived for a few more years thanks to the expensive pharmaceutical that slowed the progression of his kidney cancer. Willing to try just about anything to keep him relatively healthy, I even adopted the so-called Kelmun Protocol, which amounted to giving him a daily dose of (get this) baking soda and maple syrup. The "theory" is that the cancer cells are attracted to the sweet maple syrup and then killed by alkaline properties of sodium bicarbonate. Who knows? Maybe it helped and maybe the world is full of simple cures for things if we only knew the right combinations. But when Murdo died, it was sad for all of us and we grieved a full year before adopting a new Westie puppy from Ontario. And so it was that Kelty came into our life.

We had travelled to Italy and Greece and spent time in Cornwall during the winter on more than one occasion. We had also liked what we'd seen of the northern part of Britain — Yorkshire and the North Sea coast. In March and April one year, the frigid and unrelenting North Atlantic was keeping Nova Scotia clammy and cold and so, although you may scoff at the phrasing, we had our eye on sunny Scotland, and the shores near Aberdeen in particular.

Many years ago I had the good fortune of being writer-in-residence at the International School Aberdeen, a posh, well-appointed institution near Aberdeen for kids from many parts of the world. Aside from my rather pleasant duties of talking to students about creativity and writing, I had enough leisure time to hike along a local canal path, go bike riding the back roads and generally ramble around the most agreeable countryside my shoe leather had ever encountered.

My teacher-host, fellow Nova Scotian Andy Field, even took me surfing, first just south of Aberdeen where the water was surprisingly warm (it turned out that the sewage plant emptied into the ocean near the surf break). Later we suited up in wetsuits on a pebbly beach right in downtown Stonehaven, dropping in on small North Sea waves before a backdrop of a bustling village that dates back centuries.

Fortified with a couple of pints of Guinness, we even stole onto one of Scotland's famous public golf courses just as the sun dipped below the massive deciduous trees, and I was able to blame the diminishing light for such a poor performance at that gentleman's sport until all my balls were swallowed by those looming dark and hungry trees.

When my residency ended, I promised myself I would return to explore this northeast corner of Scotland with its sumptuous land and historical riches. And so it was that in the spring of 2015 Linda and I plotted a few adventures in that part of the world and rented a small stone cottage in the tiny village of Pitmedden. It was a converted one-room schoolhouse really, made of solid blocks of granite and conveniently located in the front yard of a newer house owned by a woman who was a professional self-help guru and drove the shiniest BMW I had ever seen.

We seek connections in this world, wherever we go, and there was another thread that brought us here, which was a sad one. An old, good friend of nearly 30 years, Jim Lotz, had recently passed away from pancreatic cancer. Jim was a brilliant independent thinker, a social activist and author, a feisty, good-natured Brit who had immigrated to Canada to roam the Arctic, fight for social justice and advise younger writers like me, "Don't ever listen to the bastards who say you can't do it. Just get on with it and bugger all." I had helped edit Jim's autobiography, *Sharing the Journey,* and the book had been at the printer as he lay dying. He had grown up in Liverpool and watched his neighbourhood get bombed by the Nazis before he was shipped off to the safer environs of Aberdeenshire, near the town of Oldmeldrum. Of the Scottish countryside, he had this to say: "This hard, barren land touched some deep, responsive chord in my nature. I enjoyed roaming through glens and over moors, happy in my own company, delighting in the scenery and the romantic history of the Highlands while coping with atrocious weather."

Our own explorations of the area actually took us farther afield from Aberdeen into a broader expanse of coast and mountains sometimes labelled the Grampian region, although this appears to be a political jurisdiction label slapped onto this part of northeast Scotland between 1975 and 1996. The name comes from the bold and somewhat bald mountains of a region of some 8700 square kilometres and, as Jim Lotz points out, it is one lovely and evocative piece of geography.

I dutifully delivered a copy of Jim's book to a state-of-the-art new library outside of Oldmeldrum and the librarian didn't quite know what to make of it (or me), but if anyone is out and about there, do check for me to see it is at least catalogued and on the shelves. Oldmeldrum itself really is quite old as the name implies. The Meldrum family built a castle here in 1236. The third Earl of Buchan reportedly found shelter for his soldiers here around Christmas of 1307 before being defeated by Robert the Bruce in a nearby battle not long after that.

In Oldmeldrum, I dutifully sampled the wares at the famous Glen Garioch Distillery but declined to purchase the more expensive vintage whiskeys with price tags in the range of US$400–$500. Linda and I did find refreshment at a downtown pub with a nautical theme. It was a wonderfully cramped and convivial establishment in one of the many grey stone buildings of the town.

Our favourite pub, however, was the more contemporary BrewDog brewery in Ellon to the east. This is one of Scotland's new breed of craft brewers whose motto appears to be "Equity for Punks." No one was quite able to explain to us what that meant, but they had a great line of hoppy beers and good hospitality. The business was founded way back in 2007 by two guys named James and Martin. James had this to say about the origins: "Martin and I were bored of the industrially brewed lagers and stuffy ales that dominated the UK beer market." And as they say, the rest was history. What on the surface appeared to be a business run by some highly creative countercultural young brewmeisters was actually on its way to becoming a very lucrative multinational corporation.

Like James and Martin, I too was weary of stuffy ales, and BrewDog's Punk IPA (my personal favourite) was proving to the quaffing masses that the new brew in town was taking over.

Hiking mountains and getting wet in salt water are always on our agenda if possible when we travel. We found our first waves for boogie boarding in the waters of Fraserburgh Bay to the north, well insulated by wetsuits of course. It was a sandy haven of hikers, surfers and kite surfers where everyone was friendly and kind. If you are in that neck of the woods, the dunes alone are worth the excursion.

Fraserburgh itself is a major bustling fishing port. We'd read reports of heavy drug use among young bored fishermen who would return from the sea with money in their pockets and a craving to get dangerously high, but we found nothing but good vibes among the Fraserburgh folk, young and old. In town we discovered a house known as Maggie's Hoosie, a traditional fishing cottage preserved for tourists like us to see. Until she died in 1950, the spinster Maggie Duthie lived there with an earthen floor, no heat or electricity and a twentieth-century life not unlike that lived by her ancestors 200 years ago.

With a good map you can find curiously named towns in this part of Scotland that are almost always worth a visit. I was curious about a place called Udny Green, which turned out to have a beautiful town commons and an upscale restaurant named Eat on the Green that appeared to be out of our league but, after much deliberation, the maître d' took pity on us and gave us a small corner table if we promised not to stay longer than an hour. On the wall were photos of the Queen, Pierce Brosnan and Sean Connery, if I recall correctly. It was that kind of place. The meal was pricey (no surprise) but good as we polished it off in the required hour and headed off to see what we could see in Pettymuick, Tillygreig, Whiterashes, Port Elphinstone, Balhalgardy and Inverurie. Then, while taking a break in Burnhervie, I spied on a map a symbol for an ancient monument nearby called the Maiden Stone.

The Maiden Stone was a bit hard to find, located in a field with no fanfare south of Pitcaple off a back road and west of a town called Chapel of Garioch. The road itself was one of those interesting rural avenues to a North American like me because it was a single lane about the width of a sidewalk but perfectly paved as if designed for elves driving miniature automobiles.

Since there was no one else on the road but us, our tires straddled the path as we made several wrong turns until we found the sought-after Maiden Stone. When approaching the stone, we met a rather excited English tourist who was snapping photographs from every possible angle. Happy to see us and eager to share his enthusiasm for what appeared to be an upright lichen-covered pink granite rock with a notch cut out of it, he told us that it dated back to the eighth century when the Picts lived here. According to legend, the daughter of a laird made some crazy bet with a man who turned out to be the devil. The impetuous young lass, on her wedding day no less, bet the stranger that she could finish her baking task quicker than he could build a road to the top of a local mountain or she would marry him instead of her betrothed. I asked the informative Englishman why someone would make such a bet, especially on her wedding day, but he had no clear explanation and seemed offended that I would even ask.

At any rate, the devil, being the devil, built that mountain road in a jiffy and came to claim his young bride. The laird's daughter made a run for it and swore she'd rather turn to stone before marrying the likes of Satan. And so she got her wish.

The tallest mountain we chose to hike upon had the curious name of Mither Tap, and we arrived just as a bus of school kids were embarking on the hike through the well-marked forest trail that led to the base of the mountain. Standing a mere 1,279 feet above sea level, Mither Tap has a commanding granite summit looking out over the other Bennachie Mountains. As the trail became steeper and steeper, we huffed and puffed our way to the glorious but barren summit as giggling Scottish schoolboys kicked pebbles down on us from above. Their harried and embarrassed schoolmistress begged them to stop and then shouted down apologies to us below. Despite the pelting of stones, the view from the top was well worth it on a clear day like this when you could see for miles.

Although I sometimes am of the opinion that if you've seen one castle, you've seen them all, Linda persuaded me that we should at least take in Castle Fraser down around Monymusk and Craigearn. I drove past it once, pretending not to see it and thought I might get away with it, but unfortunately there was a big sign at the next crossroads pointing back to the estate. I parked and grudgingly paid for admission. (It is probably unreasonable of me, but I feel that castles, ruins and ancient monuments to would-be brides of the devil should all be free as was the Maiden Stone in her grassy remote field.)

But if you are going to choose just one castle in the Grampian region, Fraser is probably as good a pick as you'll get. The grounds are beautiful and it is considered one of the "most elaborate of z-plan castles in Scotland." Most castles have stories, and if those stories are intriguing enough, most of us don't really care if they are true or not. At Castle Fraser, it is said that once upon a time a young princess was murdered (why we do not know) and as she was carried down the stairs, her blood stained the steps so badly that they had to be covered over with wood. Today, I am sure, professionals with the right tools and detergents could have solved the problem, but who are we to judge.

And, yes, it was a pretty darn good castle as castles go. As we walked back to the parking lot where a pair of swans from the castle pond seemed to be studying our rental car, I wondered out loud exactly how and why that murder happened, if it happened at all and why such stories seem to linger on for centuries while undoubtedly countless good deeds by generations of the Frasers go unremembered.

Long after that day, late one night, while starting to fall asleep in front of the TV watching Helen Mirren in *The Queen*, I thought the location in the movie looked familiar, and sure enough, Castle Fraser it was.

Before heading home, I was longing for one more foray to the sea and I noted a nature reserve named Forvie just north of Newburgh that would allow us another visit to the BrewDog in Ellon on our way home. On the way to Forvie, we passed what seemed to be miles of coastland that had been privatized and developed into a golf course.

I wondered how the people of Scotland had allowed such pristine coastal land that had remained untrampled for centuries to be developed this way. Later I would learn that none other than Donald Trump had bought up the coastline in 2014 and invested US$290 million to create the Trump International Golf Links, in the process decimating what were once legally protected sand dunes. Suffice it to say, Mr. Trump and his links did piss off a fair portion of the population of the region.

The beach and waters at Forvie, however, were providentially protected. Linda and I hiked out to the sea along the beautiful Ythan Estuary, home of "the largest breeding colony of little terns on the east coast of Scotland." The water was blue, the sky was cloudless. Helicopters scudding across the sky transporting workers to and fro from the North Sea oil rigs did nothing to detract from the beauty and sanctity of the place. The sand felt glorious on our bare feet. The terns swooped and swirled above and, at the mouth of the estuary, we began to hear an otherworldly chorus of low moaning voices drifting toward us in the wind. As we continued to walk, the sound grew louder and then we began to see a dark, undulating mass of something on the shores across the river mouth from us.

When we reached the sea, we could now realize that it was a large community of seals — perhaps a hundred — lounging on the sands across from us. Their voices were loud now, drowning out everything else, and their song stirred something within me. Young seals dove from the shoreline into the clear blue water, swam and played and then hopped back up on the sandy shoreline. That farther shore was an empty, flawless expanse of coastal wilderness. The terns, the seals, the gulls and the other creatures of the wind and sea would be free and safe here. For a while at least.

As we turned and headed back to civilization, sand sifting through our toes, we felt blessed by the birds and beasts and privileged to have encountered this pocket of pristine wilderness, here in a land where human habitation goes back over 14,000 years.

CHAPTER TWENTY

ON A BALCONY IN OSGATHORPE

Kelty was fast asleep there on the balcony at Osgathorpe as we reminisced into the sunset about Boynton, Pitmedden, Murdo, cancer and the great river of time that kept flowing. Tomorrow was another day and there was planning needed. I had wanted to drive into Atherstone, near Sibson, because they had named a street Choyce Close in honour of the nearly forgotten poet.

The Ping-Pong players were back for a last round of games at sunset and the steady staccato of the men hitting the ball was quite mesmerising as we all began to fade.

In the morning, Linda took to the roads and ran seven kilometres. She considered Osgathorpe one of her all-time favourite locales for a rural run. I preferred walking and took the dog back down the country lane, noting on this fine morning that Leicestershire may well have more birds per cubic foot of sky than anywhere on earth.

Lonely Planet suggests that "Leicestershire doesn't yet have the strongest tourist gravity," and that's just fine by me. Me and Linda and Kelty and the birds. "Tourist gravity" is a wonderful way of describing places I would prefer to ignore. I prefer anti-gravity, you might say. Like the birds above me who have a way of avoiding earthbound activity whenever they want. On our morning walk I heard the most ambitious squealy sparrows, those guttural squawking crows, unidentified single-note chirpers, some bird that sounded exactly like my old fax machine, geese invisibly honking somewhere and those large rock pigeons cooing up a storm as they flew past me at eye level. All the while, up above were silent swooping swallows.

In case that wasn't enough, if you stopped your breath long enough, you could hear squadrons of bees at work in the clover and other wildflowers. Here, in the land of my ancestors, I wondered how it was they had ever left. When they arrived in New Jersey in the eighteenth century, they would have found a veritable Garden of Eden as well, but it would change as industrialization crept over the green land, much as it had done in unluckier parts of the Midlands near here.

But, instead of constructing gargantuan sports stadiums, shopping malls and endless paved highways, places like Osgathorpe and Sibson still had vast green fields, ancient pubs, abandoned priories and birds and bees weighing in each morning with their melodic opinions about what a fine life it is in rural Leicestershire.

The next day, a perfectly fine Sunday morning, we headed into the small city with the unlikely and, I thought, highly comic name of Ashby-de-la-Zouch. *No, really?* I asked the sign welcoming us to town. I told Linda and Kelty that I thought the place was named after a Monty Python sketch, but they both thought otherwise. There was a famous castle there, possibly once owned by the Zouches, or the de la Zouches to be specific, and wasn't that indicative that they were French and, if so, how could that be the case here in the middle of the Midlands?

Ashby was bigger than I imagined and exceedingly more lively than one would expect on an otherwise quiet Sunday morning in June. Once we parked and began to scope out the town, we discovered that most people were not piously singing hymns to Jesus in the Anglican church but, instead, throngs of rowdy lads and ladies were spilling out of the several pubs along our path at 10:00 a.m.

I suppose it was the young women dressed in flamboyant red outfits waving flags and blowing kazoos that made me realize it must have something to do with football — or what we call it back on the other side of the pond, soccer. And I remembered reading yesterday's newspaper that today was the day England was pitched against Panama in the FIFA World Cup. Boisterous revellers held aloft large steins of beer, the likes of which I had not seen since sitting in the Löwenbräu Beer Garden in Baden-Baden Germany the day after Barack Obama had come to town there.

We had no inclination of joining the soccer fans but, instead, ducked down a side alley that would take us to the de la Zed castle. There we encountered an even rowdier mob of de la Zouchians wearing cut-off T-shirts and what is referred to these days as "distressed jeans" drinking yet more beer. There were no kazoo-playing women in this crowd, which must have given the lads licence to be even louder and raunchier in their beery discussions about the national qualities of Panamanians. I ushered my wife and dog along and we tried to look like innocuous tourists who had no opinions about football or Central American nations that have been dominated by the US for over a century.

Soon we were safely inside the gift shop of the castle paying the English Heritage folks admission money and studying the bottles of chili-flavoured mead for sale. When I was offered a free sample, I obliged, having never once in my

67 years tasted mead, or especially mead with hot peppers. I agreed with the sales lady that the chili did offset the sweetness of the mead but decreed that I was not prepared to pay £20 for a full bottle of it. I associated mead with *Beowulf* and thought it should only be drunk in authentic mead halls in England or Scandinavia sometime well before the birth of Christ.

The castle was what I would label a well-preserved ruin. All but one tall tower had no roof. There were large grassy grounds with sunken parts that were once gardens where aristocrats would have socialized and commented over winners and losers in jousting tournaments, or so I imagined.

According to English Heritage, the castle was "the purpose-built seat of one of the most powerful men in late 15th-century English politics, William, Lord Hastings. His adaptations to the relatively modest existing manor house at Ashby began in 1472–3, but by the time of his sudden fall from grace and execution in 1483 only about half of his grand design had been realised." The Zouches were a Breton family who had been granted the land long before that, and their name remained, but the family's ownership had slipped away. Sir Walter Scott had set a scene from *Ivanhoe* in the castle here, I read somewhere, leading me to wonder if anyone actually read Sir Walter's novels anymore, especially *Ivanhoe*.

English Heritage had dozens of informational plaques scattered about and my favourite one informed me that I could walk up to a crumbling stone wall and study the indentations made by muskets and cannons in days gone by.

I also climbed up the turret on a steep circular stone staircase that reminded me of a model of DNA I once made for a science fair back in the sixth grade. The higher I went, the grander the view, and there is something about the smell of damp stone stairs where feet have trod for hundreds of years that triggers a feeling of awe that I can't quite explain. At one of the highest narrow windows along the staircase I came across a pure white pigeon and, as I paused to catch my breath, she looked me in the eye and, through what I can only suggest is telepathy, told me that she was once a beautiful woman who had thrived here several centuries ago and now that she was reincarnated as a bird, she remained here in the turret so she could soar above the ruins each day and keep an eye on things. And then she flew off to survey the site of her former home from great heights.

Back at ground level, the three of us (yes, dogs are allowed on the grounds of ruins!) walked through roofless halls with green grass growing where aristocrats once danced and argued and drank claret in great quantities.

On our way back to the car park, the revellers had not relented one bit and, as we caught a snatch of a barroom TV, it appeared the game had only just begun.

On one of her morning runs, Linda had come upon a pub called the Queen's Head in Belton, just down the lane from Osgathorpe. I couldn't quite nail down the history except that it was once a "coaching inn" that turned into a public house. I kept wondering what the various queens of England thought about having pubs named after their heads. But this pub advertised that they "love dogs, and furry friends are welcome both in our bar area and overnight." So we liked it no matter what its history might be. Linda had seen an announcement on her run that the pub offered a Sunday Roast. And today was Sunday, so we made our way out of rowdy Ashby and drove to the sleepy little burgh of Belton.

In one room of the Queen's Head, there was a massive screen TV where football fans were shouting at it enthusiastically, but we found a quiet table outside where we could sit with our dog and enjoy the excellent food. We had roast beef, of course, pan-fried potatoes, string beans, carrots and a piece of Yorkshire pudding as big as a catcher's mitt. Even though it was early afternoon (but a bit later wherever the game was being staged), the match was ending. England won 3-1, apparently raising national aspirations of actually winning the World Cup, only to be dashed a few days later when overly ambitious Italians whipped the Brits handily.

A side trip to the east finished off our afternoon. First we drove to Shepshed and then it was on to Loughborough. Eventually, we grew weary of driving around and retired to our second-floor dwelling above the McLaren to sit on the little balcony again, play Canasta and watch the horses graze on the clover-covered fields.

By evening I was studying my AA map book and, like Rommel planning an invasion route in Africa, trying to determine the quickest and least painful way to get to our next destination, Betws-y-Coed in north central Wales. My imaginary critics were still mumbling to me their complaint about the geography of my book. "If you are going to write a book called *Around England with a Dog*, what business do you have traipsing around Wales, for God's sakes? You've already cheated and included France. And now this."

Well, yes, I would counter. It's because plans keep changing. Those pilgrims who stick to a fixed game plan miss the real possibilities of adventure. And indulge me even further if you will as I retrace a few steps.

As you may recall, I had taken a sabbatical from my university duties of teaching young writers how to write short stories and my coaxing of first-year students to try to stay awake through a 50-minute class. All our travelling was to take place in the fall — September into October. But then we learned that my daughter, Pamela, was to have twins in August and Linda's daughter, Laura, was going to have a baby at the beginning of October. So flights were cancelled and new plans hatched. A month with the dog in June would be the core of the trip.

But that wasn't quite enough to get ourselves *around* the bulk of England — and I had a craving to include some more of Scotland as well. So back in Nova Scotia in March we had hatched a plan to make a pre-Kelty trip to Glasgow in April without the dog, roam around Argyll and Edinburgh and then down to the Lake District as a pre-Kelty foray gearing up for the central dog trip. Why Argyll? Because there in Poltalloch, Edward Donald Malcolm, sixteenth Laird of Poltalloch, first bred what we now know as the West Highland White Terrier breed and it was the ancestral home of Kelty's antecedents. Why Edinburgh? Because it supposedly had great street life, was where J.K. Rowling had penned the first Harry Potter book and because it had pubs with names like the Devil's Advocate. And why the Lake District? Well, anyone who has been there knows you don't need a reason to visit there. It has mountains and lakes and the preserved home of William Wordsworth, a poet who helped me to survive graduate school.

So before we move on to me trying to overcome my grudge against the Welsh, before I write about fecklessly surfing the waves on a man-made lake, before I tell you about my $300 running shoes and our strange encounter with death in Devon, let's slip back in time by two months as we stumble out of the Glasgow airport after yet another red-eye flight across the Atlantic from Halifax, Nova Scotia.

CHAPTER TWENTY-ONE

IN SEARCH OF KELTY'S ANCESTORS AND DINNER IN DUNOON (APRIL 2018)

Just those few months earlier from our time in Leicestershire, I was offered an opportunity to write about both Argyll and Edinburgh and realized it would be a good chance to cover those very interesting parts of Scotland for the big dog book to come. In fact, we were now able to make that pilgrimage to the very origins of the West Highland White Terrier and even take a side trip down to sacred territory to me, the Lake District in England. Unfortunately, Kelty would not be allowed to take the direct flight to Glasgow given the barbaric and inhumane rules put in place by Her Majesty's government. Nonetheless, the research would help me flesh out a fuller picture of Britain and fill in some English gaps in our upcoming month-long adventure *with* our soon-to-be-famous dog.

With great sadness, we left Kelty at Country Critters in nearby Seaforth, Nova Scotia. Mary Taplin had a large fenced-in property on a hill that ran down to the sea and took in many dogs at a time. Kelty was happy there, but when we would return it would take a few days for him to recover from all the excitement of having reverted to a pack dog.

Efficient ex-principal that she was, Linda had written a document with the essentials of what any Kelty-sitter needed to know. And I quote:

Kelty MacGregor Choyce
Food

Kelty eats 1/2 cup of dry food mixed with 2 tablespoons of warm water 2 times a day. Usually around 8 and 4:30. Kelty does not have any people food. He has the potential to beg (trust me) and also has allergies and therefore we are keeping him away from any temptations. We use his kibble for treats.

Sleeping

Kelty goes to bed at the same time as we do, usually around 10:00 p.m. and sleeps with us. He is a bed hog! Wake time is usually anywhere from 6:30-7:15 but sometimes later. Also, he will often settle into bed with you after he has been outside first thing in the morning.

Pee and Poop

Here is when he will go: first thing in the morning he will definitely do both unless he gets distracted. He will go again almost immediately after breakfast guaranteed! Be sure to have a bag with you as he loves to poop on the beach! Evening poop between 8:00 and 8:30 p.m.

Kelty the West Highland TERRORIST

Kelty is a young dog and therefore a bit naughty. He is obsessed with footwear (preferably when you are wearing them) and pant legs.

Leaving Kelty Alone

Kelty is just fine left for short periods of time. If need be, we leave him for several hours at a time.

Phrases Kelty seems to know

Every meal is supper: "Let's get your supper, Kelty."

"Going to bed now."

"Going in the car."

"Going to the beach."

"No."

"Good boy."

Leash

Kelty needs to be on leash at all times while you are outdoors. He has no sense of traffic at all and would run into the road. Also, he loves to run away from you and you cannot catch him.

Tricks

He can dance. Say "Dance," while holding the treat.

"Sit." You may have to ask more than once as he will be excited.

"Give me your paw." Touch the paw you want.

Doing tricks with Kelty works best if you sit on the floor, legs out, with Kelty between them. You need a bit of patience as he is very impatient. Please just give him the tiniest bit of treat.

So, once Kelty was settled with his canine comrades at Country Critters, Linda and I headed off on our journey to the Cowal Peninsula in the Argyll region of Scotland. One travel writer described it "like a three taloned claw with the Isle of Bute clutched in its grip."

The WestJet flight from Halifax to Glasgow was as benign as an overnight flight can be, yet I felt foggy-headed as we tried to make the proper turns to find the Erskine Bridge over the Clyde River. Heading north, we saw crowds of picnickers scurrying along the shores of Loch Lomond and it looked just too civilized on this day for a man longing for some Scottish wilderness. We turned off the A83 at Cairndow to head south on the peninsula and saw the Stagecoach Inn where Dorothy and William Wordsworth had lodged in 1803 and ate fresh herring. They, of course, had done some serious hiking locally and, while "doubling and doubling with laborious walk," had found a plaque on the path that instructed them to "Rest and be Thankful," where apparently they did just that.

Linda and I didn't have an opportunity to do the same until we drove on southward along Loch Fyne to the tiny village of Uig (not to be confused with Uig, the ferry port to the Outer Hebrides on the Isle of Skye). Here we had rented a small house next door to Benmore Gardens and just down the road from Puck's Glen. From the look of the map, there was adventure aplenty nearby along Loch Eck and Loch Long, Glen Lean and the aforementioned Isle of Bute. Rowan Cottage was a bit cool and damp (No, really? In Scotland?) but it had an amazing sun room in the back with a view of a mountain named Sgorach Mor, which apparently means "the large hill rising out of the mountain," a curious double whammy of a name that puzzled us both.

Our first restaurant meal was in a tea room in nearby Dunoon that was supposedly serving "home cooked meals," but the fish on my plate and the chicken in the chicken burger were straight out of a box in the freezer. We did better stocking up on some fresh fish and garden goods at the Morrison's and found Dunoon to be a busy and lively place once we got the hang of the one-way streets and tight corners.

Dunoon is a port city of about 13,000 souls with a famous Victorian pier, and, oddly enough, during the Cold War it was the host home for US submarines carrying nuclear weapons. The subs bobbed in the harbour until 1992, after Gorbachev had almost single-handedly called off the dangerous stalemate and allowed Ronald Reagan to take all the credit for it.

Mary Campbell, often referred to as "Highland Mary," was born in Dunoon and there is a statue of her opposite Dunoon Pier. VisitScotland has this to say about it: "Erected in 1896, the statue of Robert Burns' 'Highland Mary' Campbell gazes wistfully southwards to her lover's Ayrshire home." She had been a lover of dear Robbie and he had written several poems about her, as well as *for* her, and they had hatched plans to leave Scotland for Jamaica of all places. Unfortunately, she died as a result of illness at the age of 23, yet she is revered and remembered by many in Scotland today.

Dunoon Castle sits nearby on a hill and dates back to the twelfth century, a mighty long time ago by my reckoning. It was the scene of a nasty massacre in 1646 when the Marquis of Argyll (in my opinion, a bit of a bastard) hanged "scores of prisoners."

Across Holy Loch from Dunoon is the somewhat posh suburb of Kilmun, a village founded by Saint Mun in 620, although people had been living around there since 3500

BC — again a mind-boggling long time ago to us ramblers in the twenty-first century. Saint Mun was an Irish monk, contemporary to the more famous Saint Columba, who had at one time, it was said, been "assisted" by two wolves while guarding his sheep. A hike through the graveyard behind the famous church there gave me pause as I ran my hands over the old tombstones where time and weather had erased the names of several centuries of mothers, fathers, sons and daughters.

Kilmun is on the shores of Holy Loch, which is said to be holy because soil from the Holy Land fell into the waters here when the ship carrying it for a cathedral in Glasgow foundered and sank.

The next morning, I turned on the radio to the BBC and was reminded that today was the royal wedding day of Prince Harry and Meghan Markle. I don't listen to much news, so this came as a bit of a surprise and I wondered if this day was of much importance to the inhabitants of this region of Scotland. We headed off on the delightful single-track road leading across the Cowal Peninsula through Glen Lean and discovered there was absolutely no one to ask. The scenery was both stark and glorious and we did come across one gent fishing near the dam at Loch Tarsan. He proved to have absolutely no interest whatsoever in celebrating royal weddings but instead grieved deeply that the fish were not biting.

We arrived in Colintraive at a narrow spot where cattle were once coerced to swim across the water to the Isle of Bute, which some tourist board has cleverly labelled "the most accessible of the westerly isles." For £16.50 an open-air ferry will float you, your lover and your car to the island, a crossing that takes all of four minutes. It probably took the poor cows a bit longer and, in my imagination, I could still see them today, cow-paddling themselves at the urging of their masters across the chilly strait and wondering what the hell this was all about.

It was early in the day when we landed ashore so we decided to circumnavigate the isle, heading south past Rothesay around Bogany Point, beyond Ascog and Kerrycroy and on to breezy Scalpsie Bay. The fields were ripe with barley and the sun was shining brightly on this late spring day as it should on any royal wedding day, or any wedding day really, on our small planet.

Later, while eating carbonara pasta at Harry Haw's restaurant in Rothesay, I was soundly chastised by a fellow diner, a local, florid man with a noisy family in tow, that we should have stopped off at Mount Stuart, a famous estate we had driven right past. I'd noticed the sign but was pleased that my wife had not, she being considerably more fond of paying large sums of money to the National Trust and other heritage organizations to allow us to wander through the drawing rooms of old, dead, rich people. The man's wife told me they had held the wedding of their daughter there and it had been magnificent. The man told me Mount Stuart House had the first ever indoor heated swimming pool in any private home, and I pretended to be impressed. Then he said I should turn around and drive back there at once, but I was more interested in finishing up the pasta and bacon bits on my plate.

While paying for lunch, I asked the friendly waiter if the name of the restaurant was someone famous locally, but he wasn't certain. A quick bit of research led to no easy answer, but I did discover that Harry Haw's opened for business in 2013. The owner claimed, "Our goal was to give Bute a fresh, relaxed, funky restaurant that serves a tasty menu cooked from scratch. No pre-charred chicken pieces in here!" So I give them a few stars for that alone.

We had come to Rothesay because I had read about the fame of the Victorian Toilets along the shoreline. Here tourists like me could pay 40p to pee and gawk at the glorious architecture of a bathroom of a long-gone era. Historian Lucinda Lambton once described the upscale pissoir as "jewels in the sanitarian's crown." It was built for the hordes of mainland tourists in 1899 and the water has continued to flush ever since. Nothing To See website says, "Fourteen fantastic porcelain urinals stand erect along one wall, with another six in a circular centrepiece." Based on my own research, I can confirm this to be true. Apparently, the place has won many, many awards, including multiple "Loo of the Year" designations. Nothing To See also points out, "Even Prince Charles ... has nipped in to admire a throne of a different kind."

It turns out that Prince Charles, the man whose son was being married this fine day, was the Duke of Rothesay (among other things) and, although I could not find any information about what he actually did in that role for the citizens of Rothesay, I did come across a compelling photo of him unveiling a massive statue of an Aberdeen Angus bull at a distant location. This led me to ponder, if you were just a duke and didn't wear any other hats, what exactly would your duties be except undertaking a royal flush once in a while? (Sorry.)

A quick pit stop at the Bute Brew Company revealed some intriguing-sounding pints with names like Straad Ass, Scalpsie Blonde, Jinty Red and even one called Cock Up Your Beaver intended to celebrate (what else?) Robbie Burns with a term that they insist means to "put a spring in your step." The trendy indoor-outdoor pub area was filled with lovely locals, and not one person berated me for passing up Mount Stuart House.

Back at our rental house we discovered the owners had a drawer full of games, including one called "Pass the Pigs" whereby you roll pig-shaped dice to gain points. If you roll a "razorback" you get five points, but a "leaning jowler" will win you 15, although a devastating "oinker" will set you all the way back to zero. Pass the Pigs, I believe, would be just the ticket to lure kids back to board games and away from violent video games.

The following day dawned grey, wet and blustery. We retraced our route through Glen Lean and then snaked our way down to Portavadie for a longer ferry crossing that would take us to Tarbert on the Kintyre Peninsula (as in "Mull of Kintyre"). Standing on the deck of the ferry, we were blasted by cold, salty waves once in the middle of Loch Fyne. Up front on the boat were about 20 drenched bicyclists who didn't seem the slightest bit deterred by the nasty weather. Staring at them as I received my second salty shower near the rail, I considered these middle-aged, rain-shiny adults extremely brave. I envisioned them as the modern-day versions of their ancestral Scots who once proved their mettle through bloody battle and brutality. I soon realized that I was thankful that all that courage and fortitude of the past was now being funnelled into these twenty-first-century bicyclists willing to ride through the most heinous weather on some of the most treacherous narrow roads possible.

On this day, we had left the Cowal Peninsula in search of the ancestral home of our dog. I had determined we should make a pilgrimage to the nearly non-existent village of Poltalloch, not far from the Sound of Jura. It was here that the sixteenth Laird of Poltalloch, Edward Donald Malcolm, was said to have bred the first West Highland White Terriers, originally known as Poltalloch Terriers.

Despite having a good map and the aid of satellite navigation, we had a hell of a time finding Poltalloch. We knew the estate was in ruins but thought we might be able to walk around it or at least to see it from the road. According to the Navigon, we arrived, drove through it and didn't see a village or a dog monument or anything of note. So we drove back and forth a few times and still nothing was to be seen. The rain was steady, the road was potholed and muddy and we tried several dead-end lanes before ending up at Poltalloch Farms, a dairy farm with one of the muddiest grazing fields I'd ever encountered. I did see a couple of cows and a few sorry-looking soaked chickens but not a sign of a dog or any indication that this was where Westies first came into being.

The funny thing about pilgrimages like this that we have undertaken — quests in search of little-known places that have meaning to me but not many others — is that we usually don't find what we're looking for. However, having selected a destination and remaining open to whatever adventure comes our way, we find that interesting and sometimes dramatic things happen. Even extraordinary things.

That just wasn't the case today. We found rain, mud and dead-end roads.

However, Kilmartin was just up the track from here. Kilmartin Glen is home to burial cairns, stone circles and man-made structures that are as old as 5,000 years. We braved the rain to walk into one soggy pasture and enter the Temple Wood Stone Circles. We also eventually found one of the Nether Largie South Cairns, where I tucked myself down inside, beneath the flat stone roof, and waited for voices from ancient days to whisper in my ears. They respectfully told me in their ancient dialect to stop acting like an idiot and get back into the car and out of the downpour. There is a castle and museum in Kilmartin worthy of a visitor's attention as well but, regrettably, my foray into the tomb had left me wet and without interest.

In our retreat back to the Cowal Peninsula, we stopped for lunch at the warm and inviting Argyll Inn, the only open pub we could find, in Lochgilphead. I asked the waitress what the town was famous for and she drew a blank, although later research revealed that it is an important transportation hub, being located at the head of Lochgilphead after all. The pub had a big screen TV that introduced me to my first viewing of *Ninja Warrior UK*. The food service was slow so I had the chance to watch the show where "everyday heroes take on the world's toughest obstacle course." I admit I was totally entranced. While eating my fish and chips I observed overly confident jocks tripping, falling down, bumping into obstacles, falling down some more, bouncing off both soft and hard objects and otherwise making British fools of themselves. I will definitely want the barkeep to tune it in again should I ever find myself in Lochgilphead.

Back in our Uig home, we dried off and, as the rain ended, walked through nearby Benmore Gardens — green and lush and magnificent with blooming rhododendrons exploding with colour, towering sequoia trees planted in 1863 and a delightfully chattering brook. I tried to ignore the fact that the various Dukes of Argyll (none of whom I liked very much) once used this as their hunting grounds and that the not-always-benevolent Campbells owned it in the past as well. But in my opinion, it's just a damn fine example of what man can do when he cooperates with nature in extraordinary measure.

The next day, filling up with petrol at a station in nearby Rashfield, I found myself in conversation with the proprietor concerning what he referred to as "the lack of ethics these days." I couldn't quite extract from him what prompted these concerns, since everyone we'd met in Scotland treated us quite ethically. But I think he was referring to kids stealing candy from his shelves, apparently something that would have never happened when he was a boy.

Soon after the discourse on contemporary ethics, Linda and I went hiking up nearby Puck's Glen, which the Forestry Commission calls "one of the most magical forests in Scotland, with a delightful trail along a rocky gorge." And it most certainly is. The puck in the name has nothing to do with hockey, I learned, but refers to the legendary woodland spirit, Puck, who can be friendly or mean and likes to play tricks on whomever he meets. Also known sometimes as Robin Goodfellow, he appears in literature, most famously in Shakespeare's *A Midsummer Night's Dream,* which you may have been forced to read against your will in high school. Puck was most kind to us on our visit this day, however, and provided only the best kind of magic in the form of dappled sunlight, multiple chuckling waterfalls and an amazing jungle-like trail up and down a narrow ravine.

On our last day in the area, we returned to Dunoon, where Linda bought a white bra as I toyed with the idea of buying one of those flat-topped caps (a flat cap?) like old Scotsmen like to wear. It was an old-style downtown clothing store where young children begged their mothers to buy them things the mothers did not want them to have. By five o'clock all the shops were closing and we searched for what some like to call "authentic food" but gave up after peeking into several unappealing pubs. We settled instead on a restaurant calling itself the 51st State that had "Mexican food in an American-style restaurant." I knew that the US had only 50 states and wondered at this nomenclature. Many in America thought Puerto Rico would become the fifty-first state but, looking at the menu, it seemed more likely it could be Mexico.

Nonetheless, the meal was excellent — the best Mexican food we had in Scotland.

There were sheep on the road the following morning on our way to catch the ferry from Hunter's Quay to Gourock. It was an easy drive onto the boat and I seemed to pull my car up to the front of the ferry just perfectly so that the ferry attendant complimented me on the task, rating it as "just smashing," a term I could well apply to most of our exploration of the Cowal Peninsula and places beyond.

The ferry ride across the Firth of Clyde was as good as a Caribbean Cruise as far as I'm concerned. It was everything I wanted and more. Blue skies, fresh air, sailboats afloat, fish jumping, homemade dark roast coffee still in hand from our cottage instead of the run of the mill (runoff from the hill) watered-down beverage we often encountered on the road. Our only regret was that our dog was back in Nova Scotia sound asleep at this hour at Country Critters in Seaforth.

We came ashore without fuss or muss and headed east toward Edinburgh, where I hoped desperately I might be invited someday to read at the Edinburgh International Book Festival.

There is a six-foot somewhat phallic-shaped standing stone in Gourock known as Granny Kempock that has been a bane to some and a blessing to others. Presumably it was once an altar where the ever-present mysterious Druids performed rituals. Over the years it was considered to provide good luck for sailors and fishermen — and as we all know, they are sorely in need of just that — if they walked around it seven times. A handful of Scots tried to throw it in the Clyde in 1662 and were accused of being witches. It was believed perhaps that witches favoured bad luck and were opposed to good luck. Nonetheless, it still stands today as a reminder of those people long, long ago who felt the need to move interestingly shaped rocks over great distances to use as monuments to one thing or another. In fact, it stands today in the middle of a shopping district with what the tourist advertisers like to call "traditional shops," but the term may be a bit whimsical.

I knew that many a ship over several centuries had forged out into the Atlantic from the Clyde, heading to the US or Canada with hopeful immigrants, many of them on their way to Nova Scotia.

From Gourock itself, the *Queen Mary* had plowed its way across the Atlantic many times during the Second World War, mostly back and forth to New York, carrying passengers to safety in North America and returning with fresh troops. On one such trip in 1943, she sailed to Halifax, probably in a convoy, and then on to New York, returning to Scotland with 9,000 troops on board to help fight the Nazis.

Before leaving the Clyde heading east, you pass through the larger city of Greenock, an even larger port that shipped many an immigrant to the New World. Refugees from the Highland Clearances passed through here and ended up in Nova Scotia and elsewhere.

In September 1943, my soldier father was in Camp Kilmer back in New Jersey "waiting to be put on a ship." On October 7, he wrote in his journal, "I am now on board ship. My bunk is next to the floor of ship — 8 bunks high. Chow is poor." He landed six days later in Greenock and was put on a troop train that took him south to Bedford in England. I don't exactly know why, but it gave me chills to think that we were driving through the town where my father had disembarked in uniform from a mid-war North Atlantic crossing 75 years ago.

Greenock is currently home to Wallace, the famous fire dog (1894–1902), reported by the *Sunday Post* to be "Scotland's first fire dog racing ahead of emergency teams and leading them to blazes." In April of our travel year, primary school children were campaigning to have a statue erected of the legendary Glasgow mutt. As to Wallace himself, he is sadly long gone, but not forgotten, having been stuffed and placed in the local Fire Service Museum. Miss Evelyn Gibson, head teacher at Saracen Primary School, backed her young pupils on the project, saying, "Edinburgh has Greyfriars Bobby, why shouldn't Glasgow celebrate Wallace the fire dog?" And, of course, I would agree, why bloody not? Glasgow and Edinburgh had always been in some form of rivalry with each other, and if Edinburgh had a famous dog, so should Glasgow. And, although I had not heard of Greyfriars Bobby at that point, I made a mental note to find out about him once we'd alighted in the other city.

In other dog news, two Greenock women had a falling-out not long before our travels over a failed attempt at an arranged marriage for their dogs that was publicized on a British TV show. When the rough edges were smoothed over, however, in September 2017 the pug and Shih Tzu were married by a vicar at the local cricket club and everyone lived happily ever after.

Cats and dogs seem to get a lot of press in any UK city as it turns out, and, while the deceased Wallace is safely stored behind glass in the fire museum, there have been newspaper reports of a "mysterious rat eating Catman who has been lurking around dark corners of Greenock since the 1970s." If we had not been in a bit of a rush to get on to our next destination, I would have liked to visit Wallace in person and then ask around to see if the Catman was still performing a useful public service by consuming the rat population like a good Catman should. But time was limited and we motored on. However, if the Catman and Wallace the fire dog are not enough to lure you to Greenock, then I should alert you to the fact that Jay Leno's mother was born there and if you were a late-night TV viewer this might prompt you to come visit.

And just in case you didn't know, Jay Leno bought a used McLaren F1, what he calls "the greatest car of the twentieth century," for US$800,000 and claims he's been offered $12 million today. It's really quite amazing the things your wife can tell you with a smart phone and a data package while nipping off the M74 onto the M73, then hanging a right on the M8 near Coatbridge.

CHAPTER TWENTY-TWO

DECONSTRUCTING DESTINY
(APRIL 2018)

On Linda's bucket list was a visit to Rosslyn Chapel in the town of Roslin just south of Edinburgh. I like old rural churches with their dark demeanour and musty smell and am ever thankful when we roll into some small obscure village and spy a modest kirk with a graveyard. Around the UK, I'd reckon that 50 per cent or more of such churches are unlocked and visitors are free to walk inside and time travel back to simpler centuries while the local holy ghosts whisper in their ears.

Rosslyn Chapel, unfortunately, was not such a place.

I read somewhere that the origin of the village itself goes back to nearly 200 AD when, legend has it, it was founded by the Picts. But then, there are so many "legends" about the town and the chapel that actual facts are probably hard to come by. The Catholic chapel itself was built in 1446 at the behest of William Sinclair and became both significant and controversial over time.

Sometime in the sixteenth century, a mob of unruly Protestants under the influence of none other than John Knox made their way here in a kind of rampage, wanting to destroy the "Popish" icons of the chapel, but were somehow persuaded otherwise by some cooler-headed locals who lured them away with free booze.

When we arrived, the parking lot was nearly full and there were tour buses idling on the road. I probably let out a groan, but here we were and Linda offered to pay a handsome sum in order to get in. The chapel had been featured in Dan Brown's novel *The Da Vinci Code*, which several friends had foisted upon me back when it was a bestseller. Mr. Brown had called the place "the most mysterious and magical chapel on earth," and some scenes from the movie version were filmed here as well, putting Rosslyn on the must-see map of international tourists flying in to Scotland. Tom Hanks, who produced the movie and put himself in the lead role, said that as a setting for the film, it was "all one could imagine or hope for."

The gift shop was doing a brisk business when we walked into the tourist centre attached to the chapel, and there was a lineup in the men's room to use the waterless urinals. Many Chinese visitors who had come in on one of the tour buses were queuing up outside the main chapel wearing audio guide headphones as Linda and I made our way into the beautifully restored ancient church. Inside, we lit a candle to our dead parents as we usually do in such places and we sat in a pew for a few moments of silence. Unlike in so many other sacred places I've visited, I couldn't quite locate the spiritual vibe due to the mob of tourists. I'd felt this absence in the Sistine Chapel and in Notre Dame among other famous places, so I know it is some inner flaw of my own — one of many on a long checklist of shortcomings. I knew that if I could only sneak back here after closing time and figure out the da Vinci code to the digital locks on the doors, I would be able to feel some sense of awe and breathe in the spirit of ancient holy men and women. But, for now, I'd have to settle for sitting and watching people from around the world snapping pictures on their cell phones.

We lined up to go down into the crypt below the chapel where a famous scene from the movie had been filmed. Some holy item was said to have been buried here, but I can't recall if that was just part of the movie or in real life. Perhaps it was the Holy Grail itself since there is much about the Knights Templar movement that is tied into the history of the church.

There was a fair bit of signage everywhere we turned and I was fascinated to learn that a number of writers had made pilgrimages here over the centuries. The list included Robert Burns, of course. A traveller would have a hard time to locate places in Scotland Robert Burns had not written about or visited, or partied or had a liaison with a young woman in, so it was no surprise that Robbie had been to Rosslyn. He stayed at a nearby inn, wrote a few lines of poetry there and watched the sun come up from the chapel. Samuel Johnson, with Mr. Boswell by his side, had been here, as well as Walter Scott. William and Dorothy Wordsworth both wrote about Rosslyn. In her journal, Dorothy noted, "The stone both of the roof and walls, is sculptured with leaves and flowers, so delicately wrought that I could have admired them for hours, and the whole of their groundwork is stained by time with the softest colours." While Dorothy wrote extensive descriptions about the details of the architecture, her more famous brother preferred to question the intentions of the fretwork in his sonnet where he wrote,

> From what bank
> Came those live herbs? by what hand were they sown,
> Where dew falls not, where rain-drops seem unknown?

On a more political/military note, I was surprised to learn that Oliver Cromwell left his horses here in the chapel yard to graze while taking over the castle nearby. It seemed that Cromwell did get around when he wasn't back in Ely eating eel pie or being a good family man. Hero or villain? I wonder still.

Only later did I discover a Nova Scotian thread to the mystique of Rosslyn Chapel that both Dan Brown and Tom Hanks might have missed. The grandfather of the chapel's founder was Henry Sinclair (born 1345), who is said to have travelled to Newfoundland and Nova Scotia well before Columbus. As a member of the Knights Templar, he (supposedly) carried the Holy Grail with him and possibly left it in Nova Scotia, where I may someday stumble upon it if I am lucky enough. Sinclair himself was from Roslin and it is well beyond my ability to sort out myth from fact about the man, although Frederik Pohl has written extensively about him, even suggesting that Sinclair and the legendary Mi'kmaw hero Glooscap were the same.

We left Rosslyn with my head swimming with unanswered questions, the many fragments of history surrounding this place simply not fitting together into any sensible pattern as they would in the fiction of Dan Brown or a real historian who could fathom the difference between events and myths. But as I settled back into the twenty-first-century rhythm of driving a small car on a Scottish motorway, I knew it was my duty as a writer to scribble down my two cents of imperfect wisdom about Rosslyn to add to the canon that included Johnson, Wordsworth, Scott, Burns and Brown.

Oddly enough, as we were driving past the town of Danderhall, I remembered a literary connection of my own concerning Roslin. For it was at the Roslin Institute, in 1996, that a sheep was cloned into existence and named Dolly (after Dolly Parton). In my science-fictionish YA novel *Deconstructing Dylan*, my protagonist discovers as a teenager that his parents cloned him from cells of an older brother who had died tragically. Dylan's parents were geneticists who had once worked at Roslin Institute, just down the road from the mystical chapel. Maybe the puzzle of Roslin is truly much more complex than any of us have even begun to guess, involving the mysterious Picts, the Holy Grail, the Knights Templar, the Scottish Reformation, the reverence of poets and the cloning of sheep and ultimately humans. Who's to know?

CHAPTER TWENTY-THREE

OUT AND ABOUT IN EDINBURGH
(APRIL 2018)

There's not much to say about the urban sprawl heading into Edinburgh from the south. It looked like a lot of tough neighbourhoods where it would be easy to get into a scuffle in a pub if you spoke highly of a football team from England. But once we had made our way toward Old Town and got rid of the car in a car park near Waverley Station, the city began to weave a spell over Linda and me.

We paid yet another handsome sum of money to stay at the Fraser Suites just a block from St Giles Cathedral. It was uphill from the car park (well, everything in Old Town seems to be quite up or down), and if rolling luggage over ancient cobblestones is exotic in your world, this is the place for you. And I am indeed one of those travellers, excited by the notion that famous and notorious men and women from centuries past had helped to polish these stones with the soles of their shoes the same as me.

I had a small agenda of things to seek out in Edinburgh: pubs with dogs, of course, literary connections, exploration of as many dark nooks and crannies as possible and conversations with locals about whatever was foremost on their minds.

Those conversations, as it turned out, were harder to come by than I thought. It seemed that everyone we met on the street was from somewhere else. The street in question was High Street and the section we traversed most was the famous "Royal Mile." I would later learn that 13 million tourists visit Edinburgh each year, so that explained the diverse crowd cavorting about in the city.

On a Saturday morning we hiked farther uphill to Edinburgh Castle and were not surprised to find it mobbed with visitors. The castle was built on an extinct volcano, but it hasn't erupted for 350 million years, so most of us there that day felt reasonably safe. By the entrance to the castle grounds was a plaque that read, "NEAR THIS SPOT IN 1625 Sir William Alexander of Menstrie, Earl of Stirling, received sasine, or lawful possession of the Royal Province of Nova Scotia by the ancient and symbolic ceremony of delivery of earth and stone from Castlehill by a representative of the King. Here also (1625–1637) the Scottish Baronets of Nova Scotia received sasine of their distant baronies." In essence, below our feet was a small patch of Nova Scotian land declared so that men granted free land in Nova Scotia didn't actually have to go to the trouble of travelling there to make their claim. So, there we were, over 4000 kilometres from home, yet still standing (or at least looking at) Nova Scotia soil. William Alexander, as it turned out, was a busy man and never did visit Nova Scotia. Inside the castle you will find more tourists than I was comfortable with, but if you want to see the Stone of Destiny (the rock, not the movie) you'll have to pay your money and take the tour.

The statue that made the most impression on me along the Royal Mile was that of Adam Smith. I'd never seen a statue of an economist before and, thanks to the fact I'd been reading Arthur Herman's *How the Scots Invented the Modern World*, I had learned that Smith "thought of himself primarily as a moral philosopher" and believed, unlike the church of his day, that man was primarily good rather than bad.

I hadn't made up my own mind whether Adam Smith himself was a good guy or a bad guy. He'd said things like "All money is a matter of belief." And "Man is an animal that makes bargains: no other animal does this — no dog exchanges bones with another." But Smith also said, "The real tragedy of the poor is the poverty of their aspirations."

Alas, whatever we contemporaries felt about the man, seagulls on this fine spring day had been sitting on Mr. Smith's metallic head and his face had been whitewashed by their plenteous droppings, reminding me vividly of the same fate of Winston Churchill's statue in Halifax where the old public library once stood. So goes the fate of philosophers and politicians. Later, in Glasgow, pondering the famous traffic cone covering the head of Lord Wellington, I would reflect on what a hard life it is for statues in the UK, where people and creatures can do them disservice at any time of day.

Not far from Mr. Smith, I noticed a formation of stones in the ground in the shape of a heart. This turned out to be a mosaic called the Heart of the Midlothians. Here once stood a prison built in the fifteenth century. Many executions had taken place over the years at this very spot. There is a tradition of people spitting on the stones, perhaps initiated by the lucky ones (many of them simply men who did not pay their debts) released from jail over the centuries. Mostly everyone I saw that day was too polite to spit and, in truth, the majority walked right over the spot without noticing it.

Right alongside of the Heart of the Midlothians was yet another statue, that of Walter Francis Montagu Douglas Scott, the Fifth Duke of Buccleuch. Among his other accomplishments, he is given credit for importing Labrador Retrievers from Newfoundland to Europe for the first time in the 1830s. In my mind, his other political achievements fell to the wayside and it brightened my day to see yet another Canadian connection, especially one involving dogs.

Linda thought we should lunch at the Elephant House, where it was reported that J.K. Rowling once did some writing or research for the early Harry Potter novels. The sign outside says, "The Birthplace of Harry Potter," but that may be stretching it a bit. Who knows? Inside, it was a noisy, happy little restaurant on the King George IV Bridge. The "bridge" itself confused me somewhat in that it didn't seem to be over any body of water, but outside, looking down from the bridge, was a whole other level of the city with narrow streets and ground level stores. I couldn't quite figure out how this could be since we, too, were on ground level. It was like peering into another world below us and was indeed as Harry Potteresque as a thing could be.

I still had a small grudge against Ms. Rowling because trashy newspapers in England and Scotland had claimed she had the cutest West Highland White Terrier in the UK. I thought my own Westie much cuter and soon he too would be in the UK and we would try to right this wrong. Nonetheless, there we were for lunch in her former haunt with memorabilia from herself and great gobs of Harry Potter graffiti aplenty on the walls of the loos. I ordered haggis, neeps and tatties ("Our Scottish National Dish") for lunch in honour of the occasion and found it very filling.

Back on the Royal Mile we wandered down as many narrow alleyways (or closes, as they are called) as we could. Among the many are Advocate's Close, Anchor Close, Old Post Office Close and the curiously named Fleshmarket Close, which refers to what was once a butcher's market rather than a place for street sex. Mystery writer Ian Rankin borrowed the name for the title of one of his novels where a number of dark and brutal events occur.

Down one alleyway, we came upon the Writers' Museum, which is blessedly free and open to the public. The building dates back to 1622 and displays artifacts and images of Robbie Burns, Sir Walter Scott and Robert Louis Stevenson. Behind a glass case, Stevenson's high-top shoes looked like he had just taken them off yesterday and I was rather impressed to see a photograph of the author of *Treasure Island* imbibing kava with some shirtless citizens of Samoa. I'd read *Treasure Island* as a lad and it had not occurred to me that perhaps drugs were involved in the creative process.

There was much ado in the museum about Burns's poetry and it prompted me to recite what I could remember of "A Man's a Man for a' That" until my wife grew embarrassed enough to elbow me in the ribs to make me desist. A few steps farther along, staring at a bust of Walter Scott, I couldn't for the life of me remember reading a single thing by such a famous Scottish writer and wondered why his fame lingered while his writing fell out of favour.

Stumbling upon Devil's Close, we ambled into a pub called the Devil's Advocate to quench our thirst and moved on to dinner at an establishment called the Filling Station on High Street where I ordered a curry dish, having done my duty earlier in the day to partake of the Elephant House haggis. Pubs and restaurants there are aplenty in and around the Royal Mile. Halfway through my curry, it occurred to me that in the UK I preferred Indian cuisine, in the US Mexican food, and in Canada, I preferred Thai.

The following morning, Sunday, Wetherspoon's near the train station provided nourishment for the day in the form of a tasty but lumpy egg, a couple of rashers of bacon, a delight-fully bulbous sausage and the inevitable black pudding. (It's the blood that makes it black, yes?) I couldn't help but notice that a high percentage of men were drinking large mugs of beer with their breakfast and, asking a waiter why that might be, he explained that the next day was a bank holiday.

As you can tell, I probably have not done the city full justice, having skipped or merely glanced at some of the more famous sites, both ancient and modern, of Edinburgh. The bagpipers were in tune on most corners and I confess I was shocked at the cost of an authentic kilt in the stores. During the day, buskers juggled large knives while atop rolling planks, hen parties sang a Helen Reddy song in unison and a number of young inebriated semi-clad men sang a reasonable rendition of "Wonderwall" by Oasis, then ran off, leaving one of their own behind who turned his back on the throng of curious onlookers and urinated on the wall of St Giles Cathedral, whose crown-shaped steeple dates back to the fifteenth century.

Heading back along King George IV Bridge, we stopped by Greyfriars Kirk, which has "stood in the same spot since 1620 — the first new kirk to be built in Post-Reformation Scotland." Here we came upon the shrine erected to Greyfriars Bobby that much reminded me of the statue of the loyal dog Hachikō I had once stumbled upon in Tokyo.

Bobby was a Skye Terrier (closely related to Westies, I might add) who "guarded" his owner's grave every day for 14 years after the man's death in February 1858. In a nearby bookstore, I noted that there were at least 12 children's books written about Bobby and at least two animated movies. Clearly, loyalty in dogs is admired by Scots and authors in many parts of the world. Bobby accompanied his owner, John Gray, a guard for the Edinburgh police, on his rounds every night. When John died of tuberculosis, Bobby would not leave his grave. After trying many times to evict the dog from the cemetery, the groundskeeper erected a shelter for him. Bobby would only leave for his midday meal (at the pub where he had eaten with his master). When dog licences came into effect in 1867, the Lord Provost of the city paid for the licence, and had a dog collar made for Bobby. Upon the dog's death, Baroness Angela Burdett-Coutts, head of the Ladies Committee of the RSPCA, requested city council's permission to erect a fountain with a statue at the top. Bobby's headstone reads: "Let his loyalty and devotion be a lesson to us all."

So far we had failed to find any dogs in pubs, but as luck would have it, the closest pub to Greyfriars Kirk had two large dogs, a black one and a white one, lounging on the floor, dutifully waiting for their masters, who were drinking McEwan's ale. The establishment was called Sandy Bell's pub and it purported to be famous for its folk music. A fiddler and a guitar player were tucked in a corner improvising something closer to jazz than folk, but it was a comfortable and pleasant place to ponder the story of Bobby and see how dogs behaved in the presence of Scotsmen drinking beer.

On a shelf over the bar was a bust of a man, and a note on the wall indicated it was the "head of Hamish Henderson." I wondered what a replica of this man's head was doing in a pub and later learned Hamish was a poet, songwriter and collector of folk songs and lore, as well as a soldier and a Communist — quite the list of accomplishments. I couldn't help but take a moment of reverie to wish that someday a pub owner would think enough of me to place a replica of my head over the bar to keep a watchful eye over generations of thirsty patrons. Before I could express this beer-induced daydream to Linda, I realized it was a foolish and ill-conceived idea if ever there was one.

I also noted a sign over the bar that read, "No Football Colours Allowed," and I asked a gent sipping scotch what that was all about.

"Fights," he said. "Ya can't have two different colour shirts in one pub or you have trouble." Two colours presumably indicated fans of two different teams. Combine that with enthusiasm and alcohol and inevitably you have fisticuffs. Then he pointed out the window across the street to yet another pub, an Irish one called McSorley's. "You want to see some ruckus, you should go over there." And sure enough, outside McSorley's stood two sturdy bouncers waiting for football trouble to come their way. But I found it not in our best interest to do further investigation into football team loyalty and hostility.

I liked the way drinkers casually walked over and around the lounging canines, whose weary eyes indicated they'd be much happier sleeping under the front porch. So, in the name of literary research, I asked the young tattooed barmaid with a nose piercing the following question: "How does having dogs in the pub change the nature of the place?" As you might guess, it came out sounding rather formal and stilted.

The young lady gave me a funny look but an honest answer. "Well," she said, "the dogs are much nicer than the drunks." Truth be told, I saw no drunks at Sandy Bell's, but then it was the middle of the day. After that, it was a final hike back to High Street, where a new piper provided the official soundtrack for the advancing fog rolling slowly but inexorably up the cobblestone street from the North Sea below.

CHAPTER TWENTY-FOUR

DREAMS AND DREAMERS IN THE LAKE DISTRICT (MAY 2018)

Linda and I were not at all anxious to leave Scotland, but we'd never visited the mountains, lakes and valleys of Cumbria to the south so now we were headed in that direction from our explorations of Argyll and Edinburgh. Scotland had provided more mysteries and intrigue than expected and I wondered if we should skip England altogether and gear up for a true circumnavigation of Scotland with our dog in our upcoming trip in June. After all, the Halifax to Glasgow flight was such an easy one.

But then I remembered we could not fly directly anywhere into the UK with Kelty in the cabin of the plane. British dog lovers should really do something about that rule. Most of Europe allowed dogs in plane cabins if they were as small as our Westie. Why not Britain? "Well, we are an island," I could hear the British say. "We do things our own way."

Somewhere in the government bureaucracy was some bastard or group of bastards (they had to be men in suits with really clean fingernails) who had come up with the rule. It probably started out as "no animals in with passengers on incoming flights." I do believe you can fly *out* of the UK with a dog in the cabin if the airline allows. *Just not incoming.* Okay, so I understand that some animals would be disagreeable on long plane trips. Chickens, in first class or coach, would be annoying. As would cows or other barnyard animals. One dog lover in Scotland, after sharing a story about the sadness of the death of his Yorkshire terrier, thought the ruling had something to do with mad cow disease, in fact.

So, yes, I would understand keeping cows out of planes. And snakes for that matter. And most other wild beasts. But rules are rules and stay that way (in the UK and elsewhere) until someone has the balls to change them. Perhaps when our travels were all over and I found a publisher for my book, I'd see if the Dogs Trust (formally the National Canine Defence League) might back me in my campaign to allow small dogs to sit at the feet of their owners on incoming flights to Heathrow, Glasgow, Stanstead and elsewhere.

Such are the reflections on an unexciting drive west and south from the North Sea that would take us headlong to England and into the legendary Lake District. On the way down, we were on the lookout for Hadrian's Wall. During our previous stay in Yorkshire, we never found the wall. And now, outside Carlisle, we thought we could find it or some remnant of it. I could see the dotted line on the map, but the damn thing eluded us once again.

Publius Aelius Hadrianus Augustus was a Roman emperor who lived from 76 to 138 AD. When he came into power, the empire was vast and he decided to pull soldiers out of Mesopotamia but reinforce domination of other nations, including England. So a wall in the north of England to keep out the rowdy Scottish rascals to the north seemed like a good idea at the time. Machiavelli considered Hadrian one of the "good emperors," but as with so many other historical leaders, there could be a nearly endless debate as to whether the man was a hero or villain. Anyone could guess that Roman soldiers were not always kind to the folks they conquered, although they did build some pretty snazzy baths in places like Bath and elsewhere.

It may not have come up in most British history classes, but Hadrian was also gay, and when one of his lovers drowned in the Nile he designated him a god. He was that kind of guy. Hadrian's own death, by the way, is a bit mysterious; it was either accident, suicide, murder or sacrifice. The jury is out.

Well, walls fall down, and so did much of Hadrian's, and that's probably a good thing. Good walls make good neighbours, Robert Frost once said, but even he knew that each spring when the ground thawed, rocks would tumble, and if you weren't vigilant, walls would turn to rubble soon enough without human intervention. Around Ireland and England, however, I'd noted that most roadside rock walls were amazingly intact along those narrow country roads that I both loved and loathed. Perhaps there just wasn't enough frost in the ground to do the job right. I'd lost a mirror or two to those stubborn piles of stone and had a grudge. Maybe that's why Hadrian's Wall was hiding.

In the news, Donald Trump, a president most British citizens were currently trying to keep out of Britain, was promoting his own wall between the US and Mexico, one he was asking the Mexican government to pay for. Such a wall would probably rule out Mexico from becoming the "fifty-first state," and would cause endless grief to families with ties to the south, but it does suggest a link between Trump and Hadrian. However, if Machiavelli were alive today, I would bet good money he would put Trump in the category of "bad emperor." Later that summer, the British government would grudgingly allow Mr. Trump into the country but kept him well away from his legions of detractors in London. And did I indeed detect a certain look on the Queen's face when she shook his tiny hand? Or perhaps it was just the camera angle.

And so we were headed to the heart of Cumbria, once known as Rheged in ancient Celtic times. We drove on through the gorgeously bleak empty high ground and lush lowland forests of the Lake District. Here was truly ancient legendary territory where the early Celts lived somewhat unmolested for 500 years or so until the Romans conquered them.

We rolled into the town of Windermere and needed groceries, so I stopped at the downtown Booth's store where I parked in the wrong parking lot, the bus station behind Booth's. I hung back outside while Linda went in to begin shopping. A soft-spoken man in an official uniform strolled over to tell me in the most polite manner that I was not in the store's lot but in a public space where I needed to pay £5 if I wanted to stay parked.

He was obviously someone's kindly grandfather and knew I was an outsider from the road-weary, slightly stunned look on my face. "I do apologize for the inconvenience and hope you don't mind," he said. Perhaps Donald Trump would get the same apology when he would try to visit London and accept the fact he'd have to keep his ass well outside the capital if he wanted to visit.

In the US, my minor violation of plonking my rental car into the wrong parking lot would probably have led to a fine, getting my wheel booted or my car being towed away. As I watched the parking gentleman amble away, I realized the verb I had selected in my head to describe his gait came from the fact that there was a nearby town called Ambleside, which

I assumed meant, "This is the side of the lake where we do a lot of leisurely strolling," in Anglo-Saxon or Middle English.

The streets of Windermere were confusing and crowded as I tried to wend my way to the proper parking lot for Booth's supermarket, where prim and proper men and women, all over 60 as far as I could tell, wheeled those unruly shopping carts filled with groceries and flowers to their cars.

Truth is, we rented the cottage in Windermere because I wanted to explore nearby Grasmere, home of William and Dorothy Wordsworth, but couldn't find suitably affordable digs there.

Tomorrow, we would make our way there and, as I waited in the appropriate parking lot for Linda to emerge with our supplies, I looked over some notes I had brought with me about our current locale. Wordsworth had visited Windermere often, possibly to stock up on groceries himself and have a peek at what those living in the more urbane world were up to. It's safe to say he liked the lake. Everyone did and still does. In fact, the lake gets a bit too much love. Lake Windermere stretches north–south like a long crooked finger, carved out of the land by glaciers well before the days of global warming. Towns and forests cling to the shores. Ferries shuttle tourists about and teenagers splash each other from the docks while listening to bad British rap music these days, but it's still a mighty fine lake.

Back during the Wordsworths' time here on earth, William was opposed to the building of a railway to carry outsiders to Windermere. He thought it would bring too many tourists, leading to the wholesale ruination of the place. Like Wordsworth, I'm generally in favour of keeping as much of contemporary civilization as far from my home roost as possible when I can get away with it. I admit both he and I are a couple of somewhat smug, even selfish poets in our love of nature, and we both know how easy it is for crowds of humans to quickly ruin a fine patch of wilderness.

And, of course, Mr. Intimations of Immortality was mostly correct about that damn railroad. It did bring legions of tourists and Windermere became a commercial hub of activity worth avoiding. But sitting there behind the wheel of our rental car, I vowed to overcome any prejudice Wordsworth had planted in my head and try to actually like the place. I was, after all, smack centre in one of the most magnificent lake and mountain locales on the planet.

Birthwaite Cottage was a short drive from downtown on a shady street near the shores of the lake on the outskirts of Windermere. It was located on the grounds of a large estate in a very wealthy neighbourhood with houses worth a million pounds or more each. Wordsworth would probably not approve.

I don't know about you, but I read a fair bit when I'm travelling and what I read sometimes shapes the way I experience things, the thoughts that go through my head and sometimes my dreams. In the evening at Birthwaite, I had two books on the go: *Man Seeks God* by Eric Weiner and *How the Scots Invented the Modern World* by Arthur Herman. Back in Scotland I had grown weary of reading about the religious stranglehold that Calvinism had on the population and how John Knox had preached so vehemently against Catholicism that he'd inspired followers to try to trash beautiful Rosslyn Chapel. So, instead, I turned to Weiner and his chapter about Sufism. This religion seemed appealing to me and a sharp contrast to Knox's harsh Protestantism. My experiences in Scotland, however, had led me to believe that the Scots had mostly shed their uptight religious ways. Certainly, contemporary Edinburgh appeared to me as a free-spirited place of hen parties, buskers and impromptu musical performances that ended with a young man publicly urinating on a church wall. I wondered what cultural nerve or truth Calvin and Knox had hit upon to convince their followers that the flesh is evil, man is bad and, ipso facto, restraint is paramount and, where that fails, punishment is absolutely necessary.

Sufism, on the other hand, according to Eric Weiner anyway, urges its followers to "practice pure love." Followers claim to be *in* the world but not *of* the world, and I liked the ring of that. One practitioner defines the religion as "an opening of the heart." Take that, John Knox. Weiner travelled to Istanbul to learn more about the Sufis, but I was here in England, far from the spiritual origins of most religions. Some Sufis do all sorts of things to heighten their feeling of enlightenment or euphoria or to come close to experiencing God — including whirling. You've probably heard of whirling dervishes. I could understand whirling at length would get you high, but I didn't think it would get you high enough to experience God. But there, huddled in a cottage on a fine leafy estate in Cumbria, I vowed that if the right situation presented itself, possibly during a quiet moment in a garden or on a fairly flat top of a fell, I'd give it a whirl and see what happened. And as for religion, I reminded myself, we were indeed in a sacred land. We were currently in the realm of poets and pantheists.

As I set the book aside and lay down to fall asleep, I worried that I had not made any tremendous spiritual connections so far on our pilgrimage. I thought about Wordsworth again and remembered one of my graduate professors labelling the poet, along with a few other Romantic poets, as "pantheists." Pantheists saw God or some version of spirit in nature. They worshipped nature much like their primitive Celtic counterparts who dug big chunks of granite out of the ground and set them upright in circles to praise the earth, the sun and the spirits all around.

When I was a graduate student of English literature, pantheism seemed like such a workable religion that I probably considered myself a modern-day pantheist, in league with Wordsworth and Keats and even the "diabolical" Shelley. My classes back in Manhattan were at the City University of New York Graduate Center, what I lovingly referred to as the University of Forty-Second Street, where it was located. I sopped up the Romantic poets like a sponge during three-hour lectures and then set out upon the noisy New York streets to look at it all with the eyes of a pantheist.   .

Most everything I saw on the streets was nature in retreat. It was the least Wordsworthian place one could imagine. I was in a used bookstore near the graduate school one day, looking for a copy of Thomas De Quincey's *Confessions of an English Opium-Eater*, when the clerk was held up at gunpoint. The robber got some cash and ran and I barely knew that anything had happened. The young clerk called the cops and looked more than a little rattled, so I stayed there and tried to console him until the police came, which was a full half-hour later.

When two of New York's finest finally arrived, chewing gum and looking ever so nonchalant just like those New York cops in the movies, the young clerk freaked out. "What took you so long?!" he screamed.

The stouter of the two uniformed men shrugged and said, "Hey, relax. It was only a robbery. We got our hands full around here, ya know."

I had another hour to kill before my next class on the twelfth floor of the grad school, so I went to find solace in the only real green space nearby — Bryant Park, directly behind the famous downtown public library. It was there I sat on the park bench reading the dog-eared copy of *Confessions of an English Opium-Eater* that the bookseller had told me to keep at no charge. A young, sad-sack-looking man with long shaggy hair — well, not as long as mine, but a tad shaggier — sat down on the bench beside me while I was eating my cheese and baloney sandwich. He didn't say a word but proceeded to take a small leather kit out of his coat pocket and prepare a needle of something that he then injected into his arm. It was all so matter-of-fact that I assumed he was diabetic. But when he slumped over on my shoulder I got worried and asked him if he was okay. In a dreamy, otherworldly voice that De Quincy would have automatically recognized, he answered, "Yeah, man. I'm real good. But thanks for asking." I allowed him to lean on me like a lost heroin brother until I finished my sandwich and then, as I got up to leave, I gently lowered him onto the bench to finish off whatever opium dreams would come.

It was the past and present colliding in my head as I tried to fall asleep. There in my bed in Windermere, I wanted most to connect with the spiritual element that had so far been missing in our travels. Perhaps a visit to Wordsworth's home would set us on the path. That and a journey to the Castlerigg Stone Circle, created 3,500 years ago by Celtic worshippers. Linda was already asleep as I finished reading and ruminating about the urban past and eventually fell asleep thinking about long gone family and friends.

I guess that's why I had a dream about Stan Carew. Stan was a guitar player and singer in a band I had formed in the 1990s when I was in my forties called Lesley Choyce and the Surf Poets. (Get it? Surf, poetry and music?) Stan was a fine folksinger in his own right who had performed in many rural coffee houses in the UK. He was a radio DJ by profession in the old days when real DJs gave long, deep, philosophic commentary between songs. While on air, he had famously protested the oncoming full automation of broadcasting by walking out of the station and leaving dead air.

Anyway, Stan had died a few years back and that night he appeared in a dream to me at 4:00 a.m., as vivid as a Windermere sunrise. All I remember is me asking him, "How is it where you are?" and Stan, in his usual casual radio-announcer's voice, saying, "It's like being in a video." When I asked what he meant by that, he just splayed his hands out in the air and shrugged like the New York cop and said nothing more.

Semi-awake now in the cottage with the rest of the world still happily snoring, I closed my eyes again to find that 4:00 a.m. connection that Wayne Dyer says we all could have with angels or spirits or whoever is willing to communicate from whatever other dimension. As Stan faded from view, I asked the cosmos a follow-up on the Sufi question that had been puzzling me: "What does pure love look like?"

I usually find that communication with spiritual beings is somewhat like having a really slow internet connection, but not this time. Whichever angel was monitoring my semi-dream state promptly gave me an image, that of Ozzie, my daughter Pamela's old American Staffordshire Terrier (also known as a pit bull), who had recently died from a disease passed into pond water by infected raccoons. Ozzie was a large black dog who had been found in the Ozarks of Arkansas as a puppy with a wooden stake driven into him and left to die. He had somehow been found, treated and shipped to, of all places, Nova Scotia to be adopted by my daughter and her small son, Aidan. Despite the fact that Ozzie was a breed of dog that was actually banned in some parts of Canada, he was the kindest, gentlest, most loving pet I'd ever seen and helped Pamela and Aidan weather some difficult times.

And there was old Ozzie in my early morning Windermere

vision — healthy, shiny, lying on his side in a warm pool of afternoon sunlight. Pure love. I only wish I could have taken a picture for you.

Yes, Mr. Bill Wordsworth grieved over the railway coming to the Lakes and the crowds that would follow. He wrote, "These tourists, heaven preserve us." And I suppose that would include Linda and me, here to take in the lakes and mountains and ramble about as if we owned the place. It was still dark out as I lay awake and, from the bedroom on the second floor of our cottage, listened to how ambitious the birds were, many of them joyous and cacophonous well before the sky lightened. William and Dorothy would have been out of bed by now on a day like this and headed off for a hike of many, many miles.

CHAPTER TWENTY-FIVE

IN SEARCH OF WORDSWORTH, WISDOM AND WINDERMERE BEER
(MAY 2018)

Today was our day to head north to Keswick and then back down to Grasmere itself, ground zero for Wordsworthian connections. I was giddy over the idea of simply being here in May, with my wife and my own intimations of immortality singing to me from every quarter. Already I was remembering back to my readings of *The Prelude* in Manhattan and how much the archaic language of Wordsworth's prose had resonated with me when he wrote about where his inspiration came from. "Emotion recollected in tranquility," he insisted, makes for good poetry. My graduate school professor, who actually smoked a cigarette in a cigarette holder during classes, had taken the trouble to quote T.S. Eliot's malignant view on this principle. Eliot had written, "Consequently, we must believe that 'emotion recollected in tranquility' is an inexact formula. For it is neither emotion, nor recollection, nor, without distortion of meaning, tranquility." And I had thought, Screw you, frigging Prufrock. Don't even dare to eat a peach, eh?

Accordingly, there would be no pilgrimages to Mr. Eliot's stomping grounds in East Coker. No, today was all about the Wordsworths and connecting with the deep past. I admitted to myself, though, how much tougher it had become these days to find that tranquility the poet spoke of and indulge in the luxurious licence to recollect old emotion. But he was right, of course, and I needed to remember that. Once we were young and our emotions were explosive. Once the world really was "Apparelled in celestial light, / The glory and the freshness of a dream." And did we always eventually lose sight of that, each one of us? Perhaps.

> It is not now as it hath been of yore;—
> Turn wheresoe'er I may,
> By night or day.
> The things which I have seen I now can see no more.

But enough of that, I said to birds outside my window, as I got up to make us coffee.

We passed through Grasmere first and then north along another skinny, glacially formed finger lake known as Thirlmere with the heights of Great Dodd to the right and High Seat to the left. First stop was the stone circle called Castlerigg just shy of Keswick.

Rather than driving into Keswick and following well-positioned signs on a substantial road, I took a shortcut I saw on my map that turned out to be yet another single-track lane with stone walls on either side and no pull-offs to speak of. I booted it down the road lest we encounter an advancing car, and it blessedly spilled us out the other end into a well-marked parking area and a field of visitors snapping photos with absurdly long-lensed cameras.

Wordsworth took his drug buddy Samuel Taylor Coleridge here in 1799 and the author of "Kubla Khan" wrote that here was "a Druidical circle ... the mountains stand one behind the other, in orderly array as if evoked by and attentive to the assembly of white-vested wizards." The two poets did note that some of the stones had been splashed with white paint by vandals or sloppy eighteenth-century graffiti artists, but that couldn't quite diminish the full grandeur. On another occasion, Wordsworth and Dorothy visited Castlerigg only to discover that those damn tourists from the south who had come in on the Windermere train had found it out and it had completely lost its charm due to the crowds.

More recently, *Lonely Planet* described it this way: "Set on a hilltop a mile east of town, this jaw-dropping stone circle consists of 48 stones that are between 3000 and 4000 years old, surrounded by a dramatic ring of mountain peaks." Jaw-dropping, I will admit, is not an exaggeration. And, hey, it's older than Stonehenge by a few thousand years and it has been determined the circle served some sort of astronomical purpose, as well as having a spiritual dimension, because, even today, locals see strange lights coming from the stones at night.

I was just happy to be there, sidestepping sheep poop on such a generous morning and gloating over the fact that this ancient structure was so much less commercialized than Stonehenge and had a much grander view of the country around it, as Coleridge had observed.

As we left the standing stones of Castlerigg, we took the wider, well-maintained road to downtown Keswick. My first impression was that there wasn't much of interest here. But I was wrong. For here was the Derwent Pencil Museum. Yes, a museum devoted to the history of the pencil, with its own café and gift shop. What more could a writer ask for? One reviewer online summed it up nicely. Michael Gooch wrote, "We love this place. It's a beautifully simple and happy museum — a celebration of a childhood tool. It always brings a smile to my face." Well said, Michael. I'm not sure where he is from or who he is, but I envisioned him waking up his young family on a crisp Saturday morning saying something like, "Wake up, kids. Guess what? Today we're going to the pencil museum in Keswick."

If that wasn't enough excitement for one day, then Michael would probably take his crew on over to the Keswick Museum and Art Gallery, where dogs are welcome and reviewers give it high marks for its cleanliness. Here are "musical stones," a giant xylophone and, more importantly, a display of stone axes, other "industrial artifacts," including pencils (!) and for some strange reason, Napoleon's very own teacup. How the French dictator's teacup came to Keswick is another story, but I grieved that I did not have my dog here with me so I could say to him, "Look, Kelty, there's ole Napoleon's cup from which he sipped tea."

We probably should have lingered longer in Keswick, as it seemed bubbling with possibilities, but the dead poet was whispering in my ear that it was time to pay homage. Thus, we backtracked south on A591 to Grasmere, where Wordsworth is not so much a poet as a cottage industry. I'd visited here once many years ago and what I most remembered was that there was a display of Wordsworth's shoes and socks behind glass in the museum near Dove Cottage. Well, he was a hell of a hiker, so why not? And perhaps it was just a good reminder that even legendary poets put their socks on one at a time when they awake to the symphony of songbirds on a splendid May morning in Cumbria.

Another book I had been carrying around was H.V. Morton's somewhat classic *In Search of England*. The author had visited Grasmere in the 1920s. He wrote, "No matter what opinion you have of Wordsworth as a poet, you must recognize him as a great, but unconscious, publicity agent. The solitudes he once loved are now well populated." And, by 2018, they were even more populated. Grasmere was an exceedingly busy little burgh with crowded coffee shops and discount outdoor stores where you could buy a full complement of ordnance maps. There were more than a few hiking trails hereabouts where you could see wide-brim-hatted men and women poring over those ordnance maps spread out over large boulders, trying to determine if they could get to the next tarn by hiking over the beckoning fell.

I was trying not to share Morton's cynicism as I had plenty of my own to weigh me down in a place like Grasmere. However, Morton had written, "One of England's great sights is that of a New York businessman, determined to get every cent of value from his tour, trying to work up enthusiasm for Wordsworth in the little churchyard at Grasmere." This struck me as curious in that my own enthusiasm for the great poet was formed back in my seminar room many storeys above Forty-Second Street and riveted into place later while reading *Lyrical Ballads* at lunchtime in Bryant Park.

And so it was time to park the car, pay the meter with appropriate contemporary coins recognized by the electronic machine and drop into Dove Cottage itself. It was a guided tour, which I sometimes dread, but there was an articulate, spirited and informative guide, a woman who took our small group into a dark room and said, "And there is the chair where Wordsworth sat and wrote." I was pleased to note a painting of a dog on the wall. According to our host, this was Wordsworth's dog, Pepper, given to him by none other than Sir Walter Scott. According to the BBC, "The great Scottish novelist was an amateur breeder and used to name his dogs according to their furs. The dogs were usually called Ginger, Pepper or Mustard."

Well, I was mightily pleased to see the artwork of the handsome mutt first thing as we entered. It was indeed a dark and gloomy house throughout, but then most of the Wordsworths' inspiration came from outdoors. These days, scholars recognize that Dorothy had much to do with her brother's poetry, his fame and his success. She kept extensive journals about everything and, according to our guide, tried to write down William's oral creation of his poetry as he muttered away while the two of them hiked mile after mile.

Wordsworth scholar Suzanne Stewart of St. Francis Xavier University had written to me about the ambitious hikes taken by the two Wordsworths and sent along this quote from Dorothy's 1818 journal:

> At 46 I can walk 16 miles in 4 and ¼ hours with short rests between on a blustering cold day, without having felt any fatigue except for the first ½ hour after my entrance into the house at my journey's end when my body remembered the force of the blast and I was exhausted.

Stewart notes, "I imagine her as a small woman, with little legs and wondered how she managed this," and adds that by 1820 Dorothy was frail and unhealthy and spent the last 20 years of her life indoors, "confined" in her "prison house," as she would say.

Both brother and sister loved the outdoors and they loved dogs. On a six-day "holiday ramble," Dorothy wrote, "Mrs. Luff's large white dog lay in the moonshine upon the round knoll under the old yew-tree, a beautiful and romantic image — the dark tree with its dark shadow, and the elegant creature as fair as a Spirit."

No wonder that a painting of a dog greeted the thousands of visitors as they first entered Dove Cottage.

Coleridge lived here with the Wordsworths as well for extended periods of time and, according to our cheerful guide, they rather accepted his opium habit without judgement. Robert Southey had stayed here too, she said, but the blank faces all around the dark room revealed that none of us knew a damn thing (or cared) about Southey. Poets do mostly come and go in England and elsewhere and are quickly shuffled out of the national canon like so much dandruff brushed from the shoulders of gentlemen.

The *Encyclopedia Britannica* is not exaggerating when it says, "Southey's poetry is little read today," although he wrote "lucid, relaxed, observant accounts of contemporary life." His portrait in the Wordsworth house suggested he was slightly effeminate, as were many of the Romantic poets, and he appears relaxed, yes, but somewhat aloof and full of himself — which I guess you can say of most of the well-known Romantic poets if not most twenty-first-century pop stars, who may indeed be looked upon by some as the poets of our time.

Southey was heavily influenced by Wordsworth and Coleridge, and Walter Scott liked him enough to have him installed as poet laureate rather than giving him a dog for a pet. Southey was an opinionated man and disliked Lord Byron in particular. The two of them got involved with what *Britannica* called an "imbroglio," which is a polite term that I had to look up. Apparently, an imbroglio is "an unwanted, difficult, and confusing situation, full of trouble and problems," according the *Cambridge English Dictionary*.

And before we relegate the poet laureate to the dustbins of history, do not forget (in case you ever knew) that he wrote "The Story of the Three Bears," which filtered down to your generation as the traditional children's Goldilocks tale. If Southey were alive and could still collect royalties on the silly little story, he would be wealthier than Donald Trump.

Our guide gave us the impression that William was more than a bit of a kook himself and, at times, a grumpy brother who was looked after by his sister and his sister's best friend, his wife Mary Hutchinson. And the house really was a cramped, dark dungeon of sorts that was probably quite cold much of the year, so I can see why it was preferable to be out hiking the hills soaking in as much sunshine as possible while conjuring up odes to everything under the sun. And let's face it, Wordsworth was pretty much opposed to civilization with its industrialization, urban squalor, materialism, burgeoning tourism and wholesale destruction of nature. He preferred the forest, the field, the fells, the tarns, the esks, the waters and all the wildlife therein.

And, yes, here was Wordsworth's writing desk, his favourite chair, his wash basin, his bed and, over there in the corner, his chamber pot.

We were then directed out back into the garden where the bees were buzzing and the birds singing — all so perfectly orchestrated to seem like a poem that it's possible they were staged by the foundation that kept the house in proper condition so they could rake in the cash of visitors like us.

Next up was a tour of the Wordsworth Museum that I had been looking forward to — manuscripts behind glass and whatever personal artifacts had been saved after the great poet had gone on to his next incarnation. But just as we were about to enter, a fire alarm went off inside the museum. "Oh dear," our guide said. "I'm sure it's nothing, but we can't go in until a fire official comes to give us an all-clear."

England was, after all, a country with a lot of rules and regulations and, fire or no fire, things were meant to be done properly. None of the staff were certain exactly who the proper authority was to come give the all-clear, but they would look into it. With that in mind, Linda and I decided to wander the town and come back after the appropriate inspection had taken place. I made a mental note to write a poem called "Fire Alarm at the Wordsworth Museum," as we made our way into the bustling town buzzing with tourists instead of bees but still charming and quaint — or at least as quaint as a Lake District tourist destination can be with busloads of visitors unloading near the chapel.

Linda was looking for some new sports apparel for running, so we ended up in one of a dozen outdoor-type shops that reminded me of just how much the English love to hike. Here was a treasure trove of those massive folding ordnance maps and aluminum walking sticks, folding plastic dog dishes, expensive shiny backpacks, sleeping bags that would keep you warm down to -20 degrees Fahrenheit, nylon tents with mosquito netting, endless quantities of expensive outdoor shoes and much, much more. I found myself studying a display case of compasses and found some satisfaction in thinking that not everyone afoot in the hills carries a GPS or some other device tuned in to a satellite. I almost always travel with a compass myself, on an airplane or hiking in the woods. It's a habit that goes back to Boy Scout days. If I were truly lost in the fells near here I might not be savvy enough of the lay of the land to find my way back to civilization, but I'd damn well know where north was. But then, most of the waters (lakes) here ran north–south (just like back home in Nova Scotia) thanks to the scraping of the long, powerful claws of the glaciers. So, even without a compass, I'd have a 50/50 chance of finding north.

As Linda was finishing her shopping, I noticed that on the counter was a display of smallish hobby drones that were on sale. I asked the dapper-looking clerk if the drones were popular with hikers. "Oh, yes," he said. "We just started carrying them. Folks come up from London and they either have their own or they like to buy them. One fella said that if you get yourself good and lost, you just send up your drone high enough so you can figure out where you are."

I was afraid to ask, but I'm sure that, lately, the sale of compasses was well down from previous years.

Not knowing how swiftly the fire safety bureaucrats could do their job, we decided to have an early lunch at one of those nursery/garden supply establishments that doubled as a cafeteria-style restaurant. So it was fish and chips at the Pot Shed. I had my copy of *Man Seeks God* with me and, once sated on the seafood and spuds, I thumbed through it while Linda looked over the plants and garden ornaments that we couldn't possibly take with us back to North America. I was reading the chapter titled "God Is a State of Mind" about Buddhism and noted that the author's mentor on the subject — a young Jewish man from Long Island — insisted that for Buddhists, it's all about *intentions*, not *results*. Wow, did that ever resonate with me, the sometimes king (or at least prince) of lost causes. My father, I suppose, was the one who taught me that you should always do the *right* thing — which I believe is different from the *proper* thing — even if you expect to fail. The *right* thing being the *kind* thing, the *compassionate* thing, dare I even say the *noble* thing.

Linda retrieved me from my mini-spiritual reverie just as the busloads of tourists were leaving the cafeteria line and looking for a place to sit.

Back at the museum, it was all clear as we showed our ticket stubs from the morning and were permitted entrance. Here were those artifacts and manuscripts and various quotes displayed by the poet who was either ecstatic or despondent about just about everything. William almost single-handedly launched poetry into an emotionally heightened bipolar phase where one was either higher than a kite on the positive side of living or deep down in the basement of despair and celebrating that as well. If you are ever in doubt about the manic-depressive nature of the Romantics, read Keats's "Ode on Melancholy":

> Ay, in the very temple of Delight
>   Veil'd Melancholy has her sovran shrine.

In the museum I remembered that in an old notebook of mine, I had once scribbled a quote from Wordsworth:

> Dreams, books, are each a world; and books, we know,
> Are a substantial world, both pure and good:
> Round these, with tendrils strong as flesh and blood,
> Our pastime and our happiness will grow.

I sometimes wrote those lines on the blackboard for my students to let them ponder the thought and would occasionally become despondent myself when the only questions that would arise would concern the oddness of the poet's use of punctuation and capitalization.

Among the many paintings in the museum is one of Wordsworth with his right hand held to his forehead. He was either deep in thought or he had a headache or maybe both. It is a famous painting, but to me it appeared much more human than so many of the other portraits I'd seen. "The world is too much with us," it seemed to say. I was somewhat thankful that so much of Wordsworth's world was preserved here — his letters, his handwritten manuscripts, his walking stick and — of course, there they were, shielded behind glass so they could not be touched and sullied — his shoes and his socks that I had marvelled at and written a poem about decades ago.

The world had changed greatly since the early 1980s when I had first arrived at Grasmere, but not Wordsworth's socks. They were right there where I had seen them so long ago. For me, the sight was a kind of anchor in time. I felt confident that for years in the future, those socks would still be there, stared at by visitors from around the world. I thought about my daughter Pamela, about to have twins this coming summer. Some time after the two girls turn 21, I would ask them to make a pilgrimage to Grasmere to check on those socks. When I shared this thought with Linda, possibly with moist eyes, I'm not sure, she said, "I think it's time to get you out of here."

And, as always, she was right.

We retreated south through Ambleside and drove farther down the lake to Bowness-on-Windermere but couldn't find a single place to park so returned home to Birthwaite Cottage, left the car and walked into town for a beer at the Crafty Baa with its cartoony images of sheep. (Get it? Crafty as in beer. Baa as in...) It was about as small as a pub could possibly be and a carpenter was doing some kind of repairs to the front door. He asked if he could put his hammer and level on our small round table, which was a recycled cable spool, I believe. We said he could and he was careful not to knock our twin glasses of Cumbria IPA as he worked and retrieved his tools. My head was still swimming with thinking about Wordsworth, the future and a life lived with good intentions without worrying about results.

As you can tell, I can be a bit long-winded, prone to going on tangents, mental meanderings and near-purposeless ponderings. After I went on a bit like that to my dear wife, the IPA finally settled me down. Think of a wind-up toy dancer as the spring is nearly fully unwound.

To sum up the rest of the day thereafter, I'll quote directly from my succinct wife and her notebook where she wrote, "Walked path back from town. Cod for dinner."

CHAPTER TWENTY-SIX

PETER RABBIT AND THE CONQUEST OF STICKLE TARN

(MAY 2018)

On the morning of May 24, we took the little car ferry from Bowness across Lake Windermere to Far Sawrey. On board were backpackers, bikers and people out to enjoy a day on the other side of the long lake.

Our destination was Hill Top farm in Near Sawrey. We were headed to the home of Beatrix Potter. Peter Rabbit was a long hop, skip and jump from Wordsworth and Coleridge's 1789 volume of *Lyrical Ballads* with its "Rime of the Ancient Mariner" and "Tintern Abbey," but it was a story my mother had read to me as a little boy. The names Flopsy, Mopsy and Cotton-tail still echo in my head because we raised rabbits back there in the early 1960s and had named three of our brood after these characters. Exactly *why* we were raising rabbits back then is something I am afraid to ask of my memory.

There was also a Choyce connection here. One of Potter's closest friends was a woman named Louie Choyce. They had an extensive correspondence that was later published as *The Choyce Letters*, revealing the details of their friendship and also their common interest in sheep, fungi (mycology), horticulture and all things living.

Potter herself is best known for her 28 children's books that she wrote and illustrated. They were somewhat cutesy little stories for the most part that have sold over 100 million copies and been translated into 35 languages. Like most successful authors, she initially met with rejection when trying to find a publisher for her work but, once she met up with publisher Frederick Warne, her career took off. She then met Frederick's brother, Norman, both her editor and lover — which sounds like a most unlikely combo — and things might have gone happily ever after had he not died of a disease known as pernicious anaemia.

In her heart and life, Beatrix was a lover of animals. Peter Rabbit was modelled on her own pet rabbit, Benjamin Bouncer. As a child, a somewhat homely child one might observe from the photographs, she had mice, frogs, hedgehogs and even a pet bat to keep her company.

Through the years she had dogs for pets too, of course. Perhaps her most famous is her collie Kep, who appears in a number of photographs of Beatrix, as well as in *The Tale of Jemima the Puddle-Duck*. Beatrix had feared dogs as a child but grew to love border collies as working farm dogs and always had one as her own. Kep was followed by Fleet and Nip.

In the car park at the preserved Potter home, Hill Top farm, I chatted up a man standing there with a Jack Russell Terrier. We talked about dogs for a few minutes and he grumbled about dogs not being allowed in the World of Beatrix Potter, an entertainment attraction back across the lake in Bowness. He also thought that the price tag for a family afternoon there with the show and afternoon tea was a bit steep: £84. Holy hedgehog! I agreed and lodged my own complaint as to the high price of going into Hill Top and other National Trust sites. Linda must have been off taking photos, because we two men grumbled and consoled each other like that for a while until, in the spirit of mutual male complaints, I mentioned how the unyielding British government would not allow us to fly our Westie into the country in the cabin of the plane. "It's just not fair," I said, one dog lover to another, but because he was an Englishman I added in jest, "You should have that fixed."

Instead of laughing and saying, "Yes, I'll get right on that," he frowned and said, "That and a lot of other things. It's this damn European Union thing, I bet."

Oops. He bet wrong because France and other Euronations are easy-peasy on dogs compared to Great ("We're an island, you know") Britain. After that, the conversation sort of peter-rabbitted off and he allowed his Jack Russell to tug him off toward a trash can, where the dog sniffed and then peed on the shiny metal, reminding me to avoid anything even slightly political when talking to strangers and to never, ever mention anything about the European Union, Brexit, fox hunting or the lack of proper hot water to anyone I would meet in the United Kingdom from now on.

As the parking lot continued to fill up and my wife came to rescue me from further alienating citizens of our host country, I began to wonder why Ms. Potter's fame had grown rather than diminished over the years. I had tried rereading some of those children's books recently and, well ... am I allowed to say it? I just didn't get it.

I know, I know, I know. "They're children's books, you flaming asshole, snob, jerk," you might say to my face.

So I'll say no more about the thin plots, the silly characters with even sillier names like Squirrel Nutkin, Little Pig Robinson and Mrs. Tiggy-Winkle. And, besides, it was my own dear mother who loved the stories and was willing to share them with my brother and me when we were still peeing our pants and dripping snot on the books she read from.

The Potter house itself was smallish and dark like Dove Cottage and downright austere, but the countryside around there was heavenly. Beatrix proved herself to everyone near there that she was indeed a true animal lover and a conservationist. When she died at 77, she left her 14 farms (14!!) and 4,000 acres to the National Trust. She was able to buy all that property thanks to the huge success of her book sales.

Although she ended her life as a famous writer, naturalist and philanthropist, she had begun farming here with as much difficulty as anyone else, even having to cope with a total of 96 rats in her first two years at Hill Top. Her passion extended itself to sheep farming and, for a woman in her time, this was predominantly a male domain. Yet her fame for breeding Herdwick sheep led to her election as the president of the Herdwick Sheep Breeders Association, which was a big deal in those days and in these parts.

As usual, we were channelled through the gift shop as we were leaving Hill Top Farm, and I was sorely tempted to buy a Peter Rabbit shot glass but left it there on the shelf instead for a true fan to purchase and carry home and revere.

Driving on to Hawkshead and Hawkshead Hill, it was easy to see why Potter had fallen in love with this rolling green bucolic countryside, and I was thankful that this side of Windermere was not quite as commercial as the Eastern Shore around Bowness, Windermere proper and Ambleside.

We stopped for lunch at the Old Dungeon Ghyll Hotel on our way to Great Langdale. I had the chicken and leek pie, which I would recommend. On Tripadvisor, which is always a lively place to monitor other travellers' opinions rather than facts, David L. of Preston, UK, reports that it is "a no nonsense pub, popular with climbers and walkers enjoying the Langdale Pikes. The interior consists of stone floors and bare wooden benches and tables; perfect if you're wet or muddy (fairly common in this part of the world).... Service is efficient, but I'm puzzled that the staff all appear to be from Eastern Europe. Are there no locals who need the work?"

While I can't answer his Socratic enquiry concerning the local employment situation, I would own up to the fact that we encountered many, many Eastern Europeans in the service industry while travelling in the UK and they were all super-friendly, efficient and helpful. Despite some obvious lingering resentment of the European Union that had flared into the Brexit disaster, many a British veteran pub goer will tell you that service dramatically improved throughout the land once the job-hungry immigrants from the continent were permitted entry into the kingdom.

Refreshed and restored, we motored on through Chapel Stile and on to our destination of Great Langdale. I had fussed over what mountain we should climb — something difficult but not too difficult — a steep hike that Wordsworth would approve of and something that would get us breathing heavily and challenge our abilities. In a hiking book, I'd read about the trek up to Stickle Tarn and decided that was the place. A tarn is a lake, I had learned, but when trying to determine what "stickle" meant, I could only discover it meant to have a stubborn argument about something trivial or, if you can believe the Urban Dictionary, it is "the space between you and someone else, when you don't want them touching you." I never did sort out how it applied to the mountain we were about to hike, but chalked it up to one of a myriad of small mysteries in my life that would never be unravelled. But

I would maybe use the word out loud if ever again I found myself on a subway ride in Tokyo during rush hour.

Parking the car at the foot of this most Cumbrian of the Cumbrian Mountains, we were certain Stickle was a worthy adversary and set out on the stony path behind the inn. Our first encounter was with some sort of Outward Bound–type group. About thirty 12-year-olds in safety helmets, bright sports clothes and water shoes were scrambling up a ravine through the cascading water. They were led by shouting university-age counsellors and aggressively splashing each other as they hopped from rock to rock. It was a warm day and it probably felt good to be wet. Linda and I agreed that we approved of anything challenging like this that would get a contemporary English youth out of a classroom and out from behind the screen of a dastardly video game.

Sure, there would be a few scraped knees and some damaged egos, but it was the pre-teen version of real adventure and made me think that perhaps the British Outdoors for Youth Anti-Internet Soak Your Bully in a Mountain Stream central office should require all children between the ages of 9 and 16 to be locked out of their homes at least once a week and required to commune with Mother Nature on whatever terms possible.

There was, however, in the path before us, one chubby lad sitting it out on a ledge with his (or somebody's) mother, his safety helmet in hand, his ego battered, his self-esteem damaged beyond recognition. We didn't stop to ask what the problem was as that would only have exacerbated his plight. But it was clear and universal that here was the boy who couldn't quite find the will or courage to join his peers in their wet and wild fun. Maybe he just had a bad stomach from eating too many Yorkies, Rolos, Maltesers, Milkybars or Haribo Strawbs. Or maybe he had just chickened out and his schoolmates would never, ever allow him to forget it. Scarred for life from this and several similar episodes, he would grow up to be a murderer or a terrorist. Or it could go the other way. He could turn out to be an I'll-Show-Them type who comes up with a cure for cancer and a device that can convert poisoned water into clean, healthy, life-giving fluid for free.

We left the brooding boy and the shouts of his happier classmates as we ascended a stony trail that continually became steeper and steeper. Linda was in better shape than me thanks to her running mornings, but I was successfully coaching raw oxygen into my lungs, faithfully advising my calf muscles to muster their strength and royally trying to keep up with her as best I could.

There were sheep about perched on small ledges here and there and the view of the Great Langdale Valley just kept getting grander and grander. Sure enough, the tarn was waiting for us at the top with two even higher mountains — Harrison Stickle and Pavey Ark — looming above with a spectacular blue sky behind them. All the mountains around had been scraped mostly bare by retreating glaciers. There were no trees but hearty, desert-like-looking plants and enough dry grass to keep the sparse sheep fed.

At the summit, we were rewarded with a view of a pristine mountaintop lake. It reminded me of photos I'd seen of other mountaintops with circular lakes at the summit. And then it occurred to me. It was a volcanic cone. Stickle Tarn is what's left of an extinct volcano. And here we were, me puffing heavily like a six-pack-a-day smoker and Linda still hopping from boulder to boulder like a 20-something gymnast. We had worked hard to get here and this was our reward. A dead but breathtaking volcano top.

We gorged our eyes on water, sky and distant peaks for a while and congratulated ourselves on such success at a strenuous climb, vowing that if there were more hills like this about, bring them on. We wandered a bit here in the heights and snapped some of those photographs that never do justice to such natural magnificence. Then Linda led the way down — on the far side of the tiny rivulet we had traced to the summit.

Unfortunately, the trail petered out to nothing and we found ourselves on a much steeper slope with much less stable footing. It turned out to be a path mostly used by the mountain sheep and I feared we were not quite as adept as they were. But if I knew one thing about scaling *down* mountains (and I don't know much) it is this: when in doubt, slide down on your ass. And so we shuffled and crab walked and bumped our bums ever downward on these most ancient stones until we could cross the stream again and make our way back down toward the voices of the adventure-happy kids in the lower creek.

Uncommonly proud of having scaled such a difficult climb, I would later look up the hike in a Lake District hiking book only to discover that the author referred to it as a "nice family hike," but I refused to let that diminish my sense of accomplishment. In my memory, it continues to loom large, positively Alpine or even Himalayan.

I was itching for a pint of beer from the pub below but settled on sharing an icy cold bottle of Coke purchased from the friendly barkeep. I had noticed that in most of the British hiking books, detailed descriptions of the trails invariably end with some fairly precise directions as to how a weary, thirsty hiker can find his or her way to the nearest pub. At Stickle Tarn, you don't have to look far. We were barely off the trail when we stumbled into Walker's Bar. I don't usually drink sweet fizzy drinks, but I felt like they put something special in the Coke that day, although it was probably the generous buzz provided by the mountain and the air. I was reminded that if a person needed to overcome a bout of what the Romantic poets would have called melancholy, a good challenging hike to any available stickle or tarn might do it. That and a slug of ice-cold Coke. How exactly could it be that something so natural and magnificent combined with something so commercial, crass and unhealthy could create such a small but impressive sense of euphoria? I don't quite know, but it does.

According to *Engineering Timelines*, the Langdale area "is the site of what might be called the first recognisable 'industry' in the British Isles. The scree slopes here were quarried some 5,000 years ago for the raw materials for stone axes, which were then shaped and eventually ended up distributed round the country." The stone in question was called greenstone volcanic tuff, and it really did get exported far and wide, with at least one group of diligent archeologists determining that a whopping 27 per cent of the axe heads from this period came from the Great Langdale area, and some were found as far away as Wales, Ireland and Poland.

Soon it would be time to depart from the Lake District, drive back to Glasgow airport and find our way back home to gear up for our month back in England (by way of a flight to France), this time with Kelty. I had noticed an English Facebook posting for a "Tails Trails — Events for Dogs and their Humans" coaxing everyone to "Come Join the Pack," so I knew there was plenty of dog-friendly hiking to be had in Langdale and vicinity. But I'd also read accounts of sheep farmers shooting unleashed dogs in Cumbria, blaming dogs for the death of substantial numbers of their sheep, so perhaps Kelty would be safer some place other than on the steep craggy slopes of the fells. As I went to sleep that night, I began to worry about all the things that could possibly go wrong on our upcoming journey with our beloved pet.

In the morning, over coffee, I also found myself drawn to other tragic news of this Lake District that had been so generous to us. Only a month before, a climber had died after falling at Raven Crag right behind where we'd had lunch at the Old Dungeon Ghyll Hotel.

One such tragic story led to a plethora of others with headlines reading: "Glaramara climber dies from head injuries after fall on Raven Crag," "Injured Lakeland climber airlifted from Raven Crag after 33 ft. fall," "Paraglider critically injured in crash on Tarn Crag, Great Langdale," "Great Langdale walker dies after fall in Dungeon Ghyll," and "Lake District walker dies after falling on Scafell Pike snow slope."

We were not mountain climbers, Linda and I, but I find that preparing for a long-distance flight anywhere, even when going home, sobers me to realities that haunt me from time to time. Adventure and danger are linked, as are beauty and loss.

Soon the car was packed and we were on the A592 leaving Windermere driving through the stark beauty of Kirkstone Pass and skirting the shores of Ullswater, where Dorothy and William had taken their "holiday ramble" and she had seen the vision of the white dog in moonlight. Then it was onward toward Penrith and the M6. As we crossed over Hadrian's Wall again without a trace to be seen, I fixed my thoughts on the few weeks ahead of preparation for our return to England by way of France, this time with both my wife and dog along to help me reach into the past, seek out what further hidden truths this island was willing to give up and to discover just how a dog on a journey changes the way a pilgrim encounters the world around him.

CHAPTER TWENTY-SEVEN

GOODBYE TO AN OLD GRUDGE AND HELLO TO THE FAIR FOLK

In our upstairs apartment in Osgathorpe, a little more than halfway through our primary journey around England with Kelty, it was time to firm up a few items about the rest of our itinerary. We now had a house in Devon booked and, after that, a final night at a posh old estate a few miles from the Eurotunnel entrance in Folkestone. Linda and I had travelled to Cornwall on a number of occasions before and didn't have enough time left to return there with Kelty. We would miss surf writer Chris Nelson, who had already told me he would be away doing some organization work for the London Surf / Film Festival. Who would have guessed that London was such a big surfer-friendly city? Nonetheless, he agreed to have a later email conversation with me about the surfing life in South West England. So that would have to do.

But now that we had set up our rural cottage in Devon, I emailed Tony Hawks to give him the good news that we would be in his neighbourhood and we should try to firm up a time to meet. Sadly, he emailed back almost right away to let me know that he too would be in London "for work" while we were in Devon and apologized gracefully about not being able to get together.

So there it was. I had totally struck out with my efforts to meet up with English writers of the living variety. Dead writers would have to do.

Shortly after we got on the road, we heard the news that Pamela was seriously sick as a result of an infection related to that bad tooth. She was now at least 29 weeks pregnant and this was most worrisome. We were now having some serious thoughts that all was not well at home and our first inclination was to abandon the journey. Her husband, Jason, was still away on "manoeuvres" in Fiji. Like me, you'd probably be wondering what Fiji needed from Canadian soldiers and why now of all times? Well, Pamela was not due to have her babies for another nine weeks and Jason would be home by then, having finished his work training Fijian infantrymen to build temporary quarters in swamps. But now there was this escalating dental/medical problem. Maybe it would all turn out okay. We both had faith in the Canadian medical system. Or maybe we should cut our trip short and hightail it back home where we might be needed. Linda was leaning toward making a beeline for the English Channel and the French flight home. My worries about my daughter increased as we drove, but I didn't want to say too much so as to avoid alarming Linda even further.

I had studied the map thoroughly so I thought I knew exactly what I was doing — south on the A42 and deke west on the A5 at Dordon, which would allow us to miss all the morning commuter traffic into Birmingham and the adjoining Midland cities. I had visions of the large, urban, industrial sprawl and, for the most part, we'd been good little rural pilgrims, avoiding much of that ugliness, creating for ourselves the satisfying illusion that England was still one grand big green rolling field.

But I fucked up, as we say in Canada when we can't keep our stick on the ice or when the puck flies off into the boards. I can blame parental worry over my highly pregnant dentally damaged daughter, or it could have been pure hubris. Probably a little of each. But, even as Linda was insisting, "Take this exit," I kept motoring on in the heavy morning traffic. I was like one of those lemmings you hear about or a panicked buffalo from days gone by in the middle of a herd about to go charging off a cliff at someplace that would one day be called Head-Smashed-In Buffalo Jump.

So there we were, rocketing past the turnoff to Foul End, Whitacre Heath, Hoggrill's End and Hams Hall with a mob of drivers headed to work in downtown Birmingham. There's nothing like missing a turnoff on an M class highway to quite destroy whatever hopes one might have for a pleasant journey.

Well, you might say, it's not the end of the world. Birmingham has changed its image in recent years, its citizens would argue. In fact, I think most of the old ugly cities of the Industrial Revolution have spruced themselves up quite a bit, hoping that tourists like Linda and me will read their municipal websites and say, "By God, we have to go there and see the ____ (fill in the blank: Hay Rick Museum, Luddite Monument, etc.), go on the Peaky Blinders Tour and polish it off with drinking craft beer at an infinite number of new micro-breweries."

Years ago, I'd even been invited to give a lecture on the state of Canadian writing at the University of Birmingham. All through my lecture, I kept wondering exactly why these

British English majors were interested in Canadian literature. They didn't look particularly enthused when I waxed eloquent about the small literary press movement in Atlantic Canada or the long-time national enthusiasm for the Canadian short story. So I read them a poem of mine about surfing in the winter in Nova Scotia at -20 degrees Celsius and that got a rise from the bored lads at the back of the class. So, instead of discussing the fiction of Margaret Atwood and Alice Munro, I answered questions about wetsuits, curious seals and what it feels like to have salt water freeze on your face.

So, in truth, I had fond memories of Birmingham. I just didn't want to go there this cloudy, somewhat worrisome morning. Wales was beckoning and apprehension was gnawing at me. Was it time to just keep on driving south, make a beeline for Folkestone and France and go home to Pamela?

Inevitably, we hit a big snag — a major traffic jam that seemed to have no cause other than way too many people on the road at the same time. We crawled toward Birmingham, turned west on the M6, grumbled through Birmingham and on around Wolverhampton. Now the thing about Wolverhampton that struck me was that it was so big. At a quarter-million souls, it was just slightly smaller than the largest city back home, Halifax. This in itself is no big deal. But I had never heard of it before. It just wasn't on the radar for most of us back on the Eastern Shore of Nova Scotia or even the whole Eastern Seaboard of North America. Not once had anyone said to me in my entire lifetime, "I think we'll holiday in Wolverhampton this year."

Although we didn't stop in this fine city, it did raise my curiosity enough to want to know Wolverhampton, even at a later time and from a great distance. Is it true that people living in the city are called Wulfrunians? And if so, why?

There was an abbey here as long ago as AD 659 and a "decisive battle" in 910 when the local Angles and Saxons teamed up to ward off the raiding Danes. If that doesn't stir your blood, it is worth noting that Ethelred the Unready granted the lands here to Lady Wulfrun, which must help explain the origin of Wulfrunian.

Of more modern interest to this motorist is the fact that England's first automatic traffic lights went into operation here in 1927 at Princes Square. However, more significantly, anyone with an ounce of English blood probably knows that Wolverhampton is the home of the Wanderers Football Club and, since the term "wanderer" seems a touch non-aggressive and undramatic, most fans call them the Wolves.

But there on the crowded motorway, the traffic didn't let up a speck as we passed Shifnal, Telford, Shrewsbury and Oswestry, until we crossed over into Wales with no fanfare whatsoever at Chirk.

One of my objectives in including Wales on our itinerary was to overcome that deep-seated grudge, an outright prejudice some might say, that I had against the Welsh. So, before you judge me harshly, let me explain a few more details. As a young man (well, as someone in his late thirties), I was travelling about Wales, somewhere near Merthyr Tydfil or Pontypridd, when I stopped in one late afternoon for a pint of bitter at a pub in a small town. I was alone and looking every bit the outsider. I received dark looks from working men who had obviously just finished an honest day's manual labour, I would guess, and in walks this foreigner (me) without a care in the world.

I sat at the bar and absorbed the scowls of working men with a certain amount of grace, I believe, and ordered my pint. I handed the barkeep a 20-pounder and he promptly handed back several of those weighty little pound coins. The price of a beverage to me that day seemed a bit steep here in whatever the town was. So I reminded the man behind the bar that I had handed him a 20, not a fiver or a ten. He grunted and I think so did a few of the other regulars not trying to mind their own business that afternoon. The man grudgingly opened the till again and slapped some appropriate bills with those funny pictures of the Queen before me.

As I drank my bitter, feeling a bit bitter myself, I decided then and there that here was possibly the most unfriendly pub I had ever had the displeasure to drink in. Perhaps it was the most unfriendly pub in all the UK, perhaps the Western World.

After that, even though I knew Wales to have some exquisite surfing beaches, dramatic mountains and lively culture, I couldn't shake the feeling that I had received that unwelcoming day.

But now I was a man in his sixties and it was time to bury the hatchet and forget about old grudges. And, indeed, the skies had cleared and it was a fine blue day as we drove on to Llangollen through a green valley that was untarnished by slate or coal strip mining as far as the eye could see.

Between Llangollen and Glyndyfrdwy, however, not far from Horseshoe Falls, we hit more traffic on the highway. In fact, we came to a complete halt. After a 20-minute wait, we were allowed to move forward and discovered that in the opposing lane of traffic was a monstrous-sized truck towing a mammoth blade of a wind generator that was at least four car lengths long. The truck was dead stopped and there was only a narrow laneway where it appeared he was hoping to turn off the road. We'd seen wind generators generously distributed throughout the UK and, to me, they were always symbolic of how far this nation and much of Europe had come since the energy crises of the 1970s and 1980s. Such change, however, comes at a price ... and today, I supposed those late for an appointment due to the construction of environmentally friendly energy sources would be cursing those goody-two-shoes environmentalists who were mucking up Welsh traffic flow with their damn wind machine parts.

Soon, however, we were past the truck and on our way, but for those coming from the other direction, the drivers were stuck in a dead stop traffic snarl that was at least five miles long. Maybe it is one of those disreputable North American traits, but passing those other poor sods who were going to be stuck for a really long time and not knowing even *why* they were stopped, I felt a small bubble of happiness burgeoning in me. I dare say I am not proud of the feeling, but part of my brain produced the simple adolescent equation: *they* were stuck in traffic and *I* was not. How lucky is that?

A quick glance at my AA map assured me that there was probably not another easy way through this valley and, besides, there was no place to turn around on the narrow road. Those Welsh drivers were good and screwed, if they were hoping to get home on time for their Welsh rarebit lunch. This seemingly insignificant event strangely lifted my spirits enough so that I had stopped worrying about Pamela and the soon-to-be twins.

We passed along the way a place called Ewe-Phoria Agri-Theatre and Sheep Dog Centre, although it didn't look to be open. According to Britevents, the place "details the life and work of the shepherd on a traditional Welsh farm. The Agri-Theatre has unusual living displays of sheep with accompanying lectures on their history and breed, while outside sheepdog handlers put their dogs through their paces." The BBC once declared Ewe-Phoria one of the top UK Easter destinations, coming in at number 38 just ahead of the Star Wars Museum.

I made a mental note to possibly stop there on our way back to England if we happened to be more in the mood for unusual displays of sheep, but for now we kept going and, instead, stopped for a much-needed break in Pentrefoelas. Day Out With The Kids claims there are 155 "things to do" with kids in this town, but there aren't really. However, there is a little grassy park by a chattering brook with a cool arched stone bridge. There are wood carvings here and plaques with stories about the "Fair Folk" of Welsh legend. Apparently, long ago, these mystical creatures appeared and disappeared on a regular basis and occasionally became intimately involved with the locals.

One story, recounted by author zteve t evans (zteve must really hate capital letters), tells of a young shepherd from Pentrefoelas who was staring at a peat stack one misty morning only to discover a beautiful girl standing there. It looked like she needed help and he went to aid her, eventually falling in love with this lovely person from another dimension. According to zteve, "Although the girl was not from earth they married and had children and lived a happy life. Sadly their happiness was shattered by a freak accident that broke a promise the shepherd had made to his wife's father. This meant she had to return to the Otherworld where she came from and they were parted forever." Such a sad ending to an interdimensional love story. I suppose local parents tell the tale to their children as a kind of warning not to fall in love with someone from the Otherworld. I know I wouldn't want my kids to fall for someone like that and I guess you'd have to say that becoming beguiled by one of the Fair Folk is not one of the 155 things to do in this neighbourhood.

Although we only stayed a short while in this small village, both Kelty and I felt the presence of something we could not quite name and left for the last leg of our journey refreshed and rejuvenated. I found myself thankful, as well, to all those who keep track of old legends like this, especially zteve t evans, who has this to say about himself: "I have a deep affinity with the natural world, animals, plants, trees, birds, and all other of God's creatures and a healthy respect for spiders, scorpions, snakes and anything that stings, or bites." Clearly, he and I are kindred spirits.

CHAPTER TWENTY-EIGHT

BETWS-Y-COED – DIPPING THE FEET AND DIVING THE DUMPSTER

We easily found our next temporary home, Rock Cottage, close to the centre of Betws-y-Coed. It was right behind a discount outdoor sports outlet called the Cotswold Outdoor Rock Bottom Store. "Rock bottom," I assumed, referred to prices, but to my eye, the running shoes, backpacks, BPA-free water bottles and hiking shorts all looked damned expensive. The town actually had several of these outdoor enthusiast franchises, leading me to realize that many travellers come to Betws-y-Coed to hike, climb mountains, run up and down the mountain trails and bike through the valleys, all with stylish and expensive gear. In fact, the town reminded me a lot of Grasmere back in the Lake District where such stores had been plentiful as well.

In principle, ever since I was a Boy Scout hiking through the wilds of the New Jersey Pines with my friends in the Flaming Arrow Patrol, I've believed that the really good outdoorsy stuff need not be anything special. An old pair of shoes that you'd never wear to church, some old jeans that probably had rips and paint stains, a signature faded flannel shirt with button-down pockets, an army surplus canteen with cold water, a used rucksack that had once belonged to a private in the military — and Bob's Your Uncle, as we like to say in Canada. But I could see that the world of outdoor activity had been infiltrated by commercialism like everything else on the planet. Fellow hikers here in the heart of Snowdonia National Park probably judged you by the brand name showing on your sunglasses, your self-wicking T-shirt or appropriately low rider designer white socks. I remained confident, however, that the creatures of the wild you encountered in the Gwydyr Forest didn't care a whisker about your clothes or gear as long as you left them in peace as you tromped through the valleys and along the streams.

But, by the way, did I also say that I liked Betws-y-Coed? Well, I did. The name means something like "prayer house in the woods," and it has had its share of famous visitors over the years, including Percy Shelley, Matthew Arnold, Charles Darwin, Alexander Graham Bell and the Queen of Siam. Darwin, who was born in Shrewsbury, near the Welsh border, liked to hike through the hills near Betws to find fossils. Shelley was no doubt trying to get away from the rat race of competing poets. I don't know what drew Bell or the Queen of Siam here, but the mountains of Snowdonia had a heyday of tourism that started in the eighteenth century and continues on to this day. The great news is that as soon as you walk two blocks southwest of all the hubbub of the expensive footwear stores and the organic pizza parlours you are in woods that are still as pure and pristine as the days when Wordsworth came here to wear out the soles of his latest hiking boots and mutter his latest sonnet for sister Dorothy to try to capture in writing before it drifted off into the wispy clouds of the blue Snowdonia skies.

After we'd unloaded our car, Linda wanted to shop. She reminded me that there had not been one single store, not even one tiny venue of commerce available, in Osgathorpe and now that we were back in the land of the living credit card, it was her right and duty. So Kelty and I agreed she should go her own way and have fun while we hiked about town. It was a hot day by Nova Scotia standards so we headed for the Afon Llugwy River that runs through town to connect with the River Conwy. A quick stop at the tourist bureau allowed me to pick up some brochures of nearby places we would not be going to, including Zipworld, the Conwy Valley Railway Museum, Go Below Underground Adventures and the Betws-y-Coed Golf Club. However, they did have a large bowl of water on the floor for Kelty, as did many stores, restaurants and pubs in town. In my mind, such a preponderance of this symbolic gesture made Betws-y-Coed register much higher in my travel regard than if it had 20 four-star Michelin restaurants.

I did pick up a brochure for one place already on my to-do list — Surf Snowdonia, one of the world's first inland surf parks. Tomorrow would be the day I surfed my first artificial inland wave and I was both excited and nervous at the prospect.

As Kelty slurped down half the contents of the water in the stainless steel dish near my feet, I read an item on the wall that said, "Fun Fact: Betws-y-Coed is the most misspelled word in the UK." Who would have guessed?

Kelty and I walked back and forth over the Pont-y-Pair Bridge, which was built back in the sixteenth century and still seemed in good shape today as cars and ice-cream-licking tourists passed over its stone arches. It appears in a number of famous paintings, including one by Thomas Girtin, who captured it in watercolours back in 1798 well before the bed and breakfasts and the hiking supply shops took over the town.

We found a trail leading west along the river into a forest with a high canopy of deciduous trees, and I slipped off my shoes to dangle my feet in the cold water as Kelty followed my lead and put paws to water. Back on the trail we ended up in a field of sheep that weren't the slightest bit shy around a small yappy white dog. Kelty's tail stood straight up, as did his ears as we danced around the minefield of blackish sheep shit. And soon it was time to catch up with Linda back in front of St Mary's Church.

My initial survey of the town revealed it to be busy but friendly, quaint yet commercial, dog-friendly and human-friendly as well. And so it was that I was forced to re-evaluate the national character of the Welsh and admit that my encounter with the scoundrel barman might have been an anomaly. Clearly, not all Welshmen were nasty cheats. Here was a village with water bowls for dogs, polite young smiling shopkeepers, pubs offering discounts on craft beer during mid-afternoon happy hours and balding men with serious sunburns sporting T-shirts with phrases like "I'm a Railway Nut." I was beginning to like Wales very much.

I'll get heck from Linda for including this in the book, but our first evening in our slate cottage in Betws-y-Coed, I watched as the storekeeps in the Rock Bottom shop closed up for the day and threw a number of boxes in a green dumpster that shared the same parking lot as our cottage. It immediately drew my curiosity.

My days of dumpster diving were mostly behind me, but not forgotten. My heyday was during an era when no one actually had to padlock their dumpsters. Diving into dumpsters was fun and exciting and as easy as leaning over the metal rail and doing a minor gymnastic manoeuvre to find your way inside for easy pickings of whatever a store would throw away. In North America back when I was young, vast quantities of reasonably sound goods were heaved daily and, for the most part, no one really cared if young men like me with not much money and a sense of trashy adventure came poking about. But those days were long gone. Now, garbage containers were mostly locked, and mostly to keep people from dumping their garbage in.

But the Cotswold Outdoor Rock Bottom folks didn't seem worried about who or what might creep into their big green container after hours. And so there I was, leaning far over, feet nearly straight up in the air, rooting through nifty-looking boxes that mostly had nothing until I found a very expensive-looking shoebox that, lo and behold, held a brand new pair of running shoes. A small celestial voice inside my head said, "If they are your size, then they were meant for you."

I grabbed the box and cantilevered my carcass out of the bin and looked around to see if anyone was watching. Only the chestnut trees. And they promised they wouldn't speak a word. So I lodged the magic box under my left arm like an American football and made an end run for the front door of the slate house. Inside, breathing hard as if I had just run a marathon in my newfound running shoes, I opened the box. And there they were.

My size. 9½. Kind of aqua blue with orange and white soles — a pair of elite running shoes I would never have bought in a million years. But now they were mine. I didn't recognize the markings. Not Nike, not New Balance. No. But something strange, something exotic with an upside down Q and U.

Linda immediately looked them up on the internet with some kind of program that was like facial recognition for shoes. (Who comes up with these sites? And who uses them on a regular basis, I want to know?) It turns out they were called Cloud Surfers. They were made in Switzerland and claimed to be "the world's lightest cushioned shoe for Running Remixed," whatever that meant. Back in Canada they would have cost nearly $300. I'd hit the jackpot.

I loved my new slim, ultra-chic running shoes and expected to find more booty (pardon the pun) every night thereafter. But, alas, nothing more came my way as a garbage gift from the Cotswolds. And I'll never know why this pair of shoes was in the dumpster, but they were going back to Canada with me so I could wear them on campus when I returned and so colleagues around the Faculty of Arts and Social Sciences would say to each other in the department lounge, "I think there is something different about Professor Choyce since his sabbatical." Or so I hoped.

That evening while sitting in our cozy den, me with my new footwear, I randomly picked a book from the shelves called *The Fragrant Minute for Every Day* by a writer called Wilhelmina Stitch, whose real name was Ruth Jacobs. It turned out she was English, born in Cambridge and somewhat famous in her day, although probably not as famous as Isaac Newton. But she had carved out a writing career in Winnipeg, Manitoba, Canada as "the poem a day lady." The editor of the little book had this to say about Ms. Stitch: "Most of us are of common clay. We only desire to walk in seemly paths, and live serenely. It may be that Wilhelmina Stitch recovers for us the glamour of half-forgotten days, the sweetness of memories, the buoyancy of childhood. It may be that she reminds us of something fragrant within ourselves of which contact with life is prone to rob us."

In her poem "The Gift of Day" Wilhelmina writes,

The very minute I awake,
   I find, and this is every morn,
A precious gift for me to take
   The gift of Day, newborn.

The book also included 31 sort of prose poems of a similar vein, each one more optimistic than the one before. I suppose most would find the entries pretty sappy, but the sentiment was so much like the chapter on Buddhism I was reading in *Man Seeks God*. Live in the present. Be kind. Be compassionate. Don't grieve or remain attached to losses. Celebrate each and every little thing. Right on, Wilhelmina. Her books have been relegated to those large and mouldering dustbins of literature, I am sure, but there's nothing quite like sitting in a warm slate cottage in Betws-y-Coed wiggling my toes inside some really comfortable $300 running shoes that I snatched for free, with my loving wife and dog nearby and reading a gushy early twentieth-century Winnipeg optimist who published a poem a day and became famous for it. Perhaps her work will be resurrected by some future graduate student at the University of Manitoba or even Cambridge itself and brought back into the folds of pop culture just at some distant depressing moment when all hope for humanity seems to be fading like the last pink dregs of a Prairie sunset. I can only hope.

Most books found in rental houses are pretty banal — romances and thrillers and murder mysteries in large type for old geezers like me to read without the need of reading glasses. But here were more than a few gems. Not great tomes about the history of syphilis like back in Little Walden but a good assortment, including *Born to Run* by Christopher McDougall, which is the best book on running I've ever read and contains an enlightening chapter on how the modern running shoe with all of its mechanisms to protect the human running foot has done more damage to feet than if we ran barefoot. Fortunately, the author explained why postmodern footwear like my newfound Cloud Surfers had minimal arch support and a fairly thin sole, allowing the foot-brain connection to flourish as it had with our ancestors, whose very survival depended upon the ability to outrun in bare feet whatever monstrous creatures of our shrouded past would try to eat us on a daily basis.

And as I rooted around in this wonderfully fecund little library I also found a local book titled *The A-Z of Betws-y-Coed* by Donald Shaw published by Gwasg Carreg Gwalch. (Say what?) Under "B" I discovered that the Black Plague visited the valley here in 1349 during the reign of Edward III. Did the damn plague find its way to every nook and cranny of Europe and the British Isles? I had already studied up on this Black Death or Bubonic Plague and knew it had wiped out a hundred million or more unwary people in Europe and Asia, and maybe if the locals could have kept visitors (and visiting rats that carried the infected fleas) away they might have been spared. But they weren't. Reading about the disease, I made a mental note that if I came down with vomiting, fever, headaches and swollen lymph nodes any time soon, I'd go directly for treatment, as you'd probably die from the plague within a week of exposure if not sooner.

If you'd survived the plague, you might have produced children who would have had children or grandchildren who would have been around in 1468 when the town was bashed by the Earl of Pembroke in what historians like to call the War of the Roses. You can be forgiven if that sounds like the name of a really bad movie from the 1980s you once saw pitting Kathleen Turner against Michael Douglas. The real war was not about a marital squabble that went ballistic but about two competing factions for royal domination: the Plantagenets (white rose) and the Lancasters (red rose, like the tea). I've read lengthy explanations about what this "civil" war was about, but I don't see it as my task to try to explain or make sense of the endless bloodshed and fighting that seems to have occurred on every square foot of the UK. To summarize, however, I would say the fighting was because people were unhappy, the white roses blame the red roses and vice versa, there was a certain amount of greed and lust for power, and common folk were easily duped into fighting for whichever side they sided with. History reports there was mental illness involved on the part of both families as well. If you care to know more, the library can supply you with the necessary details, but I'm just a guy with his feet up in Snowdonia looking for some background on where I am plunked down.

So I'll just jump ahead to the more important details of the twentieth century. For example, there was a "problem" with gypsies in Betws-y-Coed in the 1930s. The problem was that the "travellers" kept showing up and the locals didn't like them. I found no reports of stolen children or major crime, just minor hustling. Cheating perhaps. Maybe the mean-spirited bartender I had encountered was not even Welsh but the son of wandering gypsies who decided to stay in one place and cheat his clients, letting them come to him instead of him following in family footsteps to find new marks.

But to leave Betws-y-Coed's history on a more gentle and positive note, author Shaw writes that in 1951, "Postwoman Catherine Roberts retired. It was said that during her years of service she had walked the equivalent of twice around the world." That's a lot of walking and it led me to wonder, how many shoes had she worn out and what kind of shoes were they? This would have been in the days long before Cotswold Outdoor Rock Bottom and the other fashionable outdoor footwear establishments invaded the town like modern-day rose warriors. And 1951, I noted, was the year I was born, which, I suppose, means nothing at all, except that it was a year when some of us, me in particular, were just coming into this world. Our eager parents were hoping that all the wars were over and a bright peaceful future lay ahead, while retiree Catherine Roberts, who had served her community faithfully, was hanging up her postal walking shoes and looking forward to a quiet afternoon sipping tea beneath blooming Welsh wisteria while studying the new growth of her hydrangeas flourishing in the front yard.

CHAPTER TWENTY-NINE

THE NEOPRENE DREAMS
OF SNOWDONIA

We had reports from home that Pamela was not doing well, that the infection due to her tooth issue had gotten worse. This did not bode well for a young woman who was nine weeks from delivering twins. We stayed in contact with Pamela and her mother-in-law, Kathy Craig. Both assured us things would be fine and we should not worry. But worry we did. What were we doing off cavorting around the UK with our pet while health issues were emerging with my very pregnant daughter back home? After considerable debate, we decided to stay the course, keep in close contact and come up with a plan to head home at the drop of a hat if need be. The big problem with that is that we couldn't leave the UK with the dog in the plane. We'd have to drive to Charles de Gaulle Airport and fly home from there. Yet again, we thought that maybe all the rigmarole of travelling with Kelty was a bad idea. But we'd wait for news of what would come next. Please, angels, take good care of my daughter and granddaughters-to-be.

In the morning, Linda ran back and forth on the main drag of Betws while Kelty and I walked up into the forest behind the house. We passed Taverners — a hostel for young hikers who were sitting out at tables in the bright sun eating fresh fruit and granola. Here again was the young tribe of hikers that rather fascinated me. There were a lot of them here in town and it brightened my day. Sure, they had what looked like unwashed dreadlocks, and they were tattooed and had odd bits of metal sticking out of unlikely parts of their faces. But they were young and free (maybe) and had arrived here without cars and with only what they could carry in their voluminous nylon backpacks. Some were probably rock climbers, some bicyclists and some purebreed hikers who were about to walk to the tops of Moel Siabod or Moelwyn Mawr or climb Snowdon itself. God love them, these grano-la-munching, long-haired, eco-friendly tourists who didn't give a rat's ass about video games, designer jeans, long-term employment plans or the latest Donald Trump news gossip.

As Kelty and I breathed in the pure forest air and observed the spears of morning sunlight filtering through the hemlock branches, the heavy burden of worry about my daughter still dragged at my heart, and I had to work hard to quell the shouting voices in my paranoid parental head. But as everything seemed, while not ideal, very much under control in Canada, I reconfirmed my faith in the Canadian medical system and my trust in the support Pamela had around her. We had a backup plan for leaving if we had to. I said several more simple prayers for my child and her imminent off-springs' well-being, and then I tried to quiet my mind.

For today, at least, we'd stick with our plans. And, as for me, today I was going surfing.

And not in the ocean. Any ocean.

And that would be a first for me.

Dolgarrog is a short drive north along the River Conwy from where we were staying. It's an unlikely place for an inland surfing park, but there it is — Surf Snowdonia, "the world's first artificial surfing lake." Part of me didn't like the idea of surfing an *artificial* wave. Why? Because it's *artificial*, that's why. Those modern hippie hikers wouldn't have thought much of me, I'll bet, if they knew I was about to pay a hefty fee to surf a *man-made* wave. But I probably would not be back this way again and there was a wave here. A reportedly surfable head-high wave, so I would pay my £75 and do it. I'd been surfing since I was 13 and never given it up. In my rule book, once a surfer, always a surfer. Age would never be an issue.

Why the surf park was in Dolgarrog is a bit of a mystery to me. Travellers come here for the mountains, the climbing and the hiking. There would be skiing in the winter, of course. But there's not a great population base like other places in the world where "surf gardens" were cropping up. But I guess there was a good water supply and carloads of summer tourists willing to give predictable surfing a go. So, for one morning, I would join the inland surfers and see what it was like.

Dolgarrog itself is a small village, a bit overtaken by Surf Snowdonia with its artificial lake, its endless surf lessons, its glamping and the swarms of sunburnt surf wannabees who shell out big bucks for a chance to ride a wave. Dolgarrog was a very old town, however. Long ago, it is said that the dragon Carrog was killing local livestock and eating them and that something had to be done to stop the beast. That really pissed off Dolgarrogians, who heisted their pitchforks and set out a dead sheep as bait. When the dragon showed up on cue, they attacked it and killed it, but not before it bit off the leg of one of the farmers, who survived and became a town hero.

It was Jimmy Buffett sitting at my kitchen table with his guitar and a glass of French wine that, when I had expressed my own fears over surfing some really big gnarly waves, gave me a small Jimmy Buffett-style lecture about all of us having to confront our own dragons. This was after our communal surf session on a warm summer night in Lawrencetown, Nova Scotia. And now here I was in the land of dragons — real, imagined and symbolic. I guess I had slain a few of my own dragons in my day — surfed big waves in Hawaii, doing poorly but heroically on waves I did not understand. I guess you could say I somewhat overcame my fear of dying several times in near-death hold-down situations in large winter Atlantic waves when the north wind was roaring, the seas were thrashing and the air temperature was enough to freeze the salt water on the rocks ashore.

I envisioned those old Welsh farmers wielding their pitch-forks together, bravely attacking Carrog. Standing in my board shorts on the perimeter of the man-made lake, I looked at the wave breaking and it didn't make much sense to me. It just didn't look like any wave I'd ever ridden. The mechanics looked all wrong. In fact, everything looked wrong about it for someone used to understanding at any given moment what is going on with the hydrodynamics at my home break of Lawrencetown Point — a point break, yes, where waves line up in an orderly fashion and break left to right from the headland and out into the deeper waters to the east. I just wasn't sure I'd be able to make sense of Snowdonia waves, to catch them or to ride them. I'd likely wipe out, be in the way or get run over by other surfers who knew what they were doing here. I'd be trashed, humiliated, discouraged, and leave with a major bruise to my ego that would take weeks to heal. Did I really want to pay good money for such a privilege?

Shit yeah.

Yet this Frankenstein of a wave was something I definitely did not like. And it was somewhat ugly, to be honest. Let me try to explain.

Running the length of this artificial lake is a pier down the middle. Something like a giant wedged snowplow races down the middle of the lake on either side of the pier, gaining speed as it goes, first one way and then the other. You take off near the mesh fencing by the pier on a six-foot wall of water that just suddenly pops up, grabs you by the ankles and begins to break top to bottom before turning into a mushy, frothing four-foot gusher of white water that then carries you to the artificial edge of the lake where you need to fall off backwards before you slam into the somewhat padded but grotesquely slippery shoreline. At this point you need to grab onto your board and try to throw you and your board over a walloping bit of backwash and then get out of the way before a surfer who maybe knows what he's doing comes charging back at you from the other direction. Yes, the opposite direction where the snowplow is now proceeding from.

If you're confused by my explanation, well, so was I.

So the dragons that needed slaying here were my own fears and doubts that I would be able to surf this damned artificial wave. But then it was those very fears and doubts that had led me here ... if that makes any sense to those of you not fully familiar with the male ego.

And, yes, from now on, all such confrontations would be referred to as "Yet another Dolgarrog," but for now it was time to pay my £75 and put on a heavy 5/4 wetsuit, the only type available there for rent. That was way too much neoprene for a hot Welsh day like this. Nonetheless, I watched the silly five-minute video explaining the rules of the pool and then it was time to get wet.

Kelty was not allowed near the lake itself, but Linda could sit with him in the outdoor café area where they both might watch my heroic efforts and/or abysmal failure. Sitting on the edge of the artificial lake myself, I first watched those in the water struggling to catch the waves and then wiping out over and over. That would be me in a few minutes.

And then the time came. I knee-paddled to my position near the fencing of the pier that ran down the middle. My wave would come from behind and I'd be moving west to east. I sat and waited, feeling very, very strange. Here it comes. You hear it before you see it and, since you need to sit facing forward, you really don't have time to turn around and watch it coming. To me, it sounded like a freight train headed straight at me. Paddle, paddle, paddle. The wave arrives, jacks up from flat water to about six foot, a near vertical wall of it. And I missed it. The wave didn't care, the bastard. It just kept on going.

Paddle to the shoreline, get whomped by the head-high backwash, take a deep breath, regroup, watch your counterpart wipe out as he attempts to surf the wave back east to west. Then paddle back into position, line up your dragons, wait for the wave to come at you again. Dig hard, harder and then — aha! — I felt myself dropping down the face. I hadn't ever been on such a floaty, bouncy board like this before, so I made it to the bottom of the trough, slipped a bit to the right into the foamy white water and then lost grip of my board, did a nifty drop to my chin on the deck and got tossed around by what was left of the mechanical wave. I flopped and floundered in a manner most appropriate for a beach gremmie who didn't know the first iota about surfing. As I surfaced, opened my jaw for oxygen and tried to get my bearings, the backwash thoroughly rinsed out my mouth and drove chlorinated water effectively up both nostrils before I regained my board and paddled to shore.

The third wave was a nearly perfect imitation of the second wave, and the fourth wave reinforced my conclusion that I was not good at figuring out the dynamics of this activity. By the time I wallowed up on the shoreline again, I was hot, tired, frustrated and discouraged. If that cocktail is to your liking, then you'd admit that here was £75 well spent at Surf So-down-on-ya.

But as I paddled out again, I was reminded of the skinny 13-year-old lad I once was. I could see him in my mind's eye, trying hard to simply stay on top of his brand new nine-foot, six-inch Greg Noll slot bottom surfboard just off Long Beach Island at the (New) Jersey Shore. Learning to surf was one of the most difficult things I'd ever done in my life. But the mantra of surfing, the soundtrack of promised euphoria, had been driven into my skull by Jan and Dean and the Beach Boys. And at that instant as I sidled up to the mesh fence by the pier and awaited the watery freight train that had my number, the skinny boy inside me coached the 67-year-old geezer to take charge and tame that monster.

So I gritted my teeth, paddled like a son of a bitch, pitched forward and down, rose awkwardly to my feet, pulled off a bottom turn and drove right, ducking the offending white water as the wave collapsed around me. And, lucky me, I made the wave.

The ride was short but sweet, as they say. Linda saw me. She waved. Kelty barked his approval. I took some deep breaths and scrambled into the shallows waiting to prepare for my paddle back.

After that, I surfed a handful of waves successfully, grew tired, wiped out a goodly number of times more just to reminisce about what it felt like to learn to surf for the first time. I ended my session with a reasonable percentage of satisfaction but was quite happy to slip out of my heavy O'Neill neoprene skin and feel the warm Welsh air on my heaving pale chest.

The surfing world was changing, I well knew. Australia had a few wave parks, and in the US Kelly Slater had masterminded the creation of a wave park with a wave machine that manufactured the most perfect tubes of rolling green water that could be imagined. With artificial waves like that, surfing would soon be part of the Olympics. As an arrogant young surfer, I had despised any form of surfing competition. "Surfing is an art. It's not a sport," you could overhear me saying at weekend parties back at Montauk Point, Long Island, or Lawrencetown Beach, Nova Scotia.

Oddly enough, in 1995 the Canadian National Surfing Championship, sanctioned by the International Surfing Association, was held in Nova Scotia, just a stone's throw from my doorstep. At 44, I was at the top of my game and I had a new rule for myself: if you have a rule that you live by, you should break it and see what happens. So I broke my rule of never competing in a surf competition. And I won.

I had one good move that in those days was called a floater. Take off, bottom turn, kick to the top of the wave, let it collapse in front of you, lift, go up and then float down over the white water. It was my break, it was my move. And I got lucky.

And pretty much walked away from competition after that.

And now here in Wales I'd surfed maybe my one and only artificial wave and would walk out of Surf Snowdonia with my hair still wet, my dragons tamed if not slain and drier adventures to come with my sun-stricken loving wife and faithful white dog.

CHAPTER THIRTY

CANINE CRIMES, HOMICIDAL SUBMARINERS, MINING AND PINING

My hair was still wet by the time we reached Conwy. There was a grave here with a curious metal cage-like frame above it that supposedly inspired William Wordsworth to write a rhyming poem called "We Are Seven" about seven children, some of whom had died and were buried here. His poem begins with an encounter with a little girl:

> —A Simple Child,
> That lightly draws its breath,
> And feels its life in every limb,
> What should it know of death?

Although it's not a great poem and somewhat confusing as to which children are dead and which are alive and why there are seven spires on the metal frame, it has a great Wordsworth line or two. A child "feels its life in every limb," it's true, and so did I that day as we sat at a stoplight in Conwy waiting for our chance to drive through the single lane in what appeared to be a castle wall. Good exercise, surfing included, does indeed make you feel your life in all four of your limbs if you are lucky enough to have them.

Old Bill Wordsworth really did get around, and I was more than a little surprised to turn up in yet another location with notes about "Wordsworth was here." In 1798, the year of the publication of *Lyrical Ballads*, he visited his chum Sir George Beaumont at Benarth Hall near here. Perhaps he was out promoting his book like a good author should but, as always, the poetry just kept pouring out of him.

It turns out that what I thought was a castle wall impeding traffic flow was just that, the extended wall of Conwy Castle. The tourist guides suggest that if you can only visit a few castles in Wales, this should be one of them because of the cool suspension bridge and the fact that it looks like the classic sandcastle. And, of course, your kids would love that element. And although the builders hadn't the forethought to accommodate automobiles that would one day have to get around it, its 700-year-old walls were handy for keeping out enemies. Oddly enough, these very walls are mentioned in Max Brooks's post-apocalyptic novel *World War Z* as being effective at keeping zombies out, so perhaps those builders of yore had some foresight that went well beyond the automobile.

I was hoping to find what is supposed to be the smallest house in Britain, located here in Conwy. It is reported to be bright red and would have been easy enough to find if we had just gotten out and walked along the quay. I had already missed finding the Nutshell, "Britain's smallest pub," while walking Kelty around Bury St Edmunds and getting royally distracted by the folksingers and the affable drunks, so I guess I'm just not good at finding small things. But I have made a pact with myself to work up a list of smallest things for future trips. After all, in North America, we seem to turn largest things into tourist attractions. In Nova Scotia, we have the world's largest blueberry, I think, and a strawberry as well, although they are both made of concrete. We also have the largest fiddle and bow in Sydney, on Cape Breton Island. Somewhere there is the world's largest ball of string, peanut, motorcycle, rocking chair, and I can't forget the Sudbury Nickel, which I personally hugged on a book tour of northern Ontario. The Guinness folks, after centuries of making and drinking dark stout, keep track of more transient edible large things like the world's largest meatball, pizza, hamburger and French fry.

And exactly who are the creators of the smallest or largest things that want to make their mark in the world by such a quirky challenge? I couldn't find the name of the man who originally lived in his tiny Conwy house, but it turns out he was himself six foot three inches tall. I guess he was tired of everyone thinking he was overly tall so he decided to live in something alarmingly small. But I would hope he had other reasons.

Had I known more about recent Conwy history, I might not have even stopped at that little green park near the water to walk Kelty and stretch the tightening muscles in my legs. According to the *The Daily Post*, "People who walk their dogs off leads in Conwy were hit with a whopping 1300% more fines than in any other authority in Wales in 2015/16." Conwy has a reputation, I learned, as having the worst dog owners in all of the UK. Certainl, not much to be proud of. In 2015, 512 fines were handed out. A "dog fouling" offence will cost you £100 and a "dog control breach" will cost you £75. I don't know if they offer a twofer discount or if the fine is enhanced if your dog is both unleashed and unleashing his business.

The Daily Post turned out to be a treasure trove of important and trivial information and they obviously remained on top of the doggone news, reporting recently in May about a full-on ban of dogs on North Wales beaches from May to September. While the story to me seemed reasonable enough, it raised the ire of many readers. Someone named Movvil, for example, commented that he was more offended by parents burying "baby poo" on beaches and he resented that dogs were not allowed even though he noted that his own dog was dead. Munroemike thought the whole damn newspaper was simply "stupid" for running such a banal story that made him "winge." I really had no idea that dogs in Wales could be so controversial.

Kelty was actually leashed while we were in town and I did clean up after him in the park, which is pretty easy in Kelty's case. Still, I may have been under the watchful eye of what town councillors call "pooper snoopers," stalwart citizens who report dog crimes like this to the authorities. I wonder if there is some kind of financial compensation or honorary reward for neighbours who turn their neighbours in for such crimes.

And it's probably best that we didn't linger too long in Conwy with its big castle and tiny house and obsessive doggy laws. Back in December 2017, Bernadette Clutton and her friend Ed were trying to have a Sunday dinner at the Village Inn pub and wanted to dine in the carvery area with their assistance dog when they were told they couldn't sit there because of the canine. The pub owners said they were just "trying to balance hygiene with equality" when they attempted to move them to the bar area. This action didn't sit well at all with the diners, who soon thereafter sued the establishment for discrimination and received £2,000 in damages.

Clearly, Conwy is a most dog-sensitive town, yet I daresay it is still a rather pretty place to visit and a good place to run to once the zombie invasion begins.

If old things are to your liking, *really* old things, older than castles, I'd recommend the side trip to nearby Llangernyw just down a maze of tiny zigzag roads from Conwy. Here you'd find the Llangernyw Yew, a 4,000-plus-year-old tree, the oldest in the UK. If that's not enough to lure you there, the tree has a notch that is considered to be a gateway to the world of the dead. It was once believed to deliver a prophecy each Halloween as to which local citizens would die in the year ahead. Dogs are welcome, but I'd be careful to keep them on a lead and away from the tree itself. I was pleased to see a local news story that none other than Charles, Prince of Wales, visited the tree before he stopped off to have his picture taken several hundred times while pulling himself his own pint of bitter at a local pub. Despite worries about pooch patrols and overzealous council members, it was still a grand thing to be in the land of princes and pubs and trees that were thousands of years old.

As with so many other places on our itinerary, we really should have lingered longer around Conwy and visited nearby Little Ormes Head and Great Ormes Head and sought out some interesting stories in the towns with names like Llandudno, which sounded like something out of *Gulliver's Travels, Book III*. But instead, we ushered Kelty into the back seat of the Fiat and found ourselves suddenly on motorway A55. If you were in the Midlands of England and wanted to get yourself across Wales quickly to Holyhead to catch the ferry to Ireland, this would be your road. It skirts along the sea with some fantastic views, but as we raced along I knew we were missing some interesting towns.

Penmaenmawr, meaning Head of the Great Stone, for example. Here was a stone circle built by Druids among other ancient things, but today it is a quarry town like so many other Welsh locales. There had been a devastating train crash here in 1950 with 500 passengers aboard as the train slammed into another locomotive and 31 people were injured. And in 1976 a former submarine commander murdered four people at the Red Gables Hotel before setting the place ablaze and shooting himself.

It looked like there was a good wide beach for hiking in Penmaenmawr, but I was afraid to stop and walk the dog there given the town's bad luck and the potential fines I'd read about so we just zipped on by. Linda had commandeered the map book and discovered that there was yet another castle ahead near Bangor. She spotted it from the motorway as we skirted the coast and soon we turned off the A55 onto a leafy stretch of road that led to Penrhyn Castle. Despite the fact that it was built in the early nineteenth century as a "mock castle," intended to look like something much older, the National Trust still charges the usual hefty fee to walk inside.

It was the brainchild of architect Thomas Hopper, and the BBC once filmed a sitcom there called *It's That Man Again*. Queen Victoria had planted a tree there, but we couldn't seem to locate it as we walked around the grounds. And, of course, the castle itself was said to have ghosts. What castle doesn't, even a replica one? And there was even a ghost dog reported to roam the Ice Tower, but when we tried to enter the main edifice with Kelty, we were turned away because dogs were not allowed. Bloody hell, as the English say.

At the end of the day, back in our slate cottage in Betws-y-Coed, I dipped into a book that might unlock the meaning of some of the strange-sounding Welsh words we had encountered. Thus, I discovered that the language wasn't nearly as confounding as it seemed. I learned that a llan is a church, coed is a woods, a pont is a bridge, but a pant is a hollow. Aber means river mouth, castell is a castle, glyn is a glen or deep valley, Y or Yr means *the* and newydd is *new*. Betws means bead, referring to a rosary bead, so Betws-y-Coed means bead house or house of prayer. Very nice indeed.

I also dipped into a book called *Wild Wales* by nineteenth-century Norfolk novelist George Borrow. In his 1862 book he had this to say of the town outside my doorstep: "Crossed over an ancient bridge and passed through a small town and found myself in a beautiful valley with majestic hills on either side." Mr. Borrow would probably be appalled at the commercialization that has overtaken the "small town," but the valley itself is indeed still beautiful and I can attest to the majestic hills.

To the south of us, for example, was the town of Penrhyndeudraeth, which looked somewhat desolate at first with high barren hills all about, but I knew it held some intriguing history. Later, I would dip into *The Daily Post* again, a newspaper that serves up North Wales with both the latest gossip and some solid history, to discover there had been an explosion at the local dynamite factory there in the summer of 1998. The blast was heard up to 20 miles away, reminding me of the Halifax Explosion. Some problem, it was surmised, with the "nitroglycerine mixing house." *What town allows a dynamite factory to be built in their community?* I wondered. Well, the dynamite was used for slate mining and slate mining has been ever so popular throughout much of Wales for at least a couple of centuries. Where you have slate, apparently, you have dynamite.

Back in New Jersey when I was still in graduate school, I had a happy-go-lucky friend named Larry who worked on the night shift in an explosives plant. On breaks in the middle of the night, he owned up, he and his coworkers were in the habit of smoking marijuana — which to my mind even then didn't seem like a wise thing to do. So I thought of Larry while pondering life in a dynamite and slate Welsh town like Penrhyndeudraeth. If blokes like Larry end up working in explosives plants, then it is likely that occasionally there will be accidents like the one in 1998.

I made a to-do list of things to dig deeper into when I next returned to Wales, and first on the list was more research into the history of mining zinc, coal and slate. My guess is that it's not a pretty picture. In 1941, John Ford created a Hollywood blockbuster about the plight of Welsh miners called *How Green Was My Valley*. According to IMDB plot summary contributor Jwelch5742, "Huw Morgan [Roddy McDowall], the academically inclined youngest son in a proud family of Welsh coal miners, witnesses the tumultuous events of his young life during a period of rapid social change. At the dawn of the 20th century, a miners' strike divides the Morgans: the sons demand improvements, and the father [Donald Crisp] doesn't want to rock the boat. Meanwhile, Huw's eldest sister, Angharad [Maureen O'Hara], pines for the new village preacher, Mr. Gruffydd [Walter Pidgeon]." Who could have guessed a film set in Wales about mining and pining could be such a huge success?

Much of the devastation of Wales by mining has been erased by time and the natural healing of the land. While the hard lot of the poverty-stricken Welsh has mostly disappeared from the view of travellers like us, I am sure it is not forgotten and echoes down through generations despite our current universal obsession with the here and now.

CHAPTER THIRTY-ONE

FAIRY GLEN, THE GHOST OF SWALLOW FALLS AND DINNER FOR THE GORILLAS

I woke the next day with great fears of my own — worries about Pamela, who had now been admitted to hospital. Her offending tooth had been removed, but the wound had become severely infected. She was throwing up and had a fever. It was still eight weeks before her twins were due, but this was not good. Here were complications enough to have her admitted to hospital and hooked up to an IV drip. Her husband Jason was thousands of miles away on a military exercise in the South Pacific and we were in the heart of Wales.

We pondered yet again cutting our journey short, driving back to Paris and flying home right away. But, as noted, Linda had rented us a house in a remote area of Devon to drive to next and booked a crossing through the Eurotunnel following that. I prayed that things smoothed out back in Halifax, that Pamela regained her health and the babies understood their time to greet the world was still weeks away. We'd give it another day or so and stay in touch with Kathy, Pamela's mother-in-law.

Setting those worries aside as best we could, we set off to find a castle that allowed dogs and hoped that Dolwyddelan would do the trick. Built early in the thirteenth century, it is set in truly beautiful surroundings. We had to keep Kelty on his leash as there were sheep rambling about on our paths. It was a grand morning with dew still on the grass and the sky a striking blue. After hiking several steep dead-end paths, however, we decided we should save our energy for the trails of Fairy Glen to the south of us in Gwydir Forest Park.

With substantial difficulty, we found the tiny car park, deposited the requested entrance fee into a rusty money box and made our way across a field and into a dark woods that indeed looked like the perfect place for fairies. It reminded me a lot of Puck's Glen back in Scotland and I told Linda we should seek out as many of these glens as we could until we ultimately came face to face with some real spirits. Having the place to ourselves, it certainly felt spooky in a completely pleasant way and Kelty kept stopping to look at trees and plants, as if he could see things we could not.

Like Puck's, the narrow trail dipped down to a dazzling stream at the bottom of the forested canyon where light played tricks with the water. The stones were wet and slippery as they should be and we danced through the dappled sunlight from stone to stone until we heard the fairies singing madrigals in our attentive ears. Fortunately for us and others like us, plans to build a hydroelectric power plant here in 2016 were thwarted by tree huggers and sprite enthusiasts alike, a good reminder that magic places of nature and spirit need protection from the coalition of profiteers and pragmatists who plague the planet.

None other than Wilhelmina Stitch once wrote a poem about the place, saying that she "waits and waits to see the fairy men." I don't know why, but I'd always thought of fairies being feminine or at least childlike and I am sure I would have been accused of being sexist had I mentioned that to my wife. If there had been fairies about during our family visit, I believe they were genderless, but I made a point of wanting to find out more about this once-famous and now forgotten Stitch woman, and later, when I did some scant research, found out this.

She was born in Cambridgeshire in 1888 as Ruth Jacobs and married a Canadian lawyer, E. Arakie Cohen, and followed him to Winnipeg where she started writing for newspapers as Wilhelmina Stitch. Her prose and poetry was bubbly, full of advice and optimism and eventually found its way into international newspapers and books. In the "The Singing Kettle" she wrote, "Up to its neck in water, boiling water, too. Yet the kettle keeps on singing — that's what we ought to do!" Well, for my money that seems as good advice today as it was back in her day.

And in "Begone, Dull Care" she scolds, "No! Little, whining, fretting care, you cannot come and walk with me. So lovely is the morning air I do not want your company." Once again, her 1920s advice could still stand us in good stead today, although, as we trudged back up the steep trail surrounded by the gnarled limbs of holly and sky-reaching oak trees, I couldn't help but feel more than a twinge of worry about my own daughter and my granddaughters-to-be.

Without a doubt, the Welsh countryside around Betws-y-Coed was a spirited place. We designated our final afternoon there for a trip to one of the must-see places nearby on the River Llugwy — Swallow Falls, as it is known today, but originally called Rhaeadr Ewynnol or "foaming waterfall,"

which it truly was. You pay a gentleman in a booth some money and walk through a full-body turnstile that reminded me of something you'd go through to get in or out of a prison. Kelty was a bit perturbed by it so I had to carry him through the mechanism, prompting me to wonder what travellers do if their pet happens to be a Newfoundland dog.

Steps led to a viewpoint and then down to several other stages until you arrived at the lower reaches of the fall. Here was a clear pool with a great number of coins on the bottom, including plenty of one-pound coins. I thought it looked like easy pickings to reach into the water and scoop up enough money for the pizza we planned to buy later that day. As always, Linda reminded me that discretion was the better part of valour (did she really say that?) and, as I leaned over to touch the surface of the clear pool with my finger, she not so gently elbowed me in the ribs and pointed to a noisy family of Americans descending the stone steps discussing how hard it was on their knees.

Why do people throw money into pools and fountains? It turns out that this was an ancient European custom to repay the gods (whichever ones were popular at the time) for clean water. In return, the water would keep flowing and maybe the gift would bring a good crop of hops or wheat or string beans. If it was a well, it became a "wishing well," and I wondered how many lives were lost when young hooligans through various centuries tried climbing down into the well to steal the money.

In Rome we had observed one of the most famous of the fountains where residents and tourists alike tossed coins: Trevi Fountain. In the bright city lights of evening, the floor of the fountain pool was a skittish silver of reflected light, a complete carpet of coins reflecting tourists' dreams and wishes from around the world. According to *Business Insider*, the equivalent of US$1.5 million gets tossed into the waters there each year. The city collects the money each night and turns it over to a Catholic charity that uses the funds to feed the poor, making at least *their* minimal dreams come true. Thieves often attempt to scoop up the loot late at night but usually get caught and charged, quickly discovering that it's not the easy money they thought it would be.

As to the pool at Swallow Falls and its cache of cash, the ever-vigilant and probing *Daily Post* reported that in 2017 a "Mr. Egan and Mr. O'Neill" were apprehended collecting the coins from the Swallow Falls pool. A nosey upright citizen named Mr. Wylde who reported them said, "One of them had a spade and the other a colander and they were taking the coins, Mr. Egan sweeping up the coins with the spade and dumping them in the colander held by Mr. O'Neill." When they saw the police coming, Egan and O'Neill started throwing the money from the colander back in the river.

I'm not sure which of the men brought the colander, but I have this vision of one of their wives at home that day hoping to make spaghetti for her brood when lo and behold she can't find the damn colander and blames the fairies for hiding it. The *Post* did not report if the spade or the colander were commandeered and held as evidence. I personally have sympathy for the two men and am glad the judge was lenient and only charged them court costs for the petty crime.

Me, I only throw pennies into fountains and pools, but now we don't have pennies in Canada anymore and I might toss a nickel or two in Trevi or the fountain in the local mall, but that's it. If I want to throw away my money, I'd rather spend it on pizza and beer.

It turned out that Swallow Falls also had a spirit or two rambling about. A year before the coin heist, some paranormal investigators (men who probably held a day job) caught on video the ghost of Sir John Wynn of Gwydir walking about there. Some claim his spirit is trapped at the falls because he mistreated locals when he was alive. I presume this was John Wynn, first baronet, who lived a long and wicked life from 1553 to 1627. During his tenure on the planet, he was as nasty to his fellow man as he could be. His hobbies included quarrelling, suing and generally being unkind to his neighbours and, at one point, he was declared a public nuisance and briefly imprisoned. Why he chose to haunt the falls in modern times is puzzling, but perhaps he too was tempted by all that glittering cash in the moonlight.

But about that pizza ... Linda had read about Hangin' Pizzeria in downtown Betws-y-Coed over by the train station where all the train fanatic nutcases liked to hang out. We decided that pizza seemed like a good last supper for us in Wales since Hangin' donates a portion of their profits to two charities: Orangutan Appeal UK, which rescues and rehabilitates orangutans in Borneo, and Ape Action Africa, working to help out gorillas and chimps in Cameroon. There were plenty of photos of those lovable hairy near-human creatures on the walls for us to stare at as we waited for our gluten-free vegan pizza and shared a Death's-Head Hawk-Moth Stout. I read a poster on the wall that chided anyone who would use a plastic straw to drink their soda and it struck me as kind of preachy but, hey, here were some young tattooed health-conscious business people concerned about the fate of monkeys and great apes and I was happy to support their efforts and so should you if you ever find yourself mid-Wales with a healthy appetite for goat cheese, feta, olives and marinated leeks on your thin crust pizza slice.

CHAPTER THIRTY-TWO

AN EARLY ARRIVAL

I invested my evening in worrying about Pamela as Linda texted back and forth with Kathy Craig, who was staying with Pamela in her hospital room. I tried to let my faith in the Canadian health care system override my many worries as a parent, but I felt the inevitable fear and worry that any parent feels when they are far from their child in a time of need.

Linda ran through the town at six in the morning and I walked the dog up into the forest behind the slate cottage. As we passed the hostel, I saw a varied assortment of people young and old eating toast and granola and speaking in several languages. The $300 running shoes felt great on my feet as we left the paved road and trekked through a narrow forest trail with wet and shiny leaves on either side. Kelty was acting crazy, sniffing whatever it was that he detected.

I've lost much of my sense of smell over the years, so I probably don't have the capability to use the six million olfactory receptors in my nose, but dogs reportedly have 300 million of them in their nostrils and use 40 times more of their brain than us poor humans to process those smells. Here in the forest of Wales, Kelty's brain was on fire trying to sort out whatever traces of animals had passed through here overnight. I felt guilty every time I tugged on his leash to move us on through the forest and back to our cottage.

And soon we were on the road, headed east on the A5, with little traffic and still not quite sure if we should bail on Devon and make a run for the Eurotunnel at Folkestone. There was little traffic and the hills of Wales were green and benign beneath a blue sky hosting cotton puffs of clouds. As my troubled mind turned over and over like the drum of an old cement mixer my father once used, a guiding spirit that had no name assured me that all would be well back home in Nova Scotia. Stick with the plan.

And so the miles rolled reasonably by as we drove back toward England through Pentrefoelas, Glasfryn, Cerrigydrudion, past Ewe-phoria again, then Druid and Corwen. The traffic jam in Llangollen was long gone as we breezed through and headed toward Shropshire. And then at nine o'clock in the morning, at the very instant we crossed the border from Wales to England, Linda received a text from Kathy Craig. Pamela had given birth to twin girls: Genevieve Kathryn and Scarlett Lesley. They were eight weeks premature. Pamela's illness had triggered something, sending her into labour, and the doctors had performed a Caesarean operation to bring the babies safely into the world.

I felt both happy and sad, remorseful that we were so far away yet relieved that the babies were okay. Eight weeks premature seemed like an awfully long time ahead of schedule. What might that mean to their health, to my granddaughters' ability to survive? Linda and I drove on in silence through Oswestry and on toward Shrewsbury. A second message and a third assured us that the babies were "fine," Pamela was recovering and there was no reason to return home. The twins would, however, remain in the neonatal intensive care unit for quite some time and it was likely we wouldn't even be allowed to visit them for safety reasons even if we were home. Pamela was being well cared for and Kathy would keep us up to date on everything.

I don't remember much about the drive after that. We connected with the M5 at Wolverhampton and turned south. Worcester, Tewkesbury, Gloucester and all the rest was a bit of a blur. The urban sprawl and industrial calamity of Bristol drew my attention, but it soon gave way to more green hills on either side of the motorway and the broad blue expanse of Bristol Channel, where so many ships in centuries gone by had departed this Old World, headed across the Atlantic to America and Canada. It was a morning to give worries over to grander thoughts about births and beginnings. At least I tried.

Linda and I fussed over what we should do as we passed the familiar turnoff to Cheddar and headed toward Taunton, where my father had once stayed at a home as a soldier during the war. He and a comrade were driving a truck carrying a salvaged bomber wing from an airbase near Bedford to Land's End, presumably for it to be used to fix a plane that had crash landed there. The hosts had served them a traditional English breakfast he would never forget — eggs and greasy toast and blood sausages and fresh trout they had caught in the stream outside their door that very morning. "It was the first time I ever had fish for breakfast," I could still hear him say. And it was the voice of my dead father in my inner ear now clearly telling me that all would be okay with Genevieve, Scarlett and Pamela. And so it was that I continued to quell the voices suggesting otherwise.

I was dead tired of driving and worry when we pulled into the Tesco parking lot outside Exeter. It was hot and humid as Kelty and I made our traditional foray around the perimeter of the pavement jammed with cars, seeking out small pockets of shade and dead grass. As always, I found myself studying the trash on the ground as Kelty unleashed his 300 million olfactory receptors to do their work sniffing out the passage of other dogs, cats, squirrels, hedgehogs and humans. There were quite a few empty Skittles packages and Marlboro Gold cigarette boxes in the weeds. (Who were those idiots who still smoked and threw their garbage in the Tesco bushes while they loaded groceries into their Vauxhalls, anyway?) A condom or two indicated that not everyone in the vicinity had the luxury of a private bedroom for their sexual activity, and I wondered if the broken comb was part of the story somehow. And, yes, there were plastic cups, bright red or orange, and those damn plastic straws the Hangin' Pizza people had been preaching against.

Growing weary (and still a little more than worried), I plonked down on a patch of dead grass beneath an unhealthy-looking pine tree. A grey-haired man with a small bag of groceries was just arriving back at his Mercedes parked at my feet and saw us sitting there. Travelling with a dog almost certainly always gives strangers cause to say something to you. He must have noted the exhausted look on my face because he said in a most friendly manner, "I know just how you feel," and I wasn't sure if it was addressed to me with the sad-dog look or Kelty with his tongue hanging out as he panted from the heat. But it was an act of small kindness in a world currently populated with litter and fretting. The man made a small motion with his hand — as if he were tipping his hat, only he had no hat, as he opened the door of his grey Mercedes and sat down.

CHAPTER THIRTY-THREE

MY AFTERNOON WITH
PRINCE CHARLES (FEBRUARY 2013)

After Mr. Mercedes wheeled away, Kelty and I sat there in the heat on the dead grass studying the empty parking spot. We were perched on the curb at this point, and that must have indicated some kind of territorial right because two drivers stopped and began to pull into the spot but, spying a depleted looking man with a tired little white dog, changed their plans and went elsewhere to park their wagons.

In case I haven't said it before, I rather like the English. They are friendly, polite, witty, quirky to the extreme and give their towns wonderfully absurd-sounding names like Cheselbourne, Dewlish, Droop, Tincleton and Affpuddle. It always seemed strange to me that such a cheerful and self-effacing people could have wreaked so much havoc on the world down through the centuries. Having read more English history than is healthy for any mortal, I was well aware that the Brits had invaded every continent of the world except for Antarctica, and their soldiers had killed untold millions. Their history is filled with horror. But today, England still appeared as a cheerful and accommodating island to foreigners like me, even on a worrisome day like this. Perhaps a bit too much litter and a tad too warm today for a Canadian, but otherwise, just fine.

Linda and I had travelled to downtown Exeter, just a few miles from this Tesco, once before, and it was here we had an unlikely encounter with Prince Charles and Camilla Parker Bowles.

In the winter of 2013, while most Canadians who wanted to vacate the country were fleeing to Cancun and Punta Cana, I convinced Linda we should fly the big pond yet again and roam around a part of England we had not visited.

There are no all-inclusive sunny resorts open in February in Dorset and Devon, but I felt that part of the United Kingdom calling to me. It rains a lot in England during that time of the year (No! Really?), so we packed some substantial rain gear and headed off. The overnight flight was uneventful but left me groggy and puffy-eyed as usual as we drove east on the M25 for our first night on the legendary Isle of Wight. Apparently, signage was poor that day, so we missed the turn south on the M3 and kept driving until we were halfway to the Chunnel and France. Realizing our mistake, we made an illegal U-turn at a Little Chef rest stop at a place called Clacket Lane just outside Limpsfield and headed back toward Dorking for our proper road.

We were late arriving on the island and I will spare you details about driving around in the dark on single lane muddy back roads on the Isle of Wight. As my sweaty hands tightly gripped the steering wheel, it made me think of my father driving his lights-out excursions during the war. Eventually, we did end up at a nice overnight accommodation in a solar- and wind-powered cottage also called "Little Barn." Throughout Britain, wily Limeys have converted nearly every remnant of their stone structures to rent to visitors like us. After a number of trips to England, I've slept in converted barns, stables, grain mills, chicken sheds and other outbuildings never intended for human occupation. All of them were actually quite charming and comfortable, although I still have dents in my head from hitting it on so many low beams. But I guess that's all part of the adventure.

The next morning we left Little Barn behind for a more interesting accommodation, a converted chapel on the opulent Rousdon Estate near Lyme Regis that was once owned by the wealthy Peek family. In a previous century, Henry Peek made a fortune trading in cocoa, tea and spices. He had purchased the entire town of Rousdon and built this estate for £250,000 (roughly C$20 million today). The Peek family also made cookies, Peek Freans, which you may have nibbled on in your youth. Henry was also the governor of a local prison where he graciously allowed inmates to create floor mosaics for his new crib. It was also said that Henry had one of the finest stuffed bird collections in all England.

Nowadays, no single person could actually afford to keep up the property, so the big mansion was broken up into con-dominiums and much of the property was being turned into a subdivision. But for a week, the high-ceilinged chapel, which was really a small cathedral, was ours. It was cold and dark inside and not as much fun as it sounds, but we found ways to entertain ourselves with a great number of things I never thought I'd do in a church.

When I travel, I prefer small towns, tiny fishing villages, unpopulated hills and that sort of thing. If I could avoid cities altogether, I would gladly. Unfortunately, most large airports are in proximity to large cities like London or Paris or Rome, so grudgingly I end up having to deal with the annoyance of finding a route out of urban areas. If I had my way, I'd carry a parachute and ask to be dropped off in some rural area long before the blight of Heathrow or Charles de Gaulle or Leonardo da Vinci International. But I know that all the new security rules would never allow for that.

My wife, however, despite all her wonderful attributes, does seem to like cities. And so it was that one rainy day during our English excursion, after a dark breakfast of cheese and eggs in our sanctuary, I agreed to drive us to Exeter, what appeared to be the closest city on the map.

Those of you fond of vacationing in Varadero, Holguin and Runaway Bay have probably never had any real itch to visit Exeter, but it does have its charm. The name Exeter means something to do with a fortress and a river that is full of fish but has, at least once during its lengthy history, been miscon- strued as "fortress full of fish." Old coins found here suggest that merchants from Exeter were somehow trading with people on the Mediterranean as far back as 250 BC, and if that doesn't whet your appetite to visit, I don't know what would.

Like nearly all British cities, Exeter has a long, convoluted and often violent history, but at least one story stands out in my mind. There was a lengthy siege of the castle here in 1136 when King Stephen wanted to root out Baldwin de Redvers. De Redvers and his loyal followers were holding out fairly well until, three months in, they ran out of wine and admitted defeat.

When we arrived in Exeter that rainy day in February, we hoped to wander around the city and see what there was to be seen. Unfortunately, traffic was being diverted from the main streets and parking seemed impossible. It turned out that Prince Charles and Camilla were to be arriving that day for a ceremony of some sort at the ancient Exeter Cathedral. I knew who Prince Charles was but truly didn't know anything about this Camilla person. Once Linda explained to me who she was (apparently the Duchess of Cornwall) and the whole story behind why she would be here today with Charles, I was, yet again, both charmed and appalled at the way things go in Britain.

I insisted that we should park somewhere far away from the centre of town and the police cars lining the streets. But we decided on a whim to hike back to the cathedral to watch the royalty arrive. The cathedral, dating back to 1050, was a beauty, naturally much more elaborate and grander than our abode back at the Rousdon Estate. In a large square at the front, a crowd was gathering and we joined it. The townsfolk seemed wary of us at first but turned friendly and polite as soon as we told them we were from Canada and not the Americans we appeared to be. One exceedingly enthusiastic older woman with bad hearing was thrilled to think we had travelled all the way from Nova Scotia just to see British royalty.

I overheard a few old gents say they had forgotten their gloves and were feeling chilled. They told their wives about their plight and said they needed to find refuge in a nearby pub and the women should come find them when the hoopla was all over.

Two fashionably dressed young women came our way and asked what all the fuss was about. When we told them Prince Charles was coming, they rolled their eyes and one uttered a single word: "Wanker." Apparently, the prince is not well loved by all the citizens of the United Kingdom. The women walked off and we continued to wait in the charming English drizzle.

A limousine flanked by motorcycles arrived with the appropriate pomp one would expect. Charles and Camilla stepped out of the car, smiled and waved and shook hands with old bald men in suits as loyal citizens cheered. After about ten minutes, they disappeared into the cathedral and, since we did not have special invitations to go in, that was pretty much that. We hiked off to see how things were going with the old gentlemen in the pub. That night, we actually saw ourselves on the evening national TV news that had covered the event.

The next day we did a ten-kilometre hike along the spectacular South West Coast Path on what is dubbed, for tourist purposes, the Jurassic Coast. We couldn't help but marvel at how much untrampled wild country still exists in such a populated nation. I mused about Prince Charles and wondered what it would be like to spend your royal life smiling at strangers, waving and shaking hands for a living. It seemed to me like a royal pain in the ass but, I guess, in a monarchy, someone has to do it. Our coastal hike took us through a turnip field full of igneous rocks and finally to the picturesque seaside village of Seaton. There we found a pub, of course, with old men arguing about politics and fox hunting. I had learned on an earlier foray to Cornwall never to wade into any pub discussions involving either of those two subjects, so we simply sat back and listened to the men rant as we ate our fish and chips.

We were tired from the long trek so we cheated and took a taxi back to our chapel abode at Rousdon Estate. The driver tried his best to hit a number of pheasants that were crossing the road, reminding me that the English still might have a mean streak in them and we should be careful.

The next day, I insisted we drive to another little seaside village called Beer.

As you enter the village, there actually is a sign that reads, "Welcome to Beer. Please drive carefully." My wife thought me silly, but I had to take photos of the Beer Post Office, Beer Town Hall and, my personal favourite, the Beer Church of England.

I don't think we saw the sun that week at all. We had been warned to expect as much. But England had welcomed us as always and made me feel like this was a very livable place. We took what I thought was a shortcut on our way back to Heathrow and got lost in some more very enchanting countryside. I had to stop and ask for directions in Harcombe Bottom and was told that I should drive north to Hawkchurch and find the B3165 to Drimpton and follow it right on through to Hewish. If I wanted to stay on the back roads, I could then push on to Haselbury Plucknett or Little Wigborough and then keep on to Shepton Mallet and South Stoke. At the roundabout in Maidenhead, he said, be sure to take the third left.

CHAPTER THIRTY-FOUR

LITTLE HAZELCOTT, BOWERMAN'S NOSE, PARSLEY, SAGE, ROSEMARY AND THYME

At long last, Linda returned with a wobbly cart full of groceries and we thought we had but a short drive to our home rental — Little Hazelcott Cottage — near Manaton in Dartmoor. We had been given two sets of directions — one taking us south and one taking us north — and I chose the northerly approach, which would take us through Moretonhampstead, near the home of Tony Hawks, which was what had set the Devonian wheels in motion to begin with. This turned out to be a monumental mistake. Our directions were faulty to say the least and I had not expected the roads in this part of Devon to be so narrow and so poorly maintained, despite the fact that Mr. Hawks had well warned all his readers of this fact in his book, *Once Upon a Time in the West...Country.* He claimed that Devon has a "10,000 mile labyrinthine network of lanes," and, upon reading that book, I hoped that one day I too would be an author who could use the word "labyrinthine" effortlessly in my prose.

When we arrived in Moretonhampstead, I was of the opinion it was too busy and crowded and that we should not dawdle but push on to Manaton on the back roads described by our host as "the shortcut." The roads had no names and there were a few signs pointing toward towns like Sloncombe, Postbridge and Chagford, but none pointing us to Manaton. "Turn left at the white barn," and "At the difficult crossroads, take a sharp left" proved to be of no real help, and pretty soon we were lost.

To make matters worse, I had soldiered us on down a potholed slim donkey track of some sort with ancient stone walls on both sides, taking us deeper and deeper down into a gully with massive blackberry vines scratching the car on both sides. At the bottom of the gully there was a stream — the River Bovey, I would later learn. I found a pull-off just before a narrow ancient stone bridge but then noticed that just across the little bridge were two police cars — those miniature British versions that Americans find funny. Someone told me that these smallish cop cars are often referred to as "pandas" or "jam sandwiches," but I'm not sure I should believe that.

Tired and frustrated from too much driving and plenty of getting lost, we got out to take a breather, walk the dog and wonder what was going on there on the other side of the stream.

It was then that a man in a tweed jacket walked over to us from out of a field and eyed with some suspicion our French licence plate. The field, he said, was his property and he wondered if he could help us. I explained we were lost but asked him what the police were up to.

"I'm afraid there's been an incident," he said.

"Is someone hurt?" Linda asked.

"I'm afraid so," he said.

"I hope they'll be all right," I said.

"It doesn't look like that's the case," he said.

"What happened?" Linda asked.

"It's hard to say," he answered.

"Anything we can do?"

"Not a thing. The police have things under control."

It was then I asked for directions to Manaton and he pointed back up the steep narrow road we had just driven down. I thanked him, packed the befuddled dog back in the car and we made the ascent, slamming into one pothole after the next.

Halfway up we suddenly saw a large cube van of an ambulance headed our way, scraping itself on both sides of the narrow roadway as it approached.

"What are we going to do?" Linda asked.

"Nothing to do," I said. "I gotta back up."

"It looks impossible."

I wanted to agree, but I had little choice. Remembering my father's advice from the earliest days of driving instruction, I levered the top half of my body around, jammed the car in reverse and proceeded in a white-knuckle descent back down to the little river with the ambulance and our Fiat nose to nose. When we arrived at the bottom again, the landowner was opening a gate to his pasture to allow us to back in as the ambulance stopped in front of us, blocking us in.

Whatever tragedy had occurred in the clearing across the bridge, we will never know. Somebody died, but we don't know who or why or how. We checked the local news in days thereafter and never found out more. Someone may have drowned, but it wasn't much of a river. Or someone committed suicide out here in the woods of the Dartmoor forest. I've been told that often suicides are not reported in the news lest they promote others to copy the deed. Could this be true?

Whatever the case, it was a day of twin births and the death of an unknown person by unknown cause. When the ambulance driver returned to the truck, I apologized and asked if she could move the vehicle just enough to let us out. She did and we slowly skittered up the steep hill again.

At Little Hazelcott Cottage, we settled in and called it a day.

I checked my emails and discovered that Tony Hawks had been kind enough to provide answers to my questions in writing since we'd be unable to meet. Here would be good advice, I hoped, to put us in the proper mindset for exploring his neck of the woods.

Remember, here was an author whose spirit of adventure and witty wisdom had inspired me to write in the tradition of *Around Somewhere with a Something*. Asked what a typical day for Devon is for him, he replied, "Woken by four year old boy. Struggle with demands of four year old boy. Drop him to school. Write and work on projects if raining — putter in the garden if a beautiful day, and feel guilty. But not guilty enough to go inside and work. Long country walk. More child care. Go to bed way earlier than I ever have before!"

His response made me think yet again about being a grandparent. We would have to get to know these little ones, take them overnight to give the parents a break and care for them, maybe even be there for them at daybreak for the first bottle of the day.

And then, watch them grow, Genevieve and Scarlett, and be there to be an important part of their lives.

Tony added that he undertook quests involving refrigerators and miniature pigs "to demonstrate to people that 'play' is as necessary for adults as it is for kids." Indeed. A worthy message. He noted he had a dog as well as a child. The dog, named Coco, was a smallish mutt that he sometimes carried in a front-side pack, much like a parent kangaroo, to national book awards and such.

He reminded me that driving those "labyrinthine" roads of Devon could be frustrating and challenging, but I already knew that. Best and worst things about life near the moors: "Best — the views and the air. The worst — the pro-Brexit fervour." Another good reminder of a subject to avoid at the local pubs in Lustleigh or elsewhere.

He ended his email with some fatherly advice to a fellow earth-traveller/writer as this: "Be kind, patient and find a way to serve others." Jesus couldn't have said it much better.

I woke up in the middle of the night with that ambulance bearing down on us again on the steep, narrow road. The scene quickly shifted to driving on a paved road somewhere back in Leicestershire and me hitting those bumpy reflective knobs in the middle of the road while Linda's words echoed from the windshield: "Stop hitting the cat's eyes." That's what they were called — *cat's eyes*. One of my favourite UK road-side signs I had observed back around Alconbury was "Cat's Eyes Removed." Cat's eyes are also known as "road studs" and English drivers apparently get upset if the eye — the reflective part — is broken and not working. But why they are removed in some areas is unclear. Maybe it's just for road work, or maybe some of us found them too annoying to keep bumping into even if our vehicle was wandering onto the wrong side of the road.

Linda headed off for a run at 6:00 a.m. again and, over toast and dark roast coffee, I scanned the internet for more information about yesterday's tragedy. I found nothing but was quickly diverted by an item that caught my eye. According to *The Telegraph*, "Cat's eyes were invented by Percy Shaw in 1934 and in 2006 were voted one of Britain's top 10 designs alongside the Concorde, the Mini and the World Wide Web." Most impressive indeed. And I didn't know that the web was a British invention, did you? Later that summer, I found myself missing England so I logged back on to *The Telegraph* to see what the British were currently riled about. (They're almost always riled about something interesting.) And that's when I discovered that down in Sussex, an American tourist or two was shocked by the "Cat's Eyes Removed" signs and so local councillors changed "cat's eyes" to "road studs" on the signage. That would probably suggest to unknowledgeable travellers that the local council had cleaned up a problem with male highway hookers, so eventually linguists would need to be hired to come up with something new.

Apparently, it was a national, not a local, issue because *The Telegraph* also reported that "Rebecca Brewer, a mother from Ipswich, said that her daughter thought people were mutilating felines. 'I have a five-year-old daughter who was very upset the first time she saw the sign — she really thought that cruel people were torturing cats ... I had to explain to her what it meant — and that our pet cat was quite safe.'"

But enough of that. While Linda was improving her cardiovascular system, I did receive an email from Nova Scotia saying that all was well with Pamela and the babies — at least as well as they could be. Pamela was recovering from the Caesarean and the early twins were in incubators receiving round-the-clock care. I silently thanked the angels and the

Canadian health care system, which was not only providing excellent care to my granddaughters but doing so free of charge.

Linda returned from her run and reported she had found the village of Manaton and that it was quite lovely. There was a main road going through it and we had, most likely, found our way to Little Hazelcott by "the back way." Lucky us. Single lane. Not a cat's eye within miles and a grim tragedy in a green gully. Time to put that behind us and see what the countryside had to offer.

We drove into Manaton, parked by the church with its leafy cemetery and found the trail leading to Bowerman's Nose. Legend has it that a hunter name Bowerman liked to lead his dogs into the moors to hunt rabbits. He unwisely claimed he was not at all afraid of the witches that seemed to be as thick as thieves in this part of England. This annoyed the hell out of the witches, who plotted to trap Bowerman and turn him into a large rock. Once locals discovered what had happened, they too were angry and drove all the witches out of Devon (or so the story goes) and sent them to Wales, although I myself had not encountered a single witch during our stay there.

Such were the stories abounding in Dartmoor, a place of curious-looking hills, vast expanses of a kind of "desert," as some describe the moors, and mysteries that span the many centuries since humans immigrated here to find some rural peace and quiet.

Only the very top part of the hike to the Nose required me to lift little Kelty up the natural stone staircase. It was like some version of childhood fantasy at the top, with rocky out-croppings making a kind of fort from which to look out over the miles of moor with patches of dark and light orchestrated by sun and clouds.

I can confirm that there were no witches left here, but an odd-looking owl flew over us low enough to make a haunting whooshing sound with his wings that I can still hear if I close my eyes and drift back to Manaton.

There were more hills to be climbed, of course, and we made a quick retreat to the car park and made a brief tour of Manaton. The town is proud of the fact that the novelist John Galsworthy (1867–1933) lived here for a stint and may have written a novel or two, or at least had the inspiration for them, while in Manaton. Galsworthy would have been quite famous in his day for *The Forsyte Saga* and other works but, as with so many authors, many of his bestsellers are probably gathering dust on the library shelves.

We were crossing paths, this dead author and I, so I felt a certain kinship, too well aware that my own books would soon be gathering dust if they weren't already and I'd eventually join Galsworthy in the great crowded literary dumpster of history. But, yes, for one shining moment in June, he and I were united as Manatonians. And before the readers of the world feel a big yawn coming on, I'll remind you that Mr. G. was a vocal advocate for women's rights and kindness to animals, not to mention prison reform. He spoke out against censorship as all good writers should and turned down knighthood, stating that writing well was its own reward. While living in Manaton, he wrote a fictional story based on a girl named Kitty Jay who had hanged herself. We should forgive him for having an affair there with his cousin's wife and then using her as a character in a novel. And we should applaud him for adding a poem about a dog to the great canon of canine literature, a poem that ends with the lines

> Then through the ages we'll retrieve
> Each other's scent and company;
> And longing shall not pull my heart —
> As now you pull my sleeve!

And if you are not allergic to dust, do take a trip to the public library and check out a lonesome copy of *A Man of Property* and let me know what you think.

We walked down yet another narrow road leading out of town, where it ended and gave way to a small, stony hiking trail that took us up to Manaton Rocks, the second most notable hiking destination here. It took us across a cow pasture with a kissing gate and we kept Kelty well leashed and the cows at a distance. Linda saw a bull she didn't trust not far off and the three of us did a lively bucolic dance as we hurried on, darting this way and that around big thistle cones and sidestepping cow pies. Such exercises like this, I was certain, formed the basis for many a traditional English country dance. All that was missing was music.

Looking south from the top of Manaton Rocks revealed how truly remarkable the moors were. Here were wide-open spaces, hilltops and valleys with most towns tucked so far down in the lower regions that they appeared not to exist. It was one of those dreamlike visions you find in rural England where you realize you are looking at a landscape that, from this vantage point at least, has not changed in hundreds if not thousands of years. We scrambled around the funnily shaped boulders until the sun was high in the sky and it was time to grudgingly return to the twenty-first century and lunch.

I had eyed a town named Lustleigh not far off, so we drove there and tucked into an outdoor table at the Cleave Public

House, a thatched-roof enterprise surrounded by gargantuan chestnut trees, if I have my tree knowledge correct. I daresay it felt old and authentic but doubt that it dated back to 899 when Alfred the Great gave what is now Lustleigh to his son as a gift.

When I made my dutiful pilgrimage to the indoor loo, I peeked in the kitchen to see a cluster of young white-hatted kitchen staff watching the chef crush and sprinkle spices on a piece of roast chicken. The group was so solemn, it almost appeared as if it were a religious ceremony, but I'm sure it was meant to be a culinary educational moment. Although fish and chips still ruled the eating-out English diet, I detected that things were changing with a younger generation, who were either modern-day gourmet witches and warlocks or simply contemporary champions of parsley, sage, rosemary and thyme.

CHAPTER THIRTY-FIVE

TO THE TOP OF THE TORS, THE END OF THE ROAD AND THE SPANDEX INVASION

At the risk of sounding repetitious, I would like to say that if someone should inaugurate a special award for the most difficult roads in England, I would nominate the back roads of Dartmoor for that distinction. They are narrow, potholed and often walled on both sides with creeping blackberry vines as thick as your wrist sporting spikey thorns that will take an eye out if you or your dog decides to stick your head out the window and smell the sweet breeze.

The remains of the medieval village in Hound Tor are well documented in travel literature and you might expect a signpost or two, but we found only one as we snaked through the backcountry. But one sign in Dartmoor will lead you only so far before you come to a dozen or so more obscure unposted intersections. We spent a better part of the morning lost, zigzagging beneath one tor or another, backtracking, retracing, going north, south, east and west, sometimes in the right direction, sometimes not. "Didn't we just pass this stone house with a tidy yard ten minutes ago?" Linda would ask.

Eventually, by sheer luck, we wound up at the parking lot at Hound Tor and were properly shocked to see that it was somewhat crowded. It turned out there was a well-marked and well-maintained road that approached from the south and once again we had selected the back road route from the north, I know not why. But it was becoming clear that adventure and stupidity went hand in hand, at least in my case as a Dartmoor lane navigator.

Tors are granite rock formations throughout the region, each one with its own quirky charm and personality. The hike to the top of the Hound is fairly easy and dogs are appropriately welcomed, so we had a fine time of it, and the view from the top, like the view from most every tor in the area, is spectacular. Dartmoor is just a weird and wonderful landscape and it has fascinated visitors for centuries. Many an artist has captured it on canvas and it is said that it is the inspiration for Sir Arthur Conan Doyle's "Hound of the Baskervilles." Big Mama Thornton visited here once, it is also reported, and was inspired to write "(You Ain't Nothing but a) Hound Dog," which would eventually be a runaway hit for none other than Elvis Presley. Just kidding. It just occurred to me that a lot of "lore" about such places may or may not be true and I might as well be one of those writers to make something up and spread an unlikely but fascinating rumour.

But, no, I'll do my best to be your loyal author and stick to the truth.

There is yet another legend (I didn't make it up) that suggests a pack of hounds was turned to stone and thus the name, but that's probably not true either, even though the moor is full of any number of things that were supposedly turned to stone in ancient times. I kept wondering who it was that did all the handiwork of turning living things to granite? The devil or witches, it would appear. From the look of the landscape from atop the Hound, it seemed that whoever it was, the transformational work kept them quite busy.

Whatever the truth about the craggy rocks, Kelty, Linda and I loved clambering over them. Hound Tor was considered to be a spooky place, but it was hard to imagine this on such a sunny, blue-sky day. Certainly, Conan Doyle had been inspired by some gloomy days on the moor and even an episode of *Doctor Who* was filmed here because the place looked so otherworldly.

Alas, we saw no disappearing dogs as others before us had reported, although I once did watch a dog disappear before my eyes in a canyon in Arizona said to be a spiritual vortex of some sort. I swear I watched as it walked toward me with two brim-hatted hikers and then just vanished. So maybe these things do happen. Fortunately, Kelty remained in our sight, on the end of his sturdy leash, at all times.

And I don't doubt that the Hound has its share of mysteries, not the least of which is a geological one. In 1995, one of the granite stacks, a craggy 500 tons of granite, suddenly crashed to the ground for no apparent reason. If you like geological and mythical mysteries and scrambling around rocks for the fun of it, then this is your Devonian Disney World.

When we had enough of rock climbing, we ambled down to the parking lot and had a look at the remains of the medieval village. Here were the remains of longhouses that date back to the thirteenth century, and it is believed the village was abandoned when a plague swept the countryside. Or maybe part of the Hound had collapsed then as well and they took it as an omen to leave. We'll never know. But part of me wants to clearly imagine this isolated Bronze Age community with their animals and cultivated plants. Were they happy? Did they feel cut off from the world? Did they love their families and their dogs? My own answers are yes, no, yes. Yes, they were happy — as I imagine them at least. No, they didn't know they were isolated. They were connected to the world of the moor and drew sustenance from it. And, yes, of course, they loved their families and the family dog. Even the large, hairy dog that some still see racing across the hilltops during a full moon.

The end of the road for us was the town of Widecombe-in-the-Moor. As we drove there, we received more reports from home that the babies were doing fine — still in incubators but doing okay. And Pamela was recovering. I tried to stop worrying. Widecombe was as far *away* as we were going. Tomorrow, we'd leave Manaton and drive well across the base of England to Folkestone to rest and then retreat to France for the leg home.

H.V. Morton writes of Widecombe, "Moorland villages such as Widecombe are the oases in the desert. There are little clumps of green clustered in the hollow of the hills, sheltered, if possible, from the rougher blasts of weather — little centres of humanity in the great wildness of the desert. I imagine the beer tastes better in Widecombe than in other parts of the Dartmoor."

Parked atop a hill before descending into the town, I could see what he meant by the town being an oasis. But I didn't have a chance to see if the beer tasted any better there in either of the two pubs — the Old Inn and the Rugglestone. Like so many towns in the moor, it was rife with supernatural stories. When the church was struck by lightning in 1638, it was assumed to be the work of Satan. The American actor Daniel Stern, best known as one of the robbers in *Home Alone*, claimed to have seen 30 or more ghosts "milling about" on his honeymoon there in 1980. "They looked like extras from *Night of the Living Dead,*" he said. One of the ghosts he spoke to had "milky white" eyes that freaked him out. Apparently, the ghosts jinxed Mr. Stern and his bride because they had a blowout tire trying to get out of Widecombe and, when they arrived back at their B&B accommodation, the host told them they should not have gone to Widecombe because it was haunted.

A traditional folk song from the nineteenth century called "Widecombe Fair" features the ghost of "Tom Pearce's old mare in her rattling bones," further endorsing the fact that Widecombe has a reputation for strangeness, yet everything seemed quite normal the day we visited.

Near Widecombe in the early part of this century stood a 20-foot-tall oak chair handcrafted by sculptor Henry Bruce. It drew so much tourist traffic that local citizens (many of them fun-loathing spirits, no doubt) complained. When the authorities made Bruce take down his chair monument, he told *The Telegraph,* "It is a shame that it is health and safety that cuts these things out of life when they bring such joy and inspiration." Like Bruce, during our tenure in the UK, we did notice that the British were a bit obsessive with certain "health and safety" issues that we are a bit more lax about in fun-loving North America. They have warnings in airports letting you know your pedway is about to end and, should you travel by train anywhere in the kingdom, you'll be ever reminded to "mind the gap."

In 2010, Steven Spielberg and a fairly massive entourage found their way to Widecombe and the surrounding countryside to shoot the movie *War Horse.* Although his crew tried to keep locations a secret, invading flotillas of a hundred or more vehicles and an army of painters painting over an entire village's window frames (so that they were not white) gave away whatever secrets they were trying to maintain.

Someone over in Yelverton on the edge of the moor told the press that the famous director had been spotted buying a carton of semi-skimmed milk and that got the tongues wagging. Spielberg's film does justice to the haunting and beautiful landscape. *The Guardian* quoted him as saying, "I have never before, in my long, eclectic career, been gifted with such an abundance of natural beauty as I experienced filming *War Horse*."

Such was the scenery around Haytor on our way back to Manaton. It was an easy hike up this hill and plenty of camera-toting tourists were about, especially the men with big lens cameras that bounce off their bellies as they stride up the hill. I had to keep a close watch on Kelty as there were ponies casually grazing about as we climbed the easy rock staircase, while puffy blue clouds above kept prompting me to think this was all a dream. A woman with a charming accent working in a food truck below in the parking lot told me she wanted to adopt Kelty and would I mind if I left him behind to keep her company? I politely declined and told her we were headed to France and flying home to Nova Scotia in a couple of days. From her expression, I got the notion that she believed I was making this up. And it suddenly occurred to me that this whole business of travelling from continent to continent with a small white dog was a bit unreal — fairy tale–like, even. At the very least, the stuff of minor legends.

In nearby Bovey Tracey, Linda visited an art gallery and did some shopping while Kelty and I sniffed around town. We walked along the River Bovey and I studied the lichen growing in the grass. This may not seem a big deal to you — and Kelty could have cared less — but ever since I'd read about the longevity and resilience of lichen, I've had a special place in my heart for this clever but slow-witted living combination of fungus and algae that can thrive just about anywhere, sometimes for centuries at a time. Dog lichen, also known as dog's teeth, was believed to be a cure for rabies in the Middle Ages, so it was a pretty big deal, but I could tell that not another soul in Bovey Tracey had any enthusiasm for the dog lichen so prolific here.

The ignored lichen before me was once noted in the ancient so-called *Doctrine of Signatures*. The shape of a plant or its leaf somehow was related to what it could cure. Hence, dog lichen or dog's teeth lichen correlates to the teeth of the rabid dog that bit you so, ipso facto, if you ate the lichen, it would cure your rabies. I'm told that modern science has suppressed the notions found in the *Doctrine of Signatures*, but I did find that the dried flowers of lungwort helped me to breathe better during my I'm-more-organic-than-you period. And there's a slap-happy, good-feel approach to fostering well-being found in the doctrine. For example, walnuts are good for your brain because the nut inside looks like a human brain. Want to fix your head? Just eat a bag of walnuts. It's much cheaper than a shrink and less invasive than electrotherapy. Slice a carrot and it looks like a human eye. Mushrooms are good for the ears. Olives are good for your ovaries and kidney beans ... guess what? They're good for your kidneys. Don't just take it from me. Go read Paracelsus.

It was about then that I smelled the herbal sweet aroma of marijuana and saw a teenage boy and girl sharing a joint on a big boulder in the little river. I thought we should leave them be lest they think I was an undercover narc with a drug-sniffing Westie. I tugged at Kelty's leash and went to find Linda, since I knew we needed to get back to Little Hazelcott and start packing.

In our final night back in the cottage, with thoughts of home, babies and family swimming in my head, I realized it was the last day of June, a momentous month in a momentous year, and we had nearly concluded what we'd set out to do — travel around England with a dog.

As noted, landlords who rent vacation homes have the most unusual assortment of reading material left on the shelves for their temporary tenants. Often it's just a cheesy collection of romances or murder mysteries or large print thrillers. I had read a fair bit of "the best running book ever," *Born to Run*, back in Wales. It was the story of a little-known tribe of Indigenous people in Mexico who ran faster and longer than most any humans. I now regretted not stealing it for the flight home and became tempted to pilfer something from the shelves here at Little Hazelcott — not the valuable hiking or tattered bird guides, but some obscure paperback that no one would miss. I couldn't quite find anything that spoke to me, until I found a biography of Twiggy. I hadn't ever thought much about Twiggy. That is, she hadn't crossed my radar since sometime in the 1960s when Soho fashions were in vogue. Even then, I wasn't sure what Twiggy was famous for. I think it was just the fact she was skinny and wore currently trendy London fashions. (Or did I miss an important element of her fame?) In the end, I wasn't sure Linda would approve of me reading Twiggy's biography on the WestJet flight home, so I placed it back on the shelf.

In the morning, Linda insisted that she squeeze in a full ten-kilometre run and suggested she leave ahead of us, head to Becky Falls and on toward Bovey Tracey. Kelty and I would follow a half-hour later and pick her up on the road. The plan worried the bejesus out of me. What if for some unexpected reason we couldn't find her? What if something happened? But she insisted and quickly bolted out the door before I had a chance to complete my protest.

Little did I know that July 1 was the day of the Dartmoor Classic Sportive 2018 bicycle marathon, which was taking place on the road where I was to meet up with Linda. As I left Little Hazelcott, with thunderclouds looming overhead, I had a bad feeling in the pit of my stomach and my gut knotted up. When Kelty and I encountered the first of several displays of spandex from several dozen overzealous bike riders, I knew something was up. Side roads were closed off to traffic, but I was permitted to pass, fearing all the while that there would be a roadblock ahead, I would be shunted off onto a side road and never see my wife again.

When I encountered a man on the side of the road who looked like my high school gym teacher with a clipboard in his hand, I asked him if he'd seen a lone woman running against the incoming tide of sweaty bicyclists, he nodded and said, "Yes. She went this way and said you'd stop to ask. Keep on straight ahead, mate." And so I did.

The clouds spilled several buckets of warm rain and I kept tightly tucked to my left to stay out of the way of the rolling spandex army. But then the sun came out and the hills were at once alive with light. And there she was. Wet, slightly winded and finally dropping herself into the shotgun seat of our Fiat. And with that we were on our way to Folkestone, finding our way onto the M highways by way of Exeter, Bristol, Slough, Clacket Lane and Ashford.

CHAPTER THIRTY-SIX

THE SURF OF SENNEN COVE AND LAND'S END (APRIL 2014)

Once past Exeter and heading north, I had a twinge of regret that we would not be visiting Cornwall on this junket. Linda and I had spent a fair bit of time in Cornwall in the past — lots of bad weather and good times to be had, but Kelty had never had a Cornish hike on a sandy cove beach or a chance to fall asleep on the floor of a local pub while I sipped a Proper Job pulled straight from the tap. As we drove across the south of England, Linda and I reminisced about our days in England's boot tip, including one memorable trip from four years previous.

It was in the winter of 2014 that I first noticed photographs posted on the internet of monstrous waves crashing into the seawalls of Sennen Cove in the far southwest corner of England. These behemoth sea monsters, spawned by massive North Atlantic storms, not only slammed into the rocks but sent geysers of salt water up and over the two- and three-storey buildings near the coast. Waves like that speak to my deep subconscious, luring me with their danger, their power and their majesty.

Linda and I had explored a fair chunk of the Celtic world so far, including travels to Cornwall, but we'd never ventured this far down to the toe of that geographical boot and, with images of those winter waves still haunting me, we planned to see what magic Sennen Cove and its environs had to offer the following April.

It's an easy overnight flight to Heathrow from Halifax, but one never really gets enough sleep. The next morning found me in a familiar rental car with an equally familiar groggy, befuddled state of mind. Anyone listening in would have heard me stating out loud to myself, "Stay on the left," as we entered the multitude of busy roundabouts around Heathrow strategically located to challenge and confound sleep-deprived North Americans like me.

There was mediocre coffee and even more mediocre hamburgers from the Roadchef restaurants of the M class highways to sustain us as we fled the London suburban traffic, heading toward the wilds of Cornwall. Wisely, we didn't do the drive all in one day but spent the night at an old lopsided inn near Buckfastleigh with the babbling Dart River below our balcony singing us to sleep in the most cozy accommodations from a previous century.

We made our way onward the next day to our rental home a few miles inland from Sennen Cove, a converted stone barn on an estate situated beneath some enormous trees that hosted the largest murder of crows I'd seen anywhere on the planet. Alarm clocks were not needed here since the crows provided a lively cacophonous wakeup call at the break of dawn, most useful to rouse us from sleep and send us out on our daily adventures. Breakfast was in the upstairs kitchen, which, according to the notes provided by the owners, was once a hayloft in bucolic days gone by. It was my first breakfast in a hayloft as far as memory serves me.

We set out in the wrong direction the next morning, anxious to leave the squawking of black birds in search of coastal peace, so we ended up going south and east until the road ended at Porthcurno, where there was a busy parking lot at an outdoor theatre hanging on the edge of a cliff.

Minack Theatre, looking decidedly more ancient Greek than modern English, was created by a wealthy theatre enthusiast, Rowena Cade, in the early 1930s and host to innumerable Shakespeare plays ever thereafter. The grounds were filled with a multitude of beautiful flowers and their attending butterflies. We ventured around the clifftops and hiked a first patch of the 630-mile-long South West Coast Path, which was not far away. The British are to be commended for their hiking paths and this one is a gem. It stretches from Exmoor National Park in the north to Poole in the south and has some of the most dramatic scenery in the world by my estimation. Sure, I'd never hike the whole thing in this lifetime, but I'd pick away at a fair stretch any time I could find myself in the neighbourhood.

Mousehole (pronounced "mowsull") was not far up the shore from here, and it remains a great little seaport with narrow streets, stone buildings and old men who can offer up genuine sea stories from rugged days gone by. At a local pub, something straight out of an old pirate movie, we ate some deeply fried fish and green pea soup thick enough that the spoon could stand upright in the middle of the bowl. It was touted as a soup, but my suspicion was that it was yesterday's leftover mushy peas, a dish that bewilders even the most seasoned Anglophile.

I think my wife wanted to forge on to Penzance, but I was pretty certain it was not my kind of place — urban, touristy and the setting for a Gilbert and Sullivan musical. Instead, we headed home, picking up rations of food (hake, rice and Brussels sprouts — a feast for kings!) and beer (Hobgoblin, Cornish Knocker and Devon Dympsy) along the way.

During our time in Cornwall, we hit the trail, the afore-mentioned South West Path, at several junctures: Cribba Head, Porthcurno Sands, Logan Rock and Gwennap Head to name a few. The trail was always good, the weather always windy, the look-offs dizzying and beautiful. The hikers all seemed cheerful and self-satisfied, with their ruddy cheeks, rumpled rucksacks, telescoping hiking sticks and drippy noses. I don't mean to suggest they were snobbish; salt air does that, you see. Knowing way too much about the history of British colonialism, I kept thinking, too bad their ances-tors hadn't just stayed home and decided to go out for a good long walk instead of wanting to conquer the world. But then, hindsight is often 20/20.

Long before the British set their ambitions on making sure the sun would never set on their empire, this part of Cornwall was settled by the Cornovii, a Celtic group of people who lived here during the Iron Age. They seemed to have had this wonderful, rugged land all to themselves until the Roman armies bullied their way north.

Linda and I waited for the right wave conditions to don our wetsuits and go boogie boarding at Sennen Cove. Those winter killer waves had long since subsided and the beach adjacent to the town boasted sparkling blue water, pristine waves and hard-packed white sand. The lifeguards hassled us a bit to stay in the swimming area rather than the surfing area, and this rankled my wife, who wanted to surf the more powerful waves down the beach. Nonetheless, the sea was kind to us that day as we smashed about in the North Atlantic until our arms were limp and our spirits revived.

Aiding the surly Sennen Cove lifeguards back in 2005 was Bilbo, a Newfoundland dog who had been enlisted to help watch over swimmers and surfers alike. He was retired in 2007 when the town imposed strict regulations preventing dogs from being on the beach in the summer. This angered many locals and there was a public outcry to bring the dog back to his beach, but Bilbo was never reinstated.

Back at our hayloft one evening, we discovered we had neighbours. An elderly couple from London was renting another cottage on the property for a few days and they invited us up for gin and biscuits. I was fearful at first it might be one of those boring British social occasions that you see in old BBC programs, but thankfully I was wrong. William and Beth had already begun the party before we arrived and we deduced they had partaken more of the gin than the biscuits. Like most British folks who discovered we were from Canada, they asked if we knew their cousin in Toronto. No, we did not. But they were cheerful and full of fun and we swapped travel stories and laughed until the sun settled itself and the crows began their evening festivities, bragging and gossiping about their accomplishments of the day. At this point it was time to retire to the hayloft for some salmon, potatoes, rocket salad and a bottle of brew called Parson's Nose.

On one of our driving days, we headed to St Michael's Mount while listening to John Prine, Van Morrison and Lennie Gallant. As we were wending our way through one of the insidious roundabouts just outside Penzance (I knew it was an evil, decadent town), I must have been driving too slow because a local woman in a silver Mercedes convertible nearly rear-ended us and, as we came out of the roundabout, hammered on her horn and sped past me on the narrow roadway, lifting a finger in the air to indicate she was not appreciative of my more casual Canadian driving style. I blamed it on the inbreeding of wealthy aristocrats and thought no more about it as we drove on to Marazion.

The castle and gardens at St Michael's were glorious. It's one of those places you can only walk to at low tide, and if there is one thing I know, it is that tide and time wait for no man. So we had timed it just right. At high tide, a boat is provided for ill-prepared tourists who have not studied their tide charts. The island is a kind of twin of Mont-Saint-Michel across the water along the coast of France. St Michael's Mount is on a ley line and believed to be a place of miracles that once was a destination for pilgrims. Visions of Saint Michael himself were said to occur here and the island has had more than its share of famous visitors over the years. Even Queen Victoria and Prince Albert showed up unannounced in 1846. The owners, the St Aubyn family, were not at home, so a housekeeper kept them entertained until they sailed off on the royal yacht that had brought them there.

Back in Sennen Cove I rented a surfboard, took to the sea with some locals and was humbled as I usually am the first day surfing in unfamiliar waters. While young punks gracefully slipped into long green walls and kicked their boards high into the air on the close-outs, I dutifully did my routine. I would paddle hard, stand, hear the laughter of the wave as it drove the nose of my board into the water, then tap me on the head ever so gently before flipping me head over heels mercilessly into the watery trough beneath. I would then come up spitting sand and sea and proceed to repeat the performance until I felt that I had grown appropriately intimate with the waters of Whitesand Bay.

Of course, you don't travel to this part of the world without going to Land's End. I had been warned by *Lonely Planet* that it had been "developed" with shops and a theme park. So I was braced for the shopping mall atmosphere of the developed part. But it is one hell of a fine location. I like places on the margins and I couldn't help but like Land's End. Once you walked ten minutes beyond the tourists at the cluster of stores, museums and restaurants, it was back to the South West Path at its best. You're high up above the sea with craggy cliffs in both directions. The wide-open, rugged landscape is starkly beautiful wherever you look and the endless deep, narrow coves are my kind of places. Tiny purple brilliant flowers dot the ground, and once again, everyone you meet has a drippy nose and a smile on their face.

When you think about England, you don't usually think about rugged beauty, but the UK has a ton of it. You could probably walk the entirety of the coastline of this large island on trails established by forward-thinking men and women who understood the value of a good walk on a windy day.

From Land's End, if you had the proper boat, you could sail east to the Netherlands (rounding Gwennap Head, of course), south to France (perhaps landing at Mont-Saint-Michel), southwest to Brazil (or onward to Antarctica), northwest to Iceland and Greenland (arcing around Ireland where necessary) or west to Newfoundland and Nova Scotia (with not a darn thing in the way). And for many English sailors of centuries past, Land's End was often the last bit of England they would see before sailing off the horizon headed toward foreign lands.

For me, standing there on a high cliff, looking out past the besieged Longships Lighthouse on its tiny island of rock, I knew we had only scratched the surface in our discovery of this welcoming ancient corner of the Celtic world and would return again to see whatever we'd missed.

Before we left, we were already planning a return trip for some more surfing and boogie boarding. That other British writer, Chris Nelson, who too would be preoccupied in London during our 2018 trip, had offered me some intriguing tidbits through our correspondence about a surfer's life in Cornwall. Chris lives and surfs in St Agnes, halfway between Newquay and Land's End and famous for its tin mines and history, captured in the *Poldark* novels and TV series. As noted, we had met in Nova Scotia when he interviewed me for his book *Cold Water Souls*, about those of us around the world who surf in truly cold conditions.

Chris pointed out that "Cornish surfers are a diverse crew, riding all kinds of surfboards, with a healthy mix of the generations and sexes. There's a lot of female surfers around St Agnes. Our line-up is pretty much from seven to seventy." Surfing is year round, of course. A transplanted Australian surfer, "'Chops' Lascelles was definitely at the heart of the surf community for nearly four decades, both in and out of the water." Sadly, Chops has passed on, but surfing continues to grow.

Like so many surf locales in the world, the area was plagued by a form of localism. "This small area was known as The Badlands for many years," Chris wrote, "harking back to the heavily localised days during the seventies and eighties. Surfers from outside the area weren't welcomed and the tight knit crew made sure that they were 'discouraged' from visiting."

Those same locals, however, formed the basis for Surfers Against Sewage (SAS). According to Chris, "They played a central role in the sea change that has occurred across the EU with laws governing water quality being strengthened. For a long time no one knew what was happening to our coastal waters — but SAS helped open people's eyes to the fact that this wasn't just affecting a few surfers, their own children were paddling in this whenever they went to the beach."

Beyond the fun and lunacy of cold water surfing, "There is an interesting tradition in St Agnes that every Easter all the local dog owners take their animals to the beach at Trevaunance for 'dog racing.' All the owners line up with their dogs, someone dressed up as a rabbit goes up and down the line goading the dogs, then sets off running and the dogs are let off their leashes — first dog to catch the rabbit wins." It seems better than fox hunting in my book and just the thing to keep you in shape if the waves aren't pumping. It's on my list for a future visit to Cornwall as I've scratched off running with the bulls in Pamplona in favour of watching a bunch of English dogs chase a Cornish surfer in a rabbit suit on Easter.

CHAPTER THIRTY-SEVEN

ON TO EASTWELL IN THE GARDEN OF ENGLAND

And now here it was the beginning of July 2018, and on this trip we had more than covered a fair part of England and Wales, but my head was filled with the inevitable soundtrack of "We're going home," made all the more poignant with the worried thoughts about Pamela, Scarlett and Genevieve. The photos emailed to us showed two exquisite but fragile micro-humans with partially shaved heads, wires to their chests and tubes up their nose. These were images that would bring trepidation to any grandparent no matter how many times we'd been informed by Pamela and her mother-in-law Kathy that everything was okay. That it was all going to be all right.

We'd sworn off radio for the most part farther back when our ears were first assaulted by the "Horny Song," but it was a hellish long drive and there was not much to see on the motorways except the ass-end of endless lorries and fiendish BMW drivers who thought it their right to pass me at 80 mph like I was standing still.

I doggedly kept the radio on, giving me a final chance to analyze British colloquialisms, pop culture, the news of the day and the latest rattle of Top 40 DJs. I tried to keep a stiff upper lip. As Kelty fell into a pleasant comatose-dog-state in the back seat, his harness appropriately lashed to the seat belt anchor, I tried to comprehend what a fast-talking BBC radio host was talking about. He was either gushingly enthusiastic or extremely upset, I couldn't quite tell, but between Linda and me, we surmised he was commenting on an important news story of the day. The supermarket chain ASDA, given the recent "heat wave," had declared a stiff limit on the purchase of fizzy drinks for online shoppers due to a national shortage of carbon dioxide, the gas that makes your Coke and Fanta nice and bubbly.

Linda and I looked at each other in disbelief as neither of us had ever heard of a carbon dioxide shortage. In fact, we had thought there was too much carbon dioxide ruling the planet due to global warming brought on by reckless humans like us driving automobiles around whatever island or continent they chose.

The BBC host, and I wish I knew his name, but it was something like Reginald Townsby, said that if any listeners wanted to comment on the crisis, to "Give me a tingle on the blower." Tell me there was not some kinky not-so-hidden message there. Sadly, we soon were out of range of this particular BBC station and never had a chance to hear Mrs. Edna Corset from Shepton Mallet put in her two cents about the apocalyptic soda situation. Or Mr. Simon Berm from Weston-super-Mare for that matter. It was most unfortunate we had to motor on.

I told the windscreen of the car that I thought the whole situation was "quite daft," daft being one of my favourite terms adapted in recent weeks. "Daft" and "smashing" were at the top of my list for vocabulary enhancement. These were two appropriate terms that I would henceforward apply to just about everything — a new dualistic way of improving over terms like "evil" and "good." Think about it for a while and you can see that most all news events involving politicians, sports, the economy or simply day to day circumstances at the ASDA, Tesco, Lidl or Morrison's could be labelled one or the other.

Well, the miles rolled by quickly enough. Soon we were approaching the ring road around London and Linda's Navigon, the blighty little bastard that I never fully trusted, told us we should take a shortcut, deke down the A329 and A322 near Wokingham and skirt through Bracknell, Swinley Forest and Bagshot until we merged with the M3 at Lightwater before bumping into the M25 to take us south and east. Sadly, this decision turned a so far pleasant drive into a sour situation. I wouldn't advise it myself if you are ever on a path similar to ours. There was construction, church picnics, football events involving inadequate parking, roundabouts filled with red-faced aggressive drivers, yet another bicycle event, more construction and a traffic jam outside, yes, an ASDA store where panicked online shoppers were probably trying to get to the shelves for the last of the Pepsi before it was all gone.

It was of great interest for me to learn later that this particular side trip, the purported shortcut, took us into the very location where the Martians first invaded earth in the original H.G. Wells's *War of the Worlds*. And there may well have been Martians about as far as we could tell, but if so, they had blended in with the purposeful ordinary busybodies who make up this corner of England.

The good news was that we didn't have to go anywhere near Heathrow and we didn't make our usual wrong turns in the city of Slough. But it was beyond daft and we lost a good hour in the melee of traffic, bicycles and heedless pedestrians. And we were, in a roundabout way, on our way home.

An hour or so later, safely out of the sprawl of suburban London, we pulled into a crowded service area with a WHSmith, an assortment of hamburger shops and various retail outlets of all sorts selling trinkets, gum and video games. It was a worthy pit stop to make good use of the enormous washrooms, which seemed fitting for sports arenas. For women, I suppose, the site of a row of men standing at a wall full of urinals is something they only see in romantic comedy movies where the girl walks into the men's room to say she is leaving the romantic lead while he is taking a whizz. I myself am more than accustomed to standing before a porcelain unit made by a company named Armitage Shanks. I can't say I look forward to it, but it feels familiar.

In recent years, in North America, England and away, advertisers have begun to rent space in small placards that you find yourself eyeball to eyeball with while trying to unload whatever liquid you have been accumulating during your busy day. Back at my university in Halifax, there is a lot of information there about what constitutes date rape and that when she says no, it really means no. In Canadian pubs, as well, I've seen ads for herbal prostate remedies (what better place to flaunt your product!), online dating services (do the two go hand in hand?) and, even stranger than that, tooth whitening products.

But here before me, riveted into the ceramic tiles of the wall, was a colourful ad for something called "Shreddies." And to my surprise, it was not a breakfast cereal. You may think I invented this for a laugh, but I didn't. I studied the ad carefully to make sure it was not some road-weary hallucination and, I kid you not, it wasn't. "We Sell Freedom!" the ad read. And here was a photograph of a black pair of men's briefs. Not just any ole black underwear, mind you. Shreddies has a charcoal lining that prevents the escape of flatulence. The charcoal lining is called Zorflex.

You'll probably want to go immediately online to see if I'm making this up, but there on myshreddies.com you'll discover that any number of people whose names are "Anon," from Amsterdam, Sweden and various likely UK locations swear by them. You'll find that Dastin from Estonia reported, "I worn my Shreddies for 3 days and they are just amazing, works as promised :)."

After my excursion, while Linda and I walked Kelty around the oh-so-familiar perimeter of yet another parking lot, I told Linda about my discovery and she reported that in the women's room there were ads for something called "Stay dry for women." Clearly, there was a lot of money to be made from men with stinky farts and women with a tendency to drip.

But enough of that. This first day of July 2018 was mostly about getting from Point A — deep in the tor heart of Dartmoor — to Point B — the posh Eastwell Manor outside Ashford, a scant 15 minutes from the Eurotunnel. Linda had found us a discount online opportunity to stay here for one night, and dogs were allowed. We weren't in the main edifice, a big castle-like affair with all the trimmings, but we had a cozy condominium-style first-floor apartment with a patio that opened up onto a small golf course.

The grounds were lovely and there were plenty of mowed lawns to walk the dog around. Svelte and not-so-svelte alike wandered in and out of the nearby spa. Many carried what looked like bowling ball bags to me, but I don't think they had bowling in the spa. I honestly didn't know what people did in a spa, and Linda tried to explain what went on there and why anyone would pay a handsome sum for these procedures, but she could tell by the dumbfounded look on my face that I just didn't fully comprehend. The spa's motto, according to a sign on the door, was "Pampering done right," which indeed seemed terribly British to me. It was the echoing of the proper job motif. "Well, if you are going to bloody well pamper yourself, you bloody well should have the pampering done right," I thought I heard a gentleman say as he toted his bowling ball bag and stopped to read the signage. He concluded by saying, "Otherwise, what's the bloody point? Any daft fool can see that." At least I think that's what I heard.

So here we were, back in Kent, "the Garden of England," on a property rightfully proclaimed as being "nestled in a green lush landscape." That it was and then some. Scores of famous guests had stayed here before us. Probably not in our semi-modern but slightly rundown condo on the golf green, but here on the exquisite property.

Although there was originally a house here going as far back as 1540, the current building is classed as "Neo-Elizabethan," and has gone through a number of incarnations. Queen Victoria stayed here on a number of occasions and skated on the lake. Edward VII stayed here and I had to look him up. It turns out he was Queen Victoria's son, who succeeded her to the throne in 1901. So did Princess Marie (whoever she was) before she became Queen of Romania. "How exactly does that work?" I badgered my wife over a glass of wine in the elaborate main dining room with its old authentic paintings of aristocracy from the past who clearly spent little time out in the sun. "I mean, one day you are a princess in England and the next, you are the Queen of Romania. How does that happen?" I asked this out loud and probably a little too loud for the other supper guests.

"I don't know," Linda said. "Just pipe down and eat your leek and potato soup." So I piped down and supped my l and p soup, which was really quite good.

A booklet I had nabbed from a table gave me a bit more history of the establishment. After the First World War, the whole place, like so many estates, fell on hard times. There was a fire, and then in the 1990s Eastwell was rebuilt by a fish restaurateur named Turrloo Parrett who had bought Eastwell but later sold it. And so on. Diana, Princess of Wales, had a fondness for Eastwell and she may well have tasted the same leek and potato soup we were now enjoying. Naomi Campbell, Helen Mirren, Judi Dench, Daniel Craig and Brad Pitt had all stayed here as well. And now the Choyces.

"If an old estate like this did not have a ghost, one would have to be invented by a lively imagination," I told my wife after my second glass of Prosecco. "Most ghost stories are hearsay anyway. Perhaps we could travel around England and I could hire myself out to hotels, castles and, if desperate, bed and breakfasts and farm holiday hosts. I would create an elaborate and colourful ghost story custom-fit for each dwelling. For a price, of course." It could have been the bubbly wine speaking (no CO_2 shortage there), but I had almost forgotten we were going home, that home where the heart is, that home where there were no ghosts at all. It sank in after a minute or two of her silence. Yes, soon we would be home. Forget the ghost writing.

Besides, Eastwell had its own "real" ghost. She is a traditional "white lady," a friendly ghost who strolls about at night spooking the hotel staff. She appears, looks down at the floor and then vaporizes. Other spirits, including a horseman, appear from time to time, visiting from the village of Eastwell, which is, after all, "classed as a highly paranormal place." I would not even think to question who has deemed it highly paranormal.

I'm sad to report that back around the previous Christmas, Claire and James Goodwin-Hill stayed here after recovering from a death in the family and having to put down their ill dog. They were most dissatisfied with their stay. According to the *Daily Mail*, they splurged on a £750 night during the holidays and found their "luxury" accommodation not at all luxurious. They took their photos to the *Daily Mail*, which ran nearly a dozen images of stained walls and floors, and, to me, it all just looked like what an old room would look like, but I guess it was pretty dingy and depressing if you were looking for an uplift from hard times. Of the high price tag, Mrs. Goodwin-Hill was quoted as saying, "You can get a whole week in Dubai per person for that." But she failed to explain why anyone would want to go to Dubai. She was particularly unhappy with the bathroom. "The grouting around the bath was badly repaired," she noted.

I myself have done a lousy job with bathroom grouting, so I have sympathy for the hired hand who did his best with such difficult work. But I can see her point. And the article even included a photo of their old dog that had been put to sleep, so I think the Goodwin-Hills deserved better. Shame on Eastwell, although they did publicly apologize once all those photos of dingy walls, worn floorboards and nasty carpet stains hit the national press.

Our only complaint about Eastwell, on our very last night in England, was that the door sills leading out to the patio were well rotted and allowed for a veritable army of ants to invade during the night, crawling around the floors, taking sustenance from our travelling food stores and finding unlikely places to inhabit our luggage. They were the really small kind of ants, though, and I didn't think much of it until later.

CHAPTER THIRTY-EIGHT

LAST MORNING IN ENGLAND
AND DRIVING ANTS TO FRANCE

In the morning we packed up the freezer bag with our leftover food, our suitcases and our dog and drove to the Eurotunnel entrance. We checked in, received a little doggy-footprint permit to hang from our mirror and proceeded through French Customs here on the English side. It was a longish wait in the parking corral until cars began to move, but soon we were driving into the train again, passing from car to car until we found our spot snug in what seemed like a cattle car from on old Western movie.

Before the train began to move, we listened to the recording of a most articulate British woman explaining (what else?) safety features, rules for the 20-minute sub-Channel excursion with advice on what to do if there was a fire on board: "Proceed slowly to the next car and wait for instructions. Do not try to put the fire out." Or something like that. Then, presumably, it was repeated in French. I studied Kelty to see if he had any sense that the journey was nearing an end. He was fast asleep with his head on a backpack for a pillow. For him, I suppose, it was just another dull crossing beneath billions of gallons of salt water.

As we began to pick up speed, my final vision of England was of power lines, electricity transformers, concrete, truck containers piled six high and a final sliver of blue sky with a cloud shaped like a scimitar. And again, I had the sense of moving between worlds. England to France. An island to the larger continent. A trip into the underworld and back into (one hoped) light and living. A necessary leg on the journey home, ending a circumnavigation pilgrimage. I don't think Linda and I spoke at all during the swift rail journey. I felt good about the trip. But what had we learned? What had we accomplished? Well, we'd gone around England — at least a fair chunk of it — with our dog, fulfilling my whimsical vision from so far back in a Canadian winter that it seemed like something from another life, on another planet.

As so often happens, once you begin to put a journey behind you, you begin to physically yearn for home: your own bed, your own house, a fire in the fireplace in the evening, the dog curled up before the flame. A day doing something profoundly ordinary.

And I was anxious to meet my tiny twin granddaughters, to see both daughters — Sunyata and Pamela — and reconnect with everything familiar. We had scaled a mountain or two, I'd surfed an artificial wave, poked around the homes of legendary writers and royalty and much more. Perhaps most importantly, England, Scotland and Wales had become familiar to me as well. My father had his first taste of life beyond the shores of North America here and its citizens had treated him very kindly despite the fact the country was in a horrifying war. And now I had returned to pay my respects and to cultivate small adventures with the woman I loved and my little white dog. So ends the story?

Well, not quite.

My reverie slipped away as the light appeared again through the windows of the cattle car. And then we pulled to a complete stop. Within minutes I started the engine and we drove down the line through the train cars before us until we were back in the industrial yards of Calais. Within minutes we were out of there and onto the toll highway, the A26 on our way toward Paris. A half-hour later, I noticed the sign for Merville. My father had himself a stint here during the war as well. After D-Day, after the Germans had been driven well back from France, he was stationed there at an Allied airbase that was now a commercial airport.

In his journal, my father's notes about the war winding down here in France were always straightforward and understated. "We went through the town of Amiens — totally destroyed. Saw a lot of German equipment destroyed along the roads all along the roads.... Saw a lot of interesting things in France."

We should have taken the side trip, perhaps to Amiens or Merville, a final salute to my father's career as a military man, but I felt anxious to get us to Roissy, the Parisian suburb that was home to Charles de Gaulle airport. These towns of northern France would remain only road signs to me. Lille to the north. Arras to the south, Amiens to the west. Saint-Quentin to the east. The experience of driving such a well-designed toll motorway is almost no experience at all. The countryside slips by in anonymity as you watch the mileage numbers to your destination drop from signpost to signpost. I knew that if we stayed on roads like this, we could drive the breadth and width of Europe and in many respects not see a thing. All were roads with minimalist highlights of gas stations and rest stops. Yet it felt damn good to be going home. Nothing outside the car windows really mattered now.

I remember stopping at a commercial rest stop where you had to walk up a staircase and over a glassed-in walkway to get to the shops and bathrooms on the other side. There were French children in the elevated walkway playing, running, shouting back and forth and having the time of their lives. A shirt-sleeved father and short-haired mother were urging them on, running themselves back and forth, making the best of an otherwise ordinary travel moment while tractor trailers, motorhomes and cars sped by just a few feet beneath us. The kids stopped only to pet Kelty and laugh as he licked their faces and wagged his tail. For at least a second or two I felt like I had been stitched back into the fabric of the living, rather than lost in the meaningless, frantic vacuum of the road. Disconnected morphed back into connected. In dogs we trust. In laughter we believe.

Linda had found us an apartment in Roissy on Expedia, one with a free shuttle that would take us to the airport in the morning. We unloaded the car and, as I went to put beer and leftover food in the little apartment fridge, I noticed that the carrots were black. Not rotten, no. Just covered with ants. As Linda opened our luggage, she reported that we also had ants in the suitcases as well. We'd driven the Eastwell ants to France, probably breaking some international law, most definitely creating a migratory insect issue. Kill them or set them free? I preferred the latter. I shook the carrots out over the bushes and opened my own suitcase on the little balcony. It wouldn't be until the following day, back in our home at Lawrencetown Beach, that I'd discovered a few of the little buggers had survived the transatlantic flight and immigrated to the New World. Welcome to Canada.

The rental car was returned that afternoon and we tucked into our apartment for the night. It was a hot one. Windows and doors remained open and, as the sun set, we looked across to the other open doors throughout the compound to see mostly men sitting in shorts and dirty T-shirts — workmen, I assumed. Mostly men without women, without families. Whoever they were, they lived in these temporary accommodations for the work available here. Later, we heard televisions tuned to soccer games, and saw shirtless men in their underwear talking to their televisions and arguing with each other in many languages. We were in the world of transients.

The flight home to Halifax was a little trickier than the nighttime flight across the Atlantic. Kelty was edgier, nervous, fidgety and vocal. I had conspired to find us an aisle and a window seat near the very back of the plane, hoping no one would be between us, but that was not the case. The centre seat was an older man who was hard of hearing and not at all comfortable with a dog near his feet. An airline attendant sussed out the situation and offered him the one empty alternate seat across the aisle. We now had three seats to ourselves. Kelty did not settle and Linda and I both made a silent prayer that our plane would quickly take off before the attendants noticed our dog was not behaving. He was in his soft-sided carry bag but desperately wanting his freedom back. One of our deepest fears had been that, along our travels, something would happen to the dog or we'd be forced to send him into the baggage compartment, or worse yet, not be allowed to fly him home at all.

But soon enough, the plane lifted off from the end of the runway. Next stop was Stanfield International in Nova Scotia.

As soon as we landed, we were taken aside by Customs for an inspection of our dog and luggage. We were cleared quickly and out on the sidewalk looking for the cab we had reserved. When the cab driver saw our dog, he refused to allow us in his car. I felt like arguing with him. We had prearranged the car and told them we had a dog. The cab company had even had a dog — a ratty-looking Chihuahua as a mascot — featured on their website. I was mad. More tired than mad, but the two do stir up into a little hot-headed result sometimes.

A taxi dispatcher from inside the airport who saw me fuming and lambasting the driver came out and quickly ushered us to another waiting cab. The driver was a young large man, cheerful but incessantly talkative, who told us about his mother's illness and his Filipino wife he had met online, then gone to the Philippines to marry and get to know her family before bringing her back to Canada. He talked nonstop all the way home.

And then we were in the door. Safe and tired.

EPILOGUE

It's 4:30 a.m. on August 6. We've been home now for over a month. My granddaughters, Scarlett Lesley and Genevieve Katherine, have been finally released from intensive neonatal care for less than a week. I'm holding Genevieve in my arms and feeding her a bottle of formula as I sit in an old wooden rocker rocking back and forth. Scarlett is asleep as well across the room near the fireplace.

Babies at this age are demanding. They need to be fed at least every two hours, day and night. Parents Pamela and Jason have had their share of nights without sleep so Linda and I have agreed to keep the babies here one full night a week — at least for a while until they grow a bit and settle into a routine that does not require round the clock attention.

I'm on the second shift as Linda was up most of the night attending to the twins. I wake in the early morning darkness of the bedroom with Kelty having taken over Linda's pillow beside me. I leave the warmth of the bed to go do my job. Grandpa to the rescue. Or, in this case, Grand Dude, as I am known to 10-year-old Aidan, the twins' older brother. Groggy Grand Dude picks up Genevieve, the one who currently needs attention. As Genevieve falls back asleep, as if on cue, Scarlett wakes up. I settle one, pick up the other and go back to rocking — rocking the darkness into light.

This night, we attend to these two beautiful new souls, feeding them, changing them, enduring their cries and enjoying their smiles. On other nights in the not so distant future, we would host Ailis, baby daughter to be born to Laura (Linda's daughter) and Andy in October, the month originally intended for our travels. Andrew Connell, the father-to-be, is himself English. He met Laura as they worked together in a pub in London. More ties to the UK, more shared lives of the British and the Canadians.

Linda heads to bed and Kelty comes to keep vigil with me, not curling up dutifully at my feet but finding the most comfortable corner he can on the sofa atop two pillows and a blanket. He watches me feeding Scarlett, exhales a satisfying breath and yawns. Kelty has proven himself good with the babies, and his only fault in that regard is that he'll try to eat a poopy diaper if it is left within his reach. Dogs will be dogs. Babies will be babies. Writers will be writers.

Yes. That's what I am thinking. This is a very literary moment. Now I realize that this is where the travel story ends properly. The journey over. A fire in the fireplace. The wife safely asleep in bed after a long night. The cave secure. The dog and man keeping vigil before the dawn.

On this day in 1945, the Americans dropped the atomic bomb known as "Little Boy" from the *Enola Gay* on Hiroshima. Over 70,000 Japanese were killed instantly and untold thousands died thereafter from the effects of radiation. With the atomic bomb unleashed, the threat of all-out nuclear war would haunt my generation from the time we were born.

Toward the end of July that year, with the war over in Europe, my father was still on a military base in England. In his journal he wrote, "Had to do K.P. today in the officer's mess. First time in a long while. Got good food there to eat." And then just a few days later, on the 27th, he wrote, "Had some bad news today." The bad news was that he was being shipped out to the Pacific, where the war was still raging.

Even worse, he was being removed from his unit. On the 29th, he noted simply that they were "getting our trucks and equipment ready to ship to the Pacific. Got a package from home with my swim trunks in. Might need them where we are going." And, curiously enough, on August 6, exactly 73 years ago to this day, completely unaware of the bombing of Hiroshima halfway around the world, he had a chance to put on those swim trunks. "Went swimming with a group from the Squad. Went to a resort town & swam in the Channel — salt water. Started to rain while there."

But it wasn't until Tuesday, August 15, that he reported, "Good news — War ended. Was on pass in Bedford. Had a lot of celebrating in Bedford — shooting fireworks etc. along the river." He shipped off to Marseille after that and then Morocco and into Germany, helping to do whatever it is soldiers do when trying to tidy up after a global war. It wasn't until January 29 of the new year that he could put his feet back on American soil. "Arrived in New York Harbor Sunday morning. No one around but Red Cross Crew."

Had the Americans not dropped the Hiroshima bomb and the Nagasaki weapon that followed, there's a good chance I would not be sitting here pre-dawn watching over my two brand new granddaughters. With his time of duty not complete, my father would certainly have shipped out to the South Pacific to continue his soldierly duties in the fight against the Japanese.

That all changed when the bombs were dropped. When Japan surrendered. And so he was allowed to go home, to take off his uniform, to put the war behind him. To marry my mother. To have two sons. To build a house with his own hands in the sandy soil of southern New Jersey.

One son would move to Canada and have a daughter and adopt another with his first wife and raise them in rural Nova

Scotia. And while that son and his second wife were tramping around England with their dog, seeking foreign adventures, the younger daughter would give birth to twin girls, she and her husband welcoming more daughters into the blended family and the promise of more adventures for the future. I see the seamless weaving together of generations down the line, of parents and children and travels far and wide. But always returning home.

Such are the thoughts streaming through my head as Scarlett now falls asleep and I tuck her in under a baby blanket. As if on cue, Genevieve awakes again and I scramble into the kitchen to prepare another bottle, then pick her up and return to the rocker.

The first hint of light appears in the sky now. It's been a long while since I've experienced this. Pure darkness giving way to milky grey. I can't see the sunrise. Too many tall spruce trees. Our house on the saltwater lake faces west so the sky begins to give itself over to light ever so slowly. With Genevieve nestled against my chest, something profound settles over me, a 67-year-old man holding a baby in his arms, the dog snoring an arm's length away. I'm in the moment. I'm really here. I'm in the absolute present. I'm centred. How rare is this? Extremely rare.

As the sky brightens, I see a mist hovering over the lake, then the low sun in the east grabs at something westerly in the distance. It flashes gold on the bridge I can see spanning the Lawrencetown River. It reflects off a road sign there in the distance as well and then begins to spread a full yellow-gold veneer of light over the expanse of the lake's surface.

Three days before this I was paddleboarding with 10-year-old Aidan on the lake. There was not a breath of wind. It was all splashing and fun at first, each of us on our own stand-up paddleboard. When we stopped midlake and just sat on our boards, surrounded by the great expanse of water and not a cloud in the sky, Aidan declared, "This is really different."

"How so?" I asked.

"Peaceful," he said. "Really peaceful."

Another rarity in this peripatetic, frenzied life.

The sky is blue now, the mist coaxed away by the sun. I realize August 6 is a holiday in this province. Natal Day is the name for it. A fairly random artificial holiday recognizing the birth of the province, although who can say when a province or a nation is truly born. But it fits nicely with my task of caring for newborns here at dawn.

In the UK, I suppose this would be called a "bank holiday" and many would be ordering their first pint of beer in a restaurant along with their proper English or Scottish breakfast. Here in the early morning hours, I decide that I should send both girls to England when they turn 21. I make a commitment to hang around on this planet at least that long. I'll teach them to surf. I'll counsel them. I'll foot the bill to send them both to Cambridge University if they desire. I'll be their aging Grand Dude to the best of my ability.

When they are 21, the year will be 2039 — a distant science-fictionish year in my mind. But then so seemed 2018 back when I was a boy. Yet here we are. No flying cars, no jet packs. But cars that drive themselves and "smart" houses to